Comparative Politics

Principles of Political Science Series

Published
John T. Ishiyama   *Comparative Politics*

Forthcoming
Marijke Breuning   *International Relations*
Jeffrey S. Lantis   *US Foreign Policy in Action*

Comparative Politics

Principles of Democracy and Democratization

John T. Ishiyama

WILEY-BLACKWELL

A John Wiley & Sons, Ltd., Publication

Blackwell Publishing was acquired by John Wiley & Sons in February 2007. Blackwell's publishing program has been merged with Wiley's global Scientific, Technical, and Medical business to form Wiley-Blackwell.

Registered Office
John Wiley & Sons Ltd, The Atrium, Southern Gate, Chichester, West Sussex, PO19 8SQ, United Kingdom

Editorial Offices
350 Main Street, Malden, MA 02148-5020, USA
9600 Garsington Road, Oxford, OX4 2DQ, UK
The Atrium, Southern Gate, Chichester, West Sussex, PO19 8SQ, UK

For details of our global editorial offices, for customer services, and for information about how to apply for permission to reuse the copyright material in this book please see our website at www.wiley.com/wiley-blackwell.

The right of John T. Ishiyama to be identified as the author of this work has been asserted in accordance with the UK Copyright, Designs and Patents Act 1988.

Library of Congress Cataloging-in-Publication Data is available for this publication.

Hardback   978-1-4051-8685-8
Paperback   978-1-4051-8686-5

A catalogue record for this book is available from the British Library.

This book is published in the following electronic formats: ePDFs 978-1-4443-4295-6; ePub 978-1-4443-4292-5.

Set in 10.5 on 13pt Minion by Toppan Best-set Premedia Limited
Printed in Singapore by Ho Printing Singapore Pte Ltd

1   2012

Contents

1

Introduction
Comparative Politics and Democracy

This book is not an introduction to political science in general, but an introduction to one of the major subfields of the discipline – comparative politics. It is designed as a book that builds upon a student's knowledge of politics, and assumes that the student has some basic familiarity with some central questions in political science – questions such as: What is politics? What is the state? What is government? What is a political system? Although designed primarily as a book for students with some familiarity with politics and political science, this book can be used by both "beginners" in the field and by more advanced students. It can be used by more advanced students because rather than being about "countries," it is about *theories* and *principles* in comparative politics. By adopting a *problem-based learning* approach, this can help even those students with little innate interest in comparative politics to understand how these concepts and principles can be used to make sense of hotspots like Iraq or Afghanistan.

This book is organized around a basic pedagogical principle: that students learn best when theories and concepts are understood in application to solving a problem (or problem-based learning). Hence this book is organized around a *problem*. How does one promote the development of political democracy? What are the factors that help explain the emergence of political democracy? Although some may object to the seemingly prescriptive nature of the question (the implication that democracy should exist everywhere), I adopt this focus for two reasons. First, it is a very *practical* question. Knowing the factors that affect the development of democracy can help students understand why "building" democracy in post-war Iraq

Comparative Politics: Principles of Democracy and Democratization, First Edition.
John T. Ishiyama.
© 2012 John T. Ishiyama. Published 2012 by Blackwell Publishing Ltd.

or Afghanistan is so difficult, if not impossible. Thus, the question is not prescriptive – rather it presumes that students need to ask this question first to realize that democracy may *not* be the best institutional arrangement, given a set of historical, economic, social, cultural and international circumstances. Second, it provides an issue on which "to hang our theoretical hats" – it demonstrates that some very practical questions can be addressed using theories that students read about in texts – it makes the field relevant and real.

Comparative Politics and the Comparative Method

However, before we begin to address the question about how to build a democracy, we do need to address some preliminaries – when we talk about a text book on "comparative politics," what do we mean? How does comparative politics fit as a subfield of political science? What has characterized the evolution of comparative politics as a subfield over time and how has that evolution reflected the development of political science generally? Finally, to sum up this chapter, I offer a brief outline of how this book is organized, and why is it organized the way it is.

Turning to a definition of comparative politics, it is first important to note that comparative politics is a subfield of political science, which includes other subfields, such as International Relations, Political Thought/ Theory, Public Administration, Judicial Politics, etc. In American political science, American Politics is also considered a subfield, but this view is not shared by European scholars, for instance, who simply include American politics as a case within comparative politics. In this book I share that European perspective, and consider the United States as one of the cases among many we investigate for comparative purposes.

There have been many different definitions of comparative politics offered by a variety of political science scholars. These can be divided into at least three general types: First, there are those who think of comparative politics large as the study of "other" or "foreign" countries – in most cases, this means countries other than the United States (Zahariadis, 1997, p. 2). A second approach emphasizes comparative politics as a subject of study. For instance, David Robertson (2003) defines comparative politics as simply the study of "comparative government" whose essence is to compare the ways in which different societies cope with various problems, the role of the political structures involved being of particular interest.

Most definitions of comparative politics, however, think of the field as both a *method* of study and a *subject* of study (Lim, 2006). Thus, for example, Howard Wiarda notes that the defining feature of comparative politics is that it "involves the systematic study of the world's political systems. It seeks to explain differences between as well as similarities among countries. In contrast to journalistic reporting on a single country, comparative politics is particularly interested in exploring patterns, processes, and regularities among political systems" (Wiarda, 2000, p. 7). These topics can include:

> [The] search for similarities and differences between and among political phenomena, including political institutions (such as legislatures, political parties, or political interest groups), political behavior (such as voting, demonstrating, or reading political pamphlets), or political ideas (such as liberalism, conservatism, or Marxism). (Mahler, 2000, p. 3)

Comparative politics is thus both a subject and method of study. As a method of study, comparative politics essentially is based on learning through comparison (which is, after all, the heart of all learning). There are different ways to compare, but for now it is sufficient to say that comparative politics as a method is a way of explaining difference. As Mahler (2000, p. 3) notes, "Everything that politics studies, comparative politics studies; the latter just undertakes the study with an explicit comparative methodology in mind." As a subject of study, comparative politics focuses on understanding and explaining political phenomena that take place within a *state*, *society*, *country*, or *political system*. Defining comparative politics in this way as both a subject and method of study allows us to distinguish comparative politics, from, say, international relations which is concerned primarily (although not exclusively) with political phenomena between countries, as opposed to within countries. If we define comparative politics, at least in part, as a method of analysis, as opposed to simply the study of "foreign" or "other countries," then it does not exclude the possibility of including the United States as a country to be studied, just as one might include Germany, or Russia, or Japan or Iraq.

So what is the comparative method? As we noted above, comparison is at the heart of all analysis. When one uses terms like bigger or smaller, greater or less, stronger or weaker to analyze anything, then by definition one is comparing. Indeed, for many scholars, being comparative is at the heart of political science. For instance, for Harold Lasswell (1968, p. 3), comparative politics was identical to political science because "for anyone with a scientific approach to political phenomena the idea of an independent comparative method seems redundant," because the scientific approach is "unavoidably comparative." Similarly Gabriel Almond (1966, pp. 877–878) equated the comparative and scientific method when he argued that "it makes no sense to speak of a comparative politics in political science since if it is a science, it goes without saying that it is comparative in its approach."

Nonetheless, as others have argued, in political science the comparative method is much more than just comparison. For the notable comparative politics scholar Arend Lijphart (1971), the comparative method is a unique approach especially designed to address a methodological problem in political science. It is a set of strategies that one uses to deal with situation of having too few cases, and too many potential explanatory factors. For instance, suppose one were to try to explain why political revolutions occur? Certainly one could examine a single case, such as the Russian Revolution of 1917. What are the potential causes that precipitated that revolutionary upheaval – perhaps it was due to the strain of World War I on Russia's relatively underdeveloped economy? Perhaps it was due to the social and economic developments prior to World War I that had created working-class chaffing under the yolk of autocracy? Or perhaps it was because of the organizational capabilities of the leaders of the Bolshevik Party (particularly Vladimir Lenin)? Or maybe it had more to do with the undue influence of the monk Grigorii Rasputin over the Empress Alexandra, which paralyzed the Emperor Nicholas' ability to act decisively? How would one be able to ascertain which of the potential theoretical causes (military defeat, social and economic transformation, organizational capacity of the opposition, and the political psychology of the incumbent leadership) had the most explanatory power when one has only a single case – the answer is, of course, one cannot. This is the essence of the problem of having too many explanatory variables and too few cases.

There are ways, of course, established in the natural and social sciences, to deal with this problem. In the life sciences, a common technique is the experimental method. This method, involves the use of an experimental group and a control group. The experimental group receives the treatment, or exposure to a stimulus. In many ways the stimulus can be seen as the "causal factor" we wish to test. On the other hand, the control group is exposed to the stimulus or treatment. The composition of the experimental and control groups should be identical, or as close to identical as possible.

Table 1.1   Classical experimental design.

Experimental group	Pre-test	Stimulus/treatment	Post-test
Control group	Pre-test	Placebo	Post-test

So if one were using human subjects, then one would want an identical number of men and women in each group, an identical number of representatives of different racial and ethnic group, or socioeconomic groups, etc. In addition the members of the control group receive a "placebo" (usually an inert substance which makes it less likely that the participants in the experiment realize that they are not receiving the active treatment). Thus the use of identical experimental and control groups (and a placebo) is meant to control for alternative factors that might explain difference on the post-test scores (such as gender differences or differences due to the subjects realizing they are not receiving the active treatment). By controlling for these alternative explanatory factors, one can presumably assess the true effects of the stimulus, treatment, or primary causal factor (see Table 1.1).

However, especially in the social sciences, the subjects of study are not easily amenable to experimental control, especially in the study of countries (as is the case in comparative politics). What many scholars advocate is a *quasi-experimental approach* (see Mannheim, Rich, and Wilnat, 2002) in which the logical structure of the classical experiment is pursued, but via non-experimental means. In other words, we still seek to control for the effects of alternative factors, thus isolating the effects of the variable in which one is most interested. One quasi-experimental technique is the statistical method (Lijphart, 1971). In the statistical method, we control for the effects of other variables via techniques such as linear regression (and its variants) which simultaneously estimate the effects of a number of independent variables (causes) while controlling for the effects of others. The statistical method, however, in order to work requires a generally large number of cases relative to the number of independent variables (causes) that are included in the analysis. This is a challenge for scholars studying comparative politics, when our universe of cases is limited by the number of countries, and the existence of an almost infinite number of explanatory variables. For example, if one were to try to identify all of the possible causes of political democracy, one can imagine an extremely large number of causes, probably more than the number of countries in the world. To avoid this potential problem, one technique is to "truncate" the model, or purposely reduce the number of explanatory variables to be tested to only those "theoretically" relevant (that is, those that are mentioned in the literature). This of course is what is most often done in quantitative comparative political analysis, but the downside of this is that there are always potentially important variables that are left out of the analysis.

Another technique that is employed is the "comparative method" which Arend Lijphart (1971, p. 685) identified as a unique quasi experimental strategy used to deal with the situation of having too many potentially causal variables and too few cases. The comparative method is related to the statistical method in that it seeks to establish controls without having experimental control over the subjects of study. Thus, like the statistical method, the comparative method is "an imperfect substitute" for the experimental method (ibid., p. 685). However, unlike the statistical method, the comparative method does not exert statistical control over variables. Rather control is attained through other means. The comparative method is specifically designed for a very small number of cases (ibid., p. 684).

There are of course a number of different types of comparative designs, but the most common is the Similar Systems Design (sometimes knows as Mill's Method of Difference, named after John Stuart Mill), which consists of comparing very similar cases which only differ in the *dependent variable*. This allows one to "control" for a number of factors in order to assess which differences account for variation in the dependent variable. For example, in my own work (Ishiyama, 1993), I have examined the impact of the electoral system on party systems development during the political transition period just prior to the collapse of the Soviet Union, comparing the then republican elections in Estonia and Latvia. These two countries were selected because they were very similar in a number of key respects. First, both had been annexed by the Soviet Union in the same year (1940) and both were characterized by ethnic bipolarity (where there were two main groups in each republic, the indigenous Latvian and Estonian populations, and the Russophones); both had similar levels of economic development, and both were regarded as "advanced" republics in the USSR. In the initial competitive elections introduced in 1989, the political systems were roughly parliamentary, and both systems were unitary. The one key dimension in which they varied was the electoral system they adopted to govern the first competitive elections. In Latvia, a single-member district plurality system was employed (as was the case in the rest of the "elections" in the USSR, at least technically). In Estonia, however, the authorities there experimented with a variation of a proportional representation system called the Single Transferable Vote (STV) used in countries like Ireland and Malta. Thus, by controlling for other theoretically important variables that might explain party systems development (by selecting similar countries) one can ascertain the effect of the one variable in which they differ – in this case, the electoral system.

On the other hand, there is the Most Different Systems Design/Mill's Method of Similarity: it consists in comparing very different cases, all of which, however, have in common the same *dependent variable*. The goal is to find the common circumstance (or common denominator) which is present in all the cases that can be regarded as the cause (or independent variable) that explains the similarity in outcome.

The Evolution of Comparative Politics

The Ancients and comparative politics

Where did comparative politics come from? How has the field evolved over time? To some extent the study of comparative politics is as old as the study of politics itself. The earliest systematic comparisons of political systems were carried out by the Ancient Greeks. For instance, Plutarch tells a story, in his *Lives of the Noble Grecians and Romans*, of the scholar Lycurgus of Sparta who traveled widely around Greece and the Eastern Mediterranean recording the strength and weaknesses of the political regimes among the various city-states he encountered. However, the two most noteworthy scholars in Ancient Greece, at least in terms of their impact on comparative politics, were Plato and Aristotle. *The Republic* by Plato and *Politics* by Aristotle are widely viewed as the first great works of political science, covering such key issues as the nature of power, characteristics of leadership, different forms of government, and the relationship between state and society and economics and politics.

Although both Aristotle and Plato had much in common (particularly in terms of their desire to understand the design of the *ideal* political system), the approaches to understanding and knowledge (or epistemologies) were quite different. On the one hand, Plato was much more concerned with what *should be* and with normative issues such as justice and right than Aristotle (although Aristotle was motivated by these concerns as well). However, where the two really differed was in their understanding of how humans come to know things. For Plato, to understand involved insight. Indeed, Plato thought of understanding as much more than just observation or reality. Thus, for instance, his "Parable of the Cave" is a metaphor for ignorance and knowledge.

The parable goes something like this: Imagine a cave in which prisoners are chained to a wall so all they see are the shadows thrown on a wall in front of them by the light shining behind them from the mouth of the cave. All they have known and see are these shadows which they mistakenly perceive as reality. Yet if one were freed, and saw the daylight behind, that person would see things as they really are, and realize how limited one's vision was in the cave (Plato, 1945, p. 516). Merely observing perceived reality is thus not real. Discovering what *should* be is what is real for Plato. From Plato is derived the *normative* tradition in political science.

On the other hand, Aristotle (1958) really represents a more "empirical" tradition in the study of politics and had a much more direct impact on the development of comparative politics. Aristotle collected approximately 150 of the political constitutions of his time, mainly from the Greek city-states but from other places in the Eastern Mediterranean as well. In addition, he used these "data" to try to answer the question of what best promoted political stability, and examined the social, cultural, and economic factors that contributed to the emergence of political stability. Most noteworthy was his development of a six-part classificatory scheme where he identified "ideal" types or models of political systems, based upon the number of people ruling, and whether the rulers ruled for all or for themselves (which he considered degenerative or corrupt). The scheme is illustrated in Table 1.2.

In this scheme, there could be the legitimate rule by one (monarchy), the few (aristocracy), and the many (polity). Each of these could degenerate into different forms, especially if the rulers chose to rule to enrich themselves as opposed to the promotion of the interests of all. Thus, monarchy could degenerate into tyranny, aristocracy into oligarchy, and polity into

Table 1.2 The Greek system for classifying political systems.

Rule by	Legitimate form	Corrupt or degenerative form
One	Monarchy	Tyranny
Few	Aristocracy	Oligarchy
Many	Polity	Democracy

democracy (which Aristotle equated with mob rule). Beyond this, Aristotle also analyzed whether these political systems had forms of local governance apart from a central elite, and what the socioeconomic base of power was as well. He found that the most unstable political systems were pure oligarchies and pure democracies, but the system that had combined aspects of oligarchy and democracy with a strong "middle class" were most politically stable.

Aristotle was perhaps the first true systematic "comparativist." Aristotle derived his generalizations from the observations he made, and formulated theories (or explanations) as to what caused political stability or instability. Although primarily motivated (as was Plato) by the desire to build a better state and promote the "good life," the methodology employed by Aristotle was more akin to the empiricism that is evident in modern political science. Indeed, within Aristotle's analysis one can find all of the basic ingredients of modern political science – theory, hypotheses, analysis, and empiricism.

An early Roman political theorist who also contributed to the development of comparative politics as a field was Cicero. Cicero's primary contribution was his emphasis on natural law, or the notion that there were laws that structured the universe, including societies, that could be discovered, and act as the basis for ordering political life. As with the Greeks, Cicero was also interested in the "normative" issue of what is the best form of government. Using essentially Aristotle's framework, Cicero argued for a mixed system that employed both aristocratic and features of the "polity" system that Aristotle had identified, and contended that this was the best possible arrangement for the Roman Republic.

Comparative political scholarship in the Middle Ages and the Enlightenment

The coming of Christianity and the Middle Ages dampened the development of comparative politics as a field. This is because the most noteworthy Christian political theoreticians of the age, particularly Augustine and Thomas Aquinas, but others as well, saw little value in investigating the merits or shortcomings of "other" political systems. Rather, they argued, the goal of politics was to establish a Christian kingdom, and what that was could be accomplished best by study of history and the primary spiritual texts of the day. Augustine in particular argued that the Christian kingdom was the end product of history and human development. The work of

Augustine greatly influenced the Catholic Church (but also later Protestant thinkers like John Calvin). However, given that the answer to the best form of government was already known, there was little need for the use of systematic comparative methods favored by Aristotle and Cicero in the past to discover the ideal political system.

What really stimulated the revival of comparative politics were real world changes, particularly the discovery of the new world and the era of exploration from the fifteenth to the seventeenth centuries. It was during this time that Western Europe came into contact with a variety of different political systems, such as the "Middle Kingdom" of China, to the east, and indigenous empires of the Western Hemisphere. At about the same time, there emerged the modern nation-states in the aftermath of the Hundred Years War (the wars between Catholics and Protestants) during the sixteenth and seventeenth centuries. It was during this time that Portugal, Spain, France, England, Holland, Prussia, and Sweden, and others, emerged as separate political entities with distinct political cultures (often linked to either Catholicism or Protestantism), distinct economic systems, and distinct political forms. Further, the rediscovery of the scientific method during the Renaissance and the scientific discoveries of Newton and Galileo fundamentally altered our understanding of the universe, ushering in a new era of interest in comparative political analysis.

One of the first "political scientists" who wrote in the sixteenth century during this time of transformation in Europe was the scholar Nicolò Machiavelli. Machiavelli was most noteworthy for his contributions to political theory, particularly his analysis of power, but he was also a keen student of comparative politics. Machiavelli was primarily motivated by his desire to promote Italian political unification (at the time Italy was divided into a number of principalities, papal states, and Hapsburg/Austrian possessions), and the restoration of the glory of Rome. In particular, Machiavelli was interested in identifying models for emulation from other countries. His favorite case was that of Spain and particularly the actions of Ferdinand of Aragon, who, together with Queen Isabella of Castile, had unified Spain by manipulating the nobility, the Catholic Church and other rivals (Machiavelli, 1946).

Another major contributor to the development of comparative politics in the eighteenth century was the French political thinker Montesquieu. Unlike other earlier thinkers of the age of Enlightenment, such as Thomas Hobbes and John Locke, who examined the characteristics of one country (England) and assumed universal applicability, Montesquieu was explicitly comparative in his investigations. In particular, he is most noteworthy for his argument that the best form of government is one that involves the separation of powers (between legislative, executive, and judicial branches). However, Montesquieu also argued that a link existed between climate, culture, and political outcomes. For instance, he argued that authoritarianism was more likely in hotter climates than in colder ones, because hotter temperatures promoted laziness and passivity, thus inviting authoritarianism. Religion, he argued, could be used to combat such tendencies, particularly by instilling cultural norms of hard work and diligence (Montesquieu, 1949).

Jean-Jacques Rousseau also contributed to the development of comparative politics, particularly via his analysis of economic development on the human condition, and his attempt to understand the state of nature via his study of "primitive" nomadic societies of the time. Rousseau was especially critical of the corrupting influences of private property. Rousseau believed that private property created divisions between people, led to individual greed, and ultimately the exploitation of one by another. Thus, the naturally harmonious nature of humankind was corrupted by private property. Rousseau called for a new social contract in which social harmony would be restored via government through the general will. However, in Rousseau's ideal political system, only the small elite (who knew the general will) would rule for the benefit of all. Rousseau's political solution (although not his analysis) is often thought of as a forerunner to modern totalitarianism, where a small elite (or one person) knows what is best for all, and where the Führer, or Duce, or Vodzh, need not consult with the population to figure out was is best (Rousseau, 1964).

Two other scholars of the nineteenth and early twentieth centuries who contributed greatly to the development of comparative political theory were Karl Marx and Max Weber. Marx, along with his long-time collaborator Friedrich Engels, was a major critic of capitalism and fashioned a "scientific" approach to understanding the laws of history and the evolution and collapse of human societies. Most noteworthy is Marx's focus on economic determinism, or the idea that economic relations of production are the determining feature in the development of the social and political superstructure of society. In short, all social, cultural, and political institutions are designed to serve the economic interests of the dominant class (which class dominated varied from historical period to historical period). For Marx, whoever controlled the means of production (or the things used to make other things – such as land, water, resources, machines, etc.) dominated. During ancient times in the slave societies of Greece and Rome, the slave owners controlled the means of production (slaves). Under feudalism, the control over the land made the feudal lords the dominant class. Economic dominance translated into political dominance. Hence, for Marx, economics was the primary factor explaining political development.

It is important to note that Marx, like earlier political thinkers from the Ancients to Rousseau, was also motivated by a normative concern over what was best, despite his emphasis on scientific socialism. What really motivated Marx was a justification to explain the demise of capitalism and the end of private property, which, like Rousseau, he believed to be at the root of all human problems. Once unshackled from the chains of private property, humankind would be free to realize its greatest potential in a classless, stateless, and nationless world, where it is possible for one to do what one wills where one can: "to do one thing today and another tomorrow, to hunt in the morning, fish in the afternoon, rear cattle in the evening, criticize after dinner, just as [Marx has in] mind, without ever becoming hunter, fisherman, shepherd or critic" (Marx, in Tucker, 1972, p. 124).

Max Weber, on the other hand, contended that economic development was not all that drove political development. Indeed, cultural attributes of countries play an important role in explaining political life. Thus, for instance, he argued the importance of cultural and religious factors in explaining economic development and industrialization. In particular, he noted the importance of the Protestant Reformation in Europe in driving the Industrial Revolution, and compared Protestantism with some of the world's other great religions, such as Hinduism, Buddhism, and Islam to provide contrasts. However, Weber was also notable in arguing for the independence and autonomy of political factors in explaining societal development. Unlike Marx, who contended that all historical change could be reduced to an economic explanation, Weber argued that development was the product of multiple causes, including the political ones. For Weber, politics was autonomous from economics (unlike Marx) and for him the leaders' political choices can have a vital and independent effect on historical change (Weber, 1964).

In sum, the evolution of comparative politics from the Ancients until the twentieth century was characterized by two common features. First, there has always been a tradition of using comparative political inquiry as a means to effect improvements in the existing political system. This certainly was the goal of the Ancients as it was for Machiavelli, Montesquieu, and Rousseau, and arguably for Marx and Weber as well. Thus, scholars of comparative politics have traditionally been very interested in the practical application of what they studied. Second, there was a growing emphasis over time (in a way, a rediscovery of the Aristotelian tradition) on empiricism and a move away from the universalistic philosophical approaches of the Middle Ages. However, quite apart from these intellectual developments (which were largely concentrated in European scholarship), comparative politics scholarship in the United States developed along quite different lines.

Comparative politics and the behavioral revolution in political science

While the field of comparative politics was fairly well developed in Europe, in the United States comparative politics remained relatively underdeveloped at the beginning of the twentieth century. Very few colleges and universities even offered programs in "politics" (usually it was subsumed under History programs), let alone offer courses in the way of the study of countries other than the United States (Ishiyama, Breuning, and Lopez, 2006). Wiarda (2000) argues that this was mainly because of the isolation of the United States from world events (the product of geography) and the inaccessibility of other countries. There were of course a few exceptions, such as future President Woodrow Wilson's (1889) book *The State*, in which Wilson used cases from the European experience to investigate the evolution of the American state. However, what little comparative scholarship that existed, was limited to a few courses on European governments.

This emphasis on Europe continued well into the twentieth century. Further, most scholarship in early political science was largely descriptive of formal and legal institutions, such as descriptions of legislatures, executives, and judiciaries (see Ogg, 1915; Neumann, 1951; Finer, 1970; for a critique of this approach, see Macridis, 1955). In particular, the focus was on describing how formal political institutions operated – although other political actors were sometimes included (such as political parties), relatively little attention was paid to issues of public opinion or interest group activity, or anything beyond formal laws and governmental procedures (for some good examples of this formal institutional approach, see Ogg, 1915; Neumann, 1951; also for some of the goals advocated by the American Political Science Association regarding the study of comparative government, see Haines, 1915).

All of this was to change with the aftermath of World War II (1939–1945). As Robert Dahl (1961) noted, World War II had a profound effect on the evolution of American political science in general and the study of comparative politics in particular. The war and its aftermath created a demand for the knowledge and skills of political scientists, particularly to address issues such as how to build (or rebuild) democracy in the former totalitarian states that the allies had fought during the war, Germany and Japan. Further, with the onset of the Cold War, there emerged a need to understand the motivations of Soviet and Communist leaders, what caused the spread of communism, what led to the demise of incipient democratic experiments among the newly independent states that were spawned by decolonization, and how to promote political stability. The national security of the United States drove these concerns, and as a result, knowledge of other countries began to be valued. Along with this rising interest also there emerged more funding and money available to support comparative political research, particularly through institutions such as the Social Science Research Council (SSRC), and private funding sources such as the Ford, Carnegie, and Rockefeller Foundations (Dahl, 1961). This growing interest in politics outside the United States had also been reinforced by the influx of European scholars who had fled Fascist tyranny before and after the war (scholars like Hannah Arendt, most noteworthy for her seminal study on totalitarianism) (Arendt, 1971).

Although there was an increasing interest in the politics of other countries in American political science, by and large, the scholarship in the immediate post-war period remained largely descriptive and focused on legal institutional characteristics of countries. However, even before the war, there had been rumblings of change. In particular, the beginnings of a movement that was to fundamentally reshape American political science was emerging as early as the 1920s. This movement began as a very small group, largely concentrated in the fledgling American Political Science Association which had been founded in 1906. This group of scholars argued for a more systematic approach to the study of politics, modeling techniques of inquiry borrowed from the natural sciences. In the first half of the twentieth century, there had been several scholars, most notably Charles Merriam, Arthur Bentley, and others, who had pioneered the use of quantitative studies of politics. In particular, from 1923–1940, Merriam and his colleagues at the Department of Political Science at the University of Chicago launched a radical new approach to the study of politics – the so-called "Chicago School" of political science. The faculty of the Chicago

School produced seminal studies of voting behavior, urban politics, African American politics, political psychology, comparative politics, the causes of war, political parties, public administration, and methodology (see Heaney and Hansen, 2006). These studies were among the first to use advanced empirical methods in political science, including survey experiments; content analysis; and correlation, regression, and factor analysis. At the same time, the Chicago School's notion of "science" embraced qualitative methods and historical analysis, which often were presented side-by-side with quantitative analysis. Above all else was Merriam's view (Merriam was the chair of the political science department at the University of Chicago) that a political science should be useful, and that the findings based upon close empirical observation should be used to better government and society. Perhaps more importantly, though, were the student products of the work of that department, those students who later became the professors of the post-war era, for they were to help lead in the 1950s and 1960s what later became known as the behavioral revolution in political science. These included, among others, future luminaries in the field such as V.O. Key Jr., Harold D. Lasswell, David B. Truman, Gabriel A. Almond, and Herbert A. Simon. These graduates of the Chicago School were the vanguard of the behavioral revolution that fundamentally reshaped political science, a revolution that created the science of politics that exists today.

This desire to bring a more systematic approach to the study of comparative politics began to gain traction in the 1950s. In particular, many scholars were quite critical of the formal and legal descriptive focus of most comparative scholarship which dominated the field. In 1955, a seminal book was published by Roy Macridis of Brandeis University entitled *The Study of Comparative Government*, in which he attacked what he called the "traditional approach" in comparative politics (Macridis. 1955). In short, Macridis argued that there were five things wrong with this traditional approach. First, it was *parochial on Europe*. This is not to say that there is anything wrong with studying Europe, in fact many classic comparative texts, such as the work of Frederick Austen Ogg (1915) at the beginning of the twentieth century, were fine pieces of scholarship. However, with an almost exclusive focus on European cases, there is a tendency to use Western blinkers to study non-Western phenomena. For instance, in many of the societies of pre-colonial West Africa, there was a relatively democratic tradition of electing "kings" and these kings would serve on a rotating basis, circulating among the more notable families in the community. However, when the British arrived, they employed the same method of indirect rule they had used elsewhere (such as in India). This would involve authorizing the "king" to rule in the name of the British Crown. The "king" was then provided with the symbols of office (such as a hat) and a stipend from the colonial government. Since the British understood king to mean a hereditary title (as it was in Europe), they appointed not only the current office holder (which had been a rotating system before) for life but also all of his heirs to rule in perpetuity – thus this practice, informed only by the European experience (that is, parochialism), served to undermine indigenous African democratic institutions (Crowder, 1968). Parochialism thus undermines true understanding of "foreign" political processes, and for Macridis this was a major problem with the traditional approach in comparative politics.

Second, the traditional approach for Macridis was descriptive rather than analytical and explanatory. By this he meant that the focus of comparative politics up to that point was largely on describing how political institutions worked as opposed to explaining why they emerged in the first place, or what effect they might have on political behavior. A crucial element, "the why" question, was essentially missing from the traditional approach.

Further, Macridis argued that the traditional approach was "essentially monographic." Many works up to that point had examined "political systems" but almost exclusively on institutional actors (such as the legislature, the judiciary, etc.) rather than taking into account actors outside of institutions – such as interest groups, individuals, etc. Thus, the traditional approach for Macridis was overly formalistic and legalistic.

A fourth criticism offered by Macridis was that the traditional approach was not comparative at all, but was really dominated by the study of individual countries. Even scholarly texts that were presented as "comparative" (meaning these included studies of more than one country) did not really compare. Rather individual chapters of such works were devoted to individual cases, and relatively little effort was made to compare and contrast across countries (a good example is Ogg, 1915; see also Finer, 1970). Finally, he claimed the traditional approach was "essentially static"; in other words, formal legalistic, or institutional approaches did not attempt to explain political change. Rather, the political "organism" was merely described as it existed, with no accounting of why it emerged in the way it did, and how it would change over time.

This disquiet over the traditional approach, coupled with trends in American political science more generally, led to the "behavioral revolution" in political science (Dahl, 1961). The essence of the new behavioralist approach was characterized by the desire to employ scientific methods from the natural sciences, particularly the emphasis on theory and empiricism. Second, advocates of behavioralism emphasized the importance of interdisciplinarity. To explain political phenomena, it was now necessary to focus on non-institutional explanations for politics (that is, economics, sociology, psychology) as well as scientific method and mathematics. Perhaps most controversially was the emphasis on the value-free nature of science. From this perspective, political scientists should not be concerned with values – rather the focus should be on facts not what should be (for a critique of behavioralism on this point, see Bay, 1965). Finally, there was the idea that a common set of terms and concepts should be developed in order to more systematically examine political behavior. From this perspective, what was missing from the study of politics, as opposed to the natural sciences, was a common set of understandings and definitions regarding key concepts used in the analysis of politics, such as "power," "political system," "democracy," etc.

In comparative politics, one of the first attempts to establish a framework and a common vocabulary to facilitate a more systematic, behavioral, approach to the field was offered by David Easton (1957). Easton argued for the adoption of a "Systems Approach" to the study of politics, in which he argued that the political system could be understood in much the same way as a biological system. Like biological systems, political systems do not exist in isolation, and therefore should not be studied as such (which traditional formal-legal analysis was apt to do). Political systems are surrounded by environments – these environments are made of other systems: physical, social, economic (Figure 1.1). Also one can distinguish between

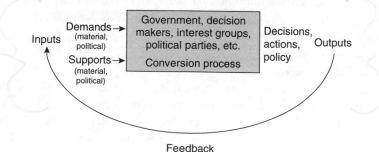

Figure 1.1   The political system.

those environments that are intra-societal versus extra-societal (or for a country, international) environments.

From these environments emerged "inputs," including demands and supports. Demands can be political – for instance, a demand to participate politically via the right to vote, the demand to recognize political freedoms, such as speech and assembly, etc. However, demands can also be for material goods and services as well (such as building a new highway, or tax breaks for industry to spur economic growth). Supports can also be material or political. Material supports include tax receipts which are revenues extracted from the environment, but also political support for actions to be taken by the political system.

The political system itself for Easton is a social system through which values are authoritatively allocated. This meant that the system includes much more than just formal governmental structures but also other actors that impact the process by which decisions are made that are binding on a society. This can include formal governmental structures, but also interest groups, political parties, individual leaders, etc. What is included in the political system would depend on what kind of regime it is – democracy, autocracy, one-party state, military junta, etc. In addition, the political system includes some kind of conversion process by which demands and supports are processed to produce policy outputs. In many ways, the political system is like an organism that processes demands (like the need to eat, procreate, etc.) takes in nutrients, and expels actions. However, these actions have a feedback effect in that they affect both the intra-societal and extra-societal environments in which the political system exists. Thus instituting tax breaks may have the effect of stimulating the economy leading to inflation and hence a demand to control inflation. Or deciding to go to war may affect the international order (as it did after World War II) which in turn creates new enemies and new challenges. For Easton, the key question is how political systems persist, and his generic conclusion is that survival requires successful conversion of demands on the system into outputs that are more or less acceptable to the environment from which the original demands originated.

Over the years there have been many critics of Easton's systems approach (for a summary, see Susser, 1992). In particular, many scholars have wondered what actually goes on inside the "black box" of the political system – that is, what is involved in the conversion process by which demands and supports are converted into policy. Second, many wonder about its utility, whether the systems approach did anything at all in helping to explain political phenomena. For instance, does it help explain the collapse of democracies? Does it explain why different kinds of political systems emerge? If theory is meant primarily as a means to explain and predict political developments, systems theory appears ill-equipped to do that.

In the late 1950s and early 1960s, Gabriel Almond and James S. Coleman (Almond and Coleman, 1960; and Almond, 1956) introduced a modification of the mechanistic theories of David Easton, a modification which they referred to as "structural functionalism." Again, like Easton, Almond sought to establish a common set of terms and concepts in order to more systematically compare political systems across very different countries. Almond's innovation was to introduce an approach to political systems that not only examined its structural components (as Easton had done) but, more importantly the *functions* performed by the political system as a whole. Structural functionalism holds that a political system is made up of structures such as interest groups, political parties, the executive, legislative and judicial branches of government, and the bureaucracy. However as Almond points out, two countries may have on the surface appear to have the same political institutions, but what differentiates these systems are the ways in which these institutions function. These functions (which all systems need to perform) can be performed by different institutions. For instance, interest groups serve to articulate political issues in many systems. However, in other systems, interests are articulated through family connections and/or patronage networks. In some systems (such as Western democratic ones), parties then aggregate and express interests in a coherent and meaningful way. On the other hand, in some military authoritarian regimes, it may be that the military aggregates interests. In some systems, government in turn enacts public policies to address these interest demands, or perhaps the Communist Party is charged with implementing policies (as was the case in the former Soviet Union); and bureaucracies finally regulate and adjudicate them differences in policy implementation. Although the functions may be the same, different structures perform these functions, and this is what differentiates types of political systems.

In addition to the "process functions" (interest articulation, interest aggregation, policy making, regulation and adjudication), there are also system-maintaining functions, that is, functions that maintain the survival of the system over the long run, by cultivating popular support for the political system and recruiting new leaders to succeed the current one. These include political socialization, political recruitment, and communication. For Almond, political socialization means the process by which a system passes down values, beliefs, and aspects of the political culture that helps sustain the system. The agents of socialization include families, schools, political parties, religion, as well as other agents that inculcate in the next generation the system's dominant political values. Political recruitment refers to the process by which new leaders are cultivated and vetted to succeed the current political generation. Finally, communication refers to the way in which the political system disseminates information to ensure its proper functioning. For instance, the media plays an important role in distributing information to citizens or those who are among the politically relevant, upon which they make political decisions. However, the media also helps to shape values and preferences.

Although a considerable advance over Easton's systems approach, structural functionalism is also plagued by some important shortcomings. First, it is at its heart, quite conservative – the centerpiece of the approach is the assumption that the primary goal of any political system is to ensure its own survival. Thus systems in this approach are not particularly adaptive or innovative (which may not really capture how political systems actually operate, some being more innovative and adaptive than others). Second, it seems to be based largely on Western democratic models and Western concepts, particularly with regard to the process functions, and may not describe these processes in non-Western and/or non-democratic systems very well. Finally, the approach itself is rather static in that it does not account for how existing systems and the structures that perform these functions came to be in the first place.

The behavioral revolution reached its zenith in the 1970s. However, at about the same time many scholars were questioning the direction in which the behavioral revolution had taken political science (Bay, 1965). In general, there have been two key criticisms of the behavioral approach. The first relates to the insistence that science is value-free. Yet how is it possible to be objective when studying something as value-laden as politics? Although there is no denying that facts do exist, analysis of what those facts actually mean often intersects with the particular preferences or values that we hold. We are human and to be human means that we have values and opinions which color what we observe as truth and evidence. To deny this is to deny political science a purpose.

Second, critics of behavioralism, like Christian Bay, have also argued that because of behavioralism's emphasis on quantification, the focus in political science has shifted in the direction of methodological trivia. Indeed, counter to the original intentions of Charles Merriam and the leading scholars in the Chicago School, behavioralism has caused political science to focus increasingly more on empirical method as opposed to application. Indeed, behavioralism, from this perspective, has caused scholars to focus on issues of methodological trivia (such as what is the best way to correct for heteroskedasticity in regression models) as opposed to focusing on big questions such as "is democracy a good thing?"

As a result of these criticisms, since the 1970s, several "post-behavioral" approaches have emerged, particularly those related to postmodern and constructivist approaches to politics. Such approaches contend that social and political realities are largely social constructions, created by humans to place order on a chaotic reality. These constructed realities are not amenable to an approach that assumes there is a reality waiting to be discovered through an "objective" science of politics. More related to comparative politics, however, is the neo-institutional movement (associated with scholars such as James March and Johan Olsen, 1984; Rein Taagepera and Matthew Shugart, 1989; and Bernard Grofman and Arend Lijphart, 1984, and others). This approach essentially argues that what has been missing from the behavioral revolution is applicability. In essence, the behavioral revolution, in its rush to identify factors affecting politics outside of political institutions and formal legal structures, had in fact abandoned the study of formal/legal political structures. Issues like the structure of the executive, or the type of electoral system adopted by a particular political system, had been largely ignored by the behavioralists, in their rush to find non-institutional explanations for political phenomena. The neo-institutionalists argue, on the other hand, that via the study of the effects of political institutions, political science can return to its historical roots, where the purpose of study was to discover something useful and applicable. Indeed, although human decision-makers have little control over the factors that may affect the development of democracy (such as political culture, or the level of economic wealth), human decision-makers do have control over rule-making and constitutions – political institutions are more malleable than cultural, economic, or social variables. This new institutionalism has given rise to a new generation of scholars who advocate a focus on the design of political institutions to affect outcomes such as political democracy, thus making political science generally (and comparative politics more particularly) relevant and applicable. Thus by the end of the twentieth century, comparative politics has, in a sense, come full circle. Like the Ancients, the new emphasis is on how to make comparative politics applicable, and applicability is best accomplished though the careful design of constitutions and political rules.

The Plan of this Book

One of the principal themes of this book is to demonstrate the applicability of comparative politics to contemporary political problems. As mentioned at the beginning of this chapter, the central problem addressed is, how does one design a system that best promotes political democracy? Of course, there is no universally applicable design, and there is no guarantee that such designs will work. The answer clearly depends on some unique historical, economic, social, cultural, and international circumstances that each country faces. Indeed, which institutional arrangements are chosen depends on whether they "fit" these circumstances.

The remainder of this book is designed with this problem in mind. The book is organized into two major sections. In the first section, I outline the contextual factors that detract from or promote the development of democracy, the "soil," if you will, in which the democratic "seed" might be planted. The second section deals with the elements of the "design" of the system – the menu of institutional choices. These include the design of the executive, the legislature, the judiciary, election laws, and the territorial arrangement of the political systems (particularly issues regarding federalism).

Thus, in Chapter 2, we examine the development of democracy in historical perspective, in particular focusing on the experiences of established, old democracies and illustrating their alternative paths to political democracy. These cases include Great Britain, France, the United States, Germany, Russia, and Japan. The use of historical cases to identify patterns of democratic development accomplishes two things. First, it underlines the "uniqueness" of the Western democratic experience, and how to some extent, democracy developed by "accident" under conditions quite different from those faced by countries in political transition now. Second, using these cases identifies the common historical, social, and economic conditions that helped to promote (or detract from) the development of democracy.

In Chapters 3 through Chapter 6, we illustrate the contextual conditions which promote or present problems for democratic development: Economics and Political Development (Chapter 3); Political Culture and

Ethnopolitics (Chapter 4); Social Structure and Politics (Chapter 5); and the Democratization and the Global Environment (Chapter 6). In each of these chapters we examine the prevailing theoretical approaches to how these dimensions affect political development and the emergence of political democracy.

In the second section (Chapter 7 through Chapter 10) we illustrate the institutional "choices" available – which electoral systems to choose (Chapter 7), how to arrange the executive, and especially the pros and cons of presidential versus parliamentary versus "mixed" systems, as well as the internal structuring of the legislative process (Chapter 8). Chapter 9 then deals with the design of the judicial system and the issues related to territorial arrangement of the political system (including issues such as federalism and varieties of local empowerment). Chapter 10 will sum up the principles identified in the book and apply these principles to a set of illustrative cases.

References

Almond, Gabriel (1956) "Comparative Political Systems," *Journal of Politics*, 18 (August): 391–409.

Almond, Gabriel (1966) "Political Theory and Political Science," *The American Political Science Review*, 60 (December): 869–879.

Almond, Gabriel and Coleman, James S. (1960) *The Politics of Developing Areas*, Princeton, NJ: Princeton University Press.

Arendt, Hannah (1971) *The Origins of the Totalitarian State*, New York: Harcourt Brace.

Aristotle (1958) *The Politics of Aristotle*, trans. Ernest Barker, New York: Oxford University Press.

Bay, Christian (1965) "Politics and Pseudo-Politics," *American Political Science Review*, 65 (January): 39–51.

Crowder, Michael (1968) *West Africa under Colonial Rule*, London: Hutchinson.

Dahl, Robert (1961) "The Behavioral Approach in Political Science: Epitaph for a Monument to a Successful Protest," *American Political Science Review*, 55: 763–772.

Easton, David (1957) "An Approach to the Study of Political Systems," *World Politics*, 9 (April): 383–400.

Finer, S.E. (1970) *Comparative Government*, Baltimore, MD: Penguin.

Grofman, Bernard and Lijphart, Arend (eds.) (1984) *Electoral Laws and Their Political Consequences*, New York: Agathon.

Haines, Charles G. (1915) "Report of Committee of Seven on Instruction in Colleges and Universities," *American Political Science Review*, 9 (May): 353–374.

Hall, Peter A. and Taylor, Rosemary C.R. (1996) "Political Science and the Three New Institutionalisms," *Political Studies*, 44 (December): 936–957.

Heaney, Michael T. and Hansen, John Mark (2006) "Building the Chicago School," *American Political Science Review*, 100 (November): 589–596.

Ishiyama, John (1993) "Founding Elections and Transitional Party Development: The Cases of Estonia and Latvia," *Communist and Post-Communist Studies*, 26 (October): 277–299.

Ishiyama, John, Breuning, Marijke, and Lopez, Linda (2006) "A Century of Continuity and (Little) Change in the Undergraduate Political Science Curriculum," *American Political Science Review*, 100 (November): 659–665.

Koeble, Thomas A. (1995) "The New Institutionalism in Political Science and Sociology," *Comparative Politics*, 27 (January): 231–243.

Lasswell, Harold D. (1968) "The Future of the Comparative Method," *Comparative Politics*, 1 (October): 3–18.

Lijphart, Arend (1971) "Comparative Politics and the Comparative Method," *The American Political Science Review*, 65 (September): 682–693.

Lim, Timothy C. (2006) *Doing Comparative Politics: An Introduction to Approaches and Issues*, Boulder, CO: Lynne Rienner.

Machiavelli, Nicolò (1946) *"The Prince" and Other Works*, trans. Allan Gilbert, New York: Hendricks House.

Macridis, Roy (1955) *The Study of Comparative Government*, New York: Random House.

Mahler, Gregory (2000) *Comparative Politics: An Institutional and Cross-National Approach*, Upper Saddle River, NJ: Prentice Hall.

Mannheim, Jarol, Rich, Richard C., and Willnat, Lars (2002) *Empirical Political Analysis*, 5th edition, New York: Longman.

March, James G. and Olsen, Johan (1984) "The New Institutionalism: Organizational Factors in Political Life," *American Political Science Review*, 78 (September): 734–749.

Montesquieu (1949) *The Spirit of the Laws*, trans. Thomas Nugent, New York: Hafner.

Neumann, Robert Gerhard (1951) *European and Comparative Government*, New York: McGraw-Hill.

Ogg, Frederic Austin (1915) *The Governments of Europe*, New York: Macmillan.

Plato (1945) *The Republic of Plato*, trans. Francis M. Cornford, London: Oxford University Press.

Robertson, David (ed.) (1993) *A Dictionary of Modern Politics*, 2nd edition, London: Europa Publications Limited.

Rousseau, Jean-Jacques (1964) *The First and Second Discourses*, eds. Roger D. Masters and Judith Masters, New York: St. Martin's Press.

Susser, Bernard (1992) "Introductory Essay to David Easton, 'Categories for the Systems Analysis of Politics,'" in Bernard Susser (ed.) *Approaches to the Study of Politics*, New York: Macmillan, pp. 180–188.

Taagepera, Rein and Shugart, Matthew (1989) *Seats and Votes*, New Haven, CT: Yale University Press.

Thelen, Kathleen (1999) "Historical Institutionalism in Comparative Perspective," *Annual Review of Political Science*, 2: 369–404.

Tucker, Robert C. (1972) *The Marx-Engels Reader*, New York: Norton.

Weber, Max (1964) *The Theory of Social and Economic Organization*, ed. Talcott Parsons, New York: Macmillan.

Wiarda, Howard (2000) *Introduction to Comparative Politics: Concepts and Processes*, New York: Wadsworth.

Wilson, Woodrow (1889) *The State*, New York: Heath.

Zahariadis, Nikolaos (1997) *Theory, Case, and Method in Comparative Politics*, New York: Harcourt Brace College Publishers.

2

Democracy and Democratization in Historical Perspective

Introduction

In this chapter, we begin our examination of the process of democratization by adopting a long-term historical perspective – why did some states of the world become democratic as they entered the twentieth century whereas others did not? Whatever one's perspective on the development of comparative politics as a discipline, there is no denying that the discipline itself emerged largely as the result of a somewhat parochial focus on the West in general and Europe in particular. Most of the early studies of democratization and democracy were almost entirely based on the Western experience. Thus, most of our existing theories of democracy are based largely upon the historical experiences of a very few states.

In order to understand the evolution of comparative political theories of democratization, it makes sense to examine their historical roots. In the first section of this chapter I examine, from a historical perspective, the factors which affected the long-term political developments in a selected group of states – England, the United States, France, Germany, Russia and Japan. Although each state's history has elements that make it unique, the trajectories of these six societies outline very different models by which states became democratic; England is held up by many scholars as the archetype of gradual democratization; the United States represents a less stable variant of democratization, that was punctuated by a major civil war; France's history has been characterized by periods of rapid democratization followed by periods of reaction; Germany democratized only very late and its first attempt at democratization was arrested by the horrors of

Comparative Politics: Principles of Democracy and Democratization, First Edition.
John T. Ishiyama.
© 2012 John T. Ishiyama. Published 2012 by Blackwell Publishing Ltd.

Nazism, only to have democracy partially imposed by victorious allies later, as was also the case in Japan; Russia's democratic experiment has only just begun and its history has been marked by extended periods of autocratic and totalitarian rule.

The classic literature on democratization and political development in European politics has tended to focus on "long-wave" historical factors such as the socioeconomic transformation of society to explain the rise of European democracy (Bendix, 1964; Moore, 1966; Gerschenkron, 1979). Although it is tempting to think of historical factors as *determining* the process of democratization, such an approach, while useful in describing "background conditions" or "context," leaves little room for human choice. Indeed, as Giovanni Sartori (1968) reminds us, we often forget in most countries in Europe, democracy did not just "emerge," but was in fact the product of human choices made at critical moments in time. Granted, these choices were constrained by circumstances – political leaders cannot simply engineer democracy when no social or economic bases exist which can support it. Nonetheless, it is important to remember that democracy did not *just happen*, nor was it predetermined by history or culture. Rather, the emergence of democracy was the product of both long-term trends *and* short-term institutional choices made by very human political leaders.

Nonetheless long-term historical trends *do matter* and *do affect* the "constraints" facing democratizing (or non-democratizing) states. In this chapter, we will explore how theories of democratization which have been built largely on the historical experiences of a few key countries are instructive in our efforts to understand the challenges facing states in the developing world.

Democracy and Democratization

If our focus is on democracy and democratization, what then is democracy and what is democratization? The literal meaning of democracy comes from a combination of two Greek words *demos* (people) and *kratos* (rule) and, at its core, "democracy is a form of government in which the people rule" (Sørenson, 1993, p. 3). However, beyond the literal meaning of democracy, there has been considerable debate as to the criteria which distinguish democracies from non-democracies. A relatively narrow definition of democracy has been offered by Joseph Schumpeter, who viewed democracy as simply a method for choosing political leadership: "The

democratic method is that institutional arrangement for arriving at political decisions in which individuals acquire the power to decide by means of
a competitive struggle for the people's vote" (Schumpeter, 1950, p. 260).
Another, more exclusive definition is offered by David Held who argued
that, "Democracy entails a political community in which there is some
form of *political equality* among the people" (Held, 1996, p. 1, italics in
original). The existence of equal rights (and, accordingly, equal obligations)
is the principal feature of political democracy.

Between the rather inclusive conception of political democracy offered
by Schumpeter and the exclusive definition offered by Held is that
offered by Robert Dahl (1989). For Dahl, "democracy" was an ideal-type
political system where citizens have the opportunity: (1) to formulate their
preferences; (2) to signify their preferences to their fellow citizens and the
government; and (3) to have their preferences weighed equally in the
conduct of government. However, since no system can fully approximate
democracy as an ideal type, Dahl prefers to use the term "polyarchies" to
refer to existing "non-ideal" democracies. Polyarchies are characterized by
the following:

1   Control over government decisions is constitutionally vested in elected
    officials.
2   Elected officials are chosen in free, fair and frequent elections.
3   Practically all adults have the right to vote in elections.
4   Practically all adults have the right to run for elective offices.
5   Citizens have the right to express themselves freely on political matters.
6   Alternative sources of information are freely and legally available.
7   Everyone has the right to form parties, pressure groups and other asso-
    ciations independent of the state.

(Dahl, 1989, p. 10ff)

One could distinguish empirically between different kinds of polyarchy in
terms of two dimensions: competition for office and political participation.
Systems that approached the democratic ideal (polyarchies) are characterized by high degrees of competition and high degrees of participation.
Systems that have lower degrees of competition and participation are more
autocratic.

Yet, critics of this approach argue that this conceptualization is "static"
and cannot distinguish between democratic and non-democratic regimes,
but only varying degrees of polyarchy. Furthermore, this conceptualization

of democracy cannot identify how democracies emerge from non-democratic regimes, which is the case in most European countries. What Richard Rose, William Mishler, and Christian Haerpfer (1998) prefer is the "democracy in competition" approach to conceptualizing democracy, or the notion that democracy is defined not relative to an "ideal" as is polyarchy, but relative to other non-democratic alternatives. Thus they opt for a definition based on Linz and Stepan's work (1996), who identify four characteristics of central importance in characterizing any regime: (1) the rule of law; (2) the institutions of civil society; (3) free and fair elections; and (4) the extent to which governors are held accountable. *Rule of law* means that no individuals, including rulers, stand above the law. *Civil society* relates to the existence of socio-political groups, autonomous from the state, which allow for the free articulation of popular interests and keep in check the uncontrolled growth of the state (see Diamond, 1994; Fine and Rai, 1997). *Free and fair elections* refer to the existence of real competition for office. Finally, *accountability* refers to the extent to which those who govern are responsible to others for their political actions. Taken individually, none of these criteria are sufficient to define a democracy, or any other regime, for that matter. Only in combination do these characteristics define different kinds of regimes.

Perhaps one way to combine these two very different conceptions of democracy is to think to them as measuring two very different things. On the one hand, the Dahlian definition of polyarchy is useful in distinguishing between different *varieties* of democracy – some systems are closer to the democratic ideal than others. On the other hand, the conception of democracy favored by Rose, Mishler, and Haerpfer (1998) and Linz and Stepan (1996) provides the minimalist criteria for democracy, and is useful not only in distinguishing between democracies and non-democracies, but also regimes that are *democratizing*. From this conception we can identify the minimal thresholds that countries pass in order to qualify as democracies – the rule of law, the development of the institutions of civil society, the existence of free and fair elections, and the extent to which governors are held accountable. In order to gain a comparative understanding of existing political systems in all, we need to account for differences among countries which have *already passed the minimal thresholds which qualify it as democratic* (that is, differences in levels of participation and competition) and those countries which have only partially met the minimal criteria for democracy, are approaching the minimal criteria, and those which are very far away from the minimal criteria.

If this is what we mean by *democracy*, what, then, do we mean by the process of *democratization*? *Democratization* is the process by which societies develop toward democracy. Some, like Freeman and Snidal (1982, p. 300) define democratization as the extension of citizenship and the franchise. Yet, this presupposes that meaningful elections take place and that political elites will abide by outcomes of such elections, which implies at least the notion that a rule of law exists and that leaders are accountable to someone. On the other hand, if we consider the minimal definition of democracy as the rule of law, the development of the institutions of civil society, the practice of free and fair elections and the establishment of accountability of those who govern, then democratization is the process by which the rule of law, elections and leadership accountability is established, and where civil society develops. Once established, the *expansion of democracy* involves extending the degree of competition and participation, through such mechanisms as broader enfranchisement (participation) and greater competition.

A Historical Approach to Democratization

Although different scholars emphasize different aspects of the historical development of democracy, nearly all note the socially and politically disruptive character of industrialization and economic modernization. Industrialization, it is argued, is a disruptive force which unleashes new social forces that can overwhelm existing political systems (Deutsch, 1961; Huntington, 1968; Gerschenkron, 1979). Industrialization creates "progressive" social classes such as the industrial bourgeoisie and the industrial proletariat, who lead the way to the construction of modern society. This creates political tensions for the old regime – these new social classes place demands for political participation on the existing political order, and challenge the right of the traditional elite (the landed nobility) to rule. In addition, industrialization also created social tensions between these new classes and the classes of the old feudal order, the peasantry and the landed nobility. Further, as French sociologist Emile Durkheim noted in his study of *social anomie*, industrialization and modernization stripped away the comforting myths which had sustained the old regime (such as the reliance on mysticism to explain social reality), leaving people with a sense of groundlessness and helplessness in the face of the modern world. Further, as many scholars of nationalism (such as Deutsch, 1953) note, industrialization and modernization gave the impetus for the development of modern nationalism. Although nationalism can be a constructive force in that it brings people together, it can also be a centrifugal force, particularly in societies which are multiethnic in nature.

A key argument made from this historical perspective has to do with the *timing* of political and economic transformations (Moore, 1966) or whether or not certain transformations had taken place prior to the coming of industrialization. To use a crude analogy, we can think of industrialization as the onset of a very turbulent storm at sea; whether or not the ship (in this case the existing political system) survives and makes the passage to democracy depends a great deal on how it was built prior to the coming of the storm. In general, we can distinguish between three different kinds of explanations which deal with the pre-industrial transformations – those that focus on social explanations (largely based on class analysis); those that concentrate on political transformations prior to industrialization; and those that focus on the importance of culture and national identity.

An example of the historical approach is the work of Barrington Moore (1966). He holds that the key to understanding the process of political development (and the emergence of both democracy and non-democracy in the twentieth century) is whether or not the social and economic system of feudalism had been transformed *prior* to the coming of industrialization. For Moore, industrialization created the social forces (such as the industrial bourgeoisie and the proletariat) which paved the way for the construction of modern society. However, if the remnants of the old social order persist, then the transition to modernity is likely to be difficult. Indeed, whether or not a democratic outcome ultimately emerges depends on whether the old order had been swept away prior to the shock of industrialization. Essentially, Moore argues that feudalism was made up of social classes who were inherently "anti-modern": the feudal lords who sought to protect their privileges based on land ownership, and the peasantry, who yearned for independence and land of their own, but who did not challenge the basis of feudal society. The more they remained important social forces, the more difficult was democratic development.

In addition to the approach which focuses on the development of class relations, there are those who focus on political developments, particularly the relationship between monarchs and people (Bendix, 1964). From this perspective, the key factor explaining the development of democracy in Europe lay in the struggle for supremacy between the monarch and the nobility (prior to industrialization). If the monarch "won" and established absolutism, then the principle of "accountability" and the rule of law, so important to the development of democracy, were not established prior to industrialization and social mobilization. On the other hand, if the monarch "lost" and the nobility won, then the principle of accountability was established prior to industrialization. Countries which had established the rule of law and accountability of the monarch were likely to have a much easier time making the transition to democracy during the period of industrialization than those which had not.

A third factor which affects the historical development of democracy was the extent to which a national identity had developed (see, for instance, Charles Tilly, 1975). To a large degree, the existence of a strong sense of community binding people together which transcended class and other social lines, mitigated the centrifugal, divisive forces generated by industrialization. From this perspective, a French worker and a French aristocrat might think of themselves as French first, as opposed to their social class affiliation, if a strong sense of national identity had already been developed. This identity might have a dampening effect on the divisive pressures generated by industrialization and modernization. However, if that identity was weak or non-existent, then the divisive pressures generated by modernization were likely to be quite acute, making the smooth transition to democracy quite problematic.

Yet national identity is not simply the sense of having something in common with others – be it racial, ethnic, religious or otherwise. Indeed, scholars have distinguished between cultural national identities and political national identities. Friedrich Meinecke spoke of the *Kulturnation* (the largely passive cultural community) distinct from the *Staatsnation*, the active self-determining political nation (Smith, 1991, p. 8). Smith (ibid., p. 9) argues that any national identity involves some sense of "political community however tenuous." Such a political community in turn implies at least "some common institutions and single code of rights and duties for all members of the community." Liah Greenfield suggests that nationalism and a political national identity are best understood as an umbrella term for the variety of ways a group can be self-constituted as a "people"; in other words, as a territorially and socially defined collectivity that see themselves as "the bearer of sovereignty, the central object of loyalty, and the basis for collective solidarity" (1992, pp. 3–4). Thus a national community is not defined as simply allegiance to the state, but the recognition that the community, held together by some cultural or political bond, is sovereign. In practical terms, then, a national political identity persists beyond loyalty to a king, or prince, or emperor. This sense of common political purpose is what helps a polity weather the storm of modernization.

Hence three questions are key to explaining why democratization was relatively painless for some European states and why it was painful in others. These are:

1 To what extent had the principle of accountability and the rule of law been established prior to the coming of industrialization?
2 To what extent had a mass national identity been established prior to the Industrial Revolution?
3 To what extent had the old social order been swept away prior to the coming of industrialization?

These three questions are addressed in the follow case studies of Britain, France, the United States, Germany, Russia, and Japan.

Six Historical Cases

Britain

The contemporary British political system emerged out of seven hundred years of gradual change, beginning with the Magna Carta of 1215 which placed some limits on the Norman kings, to the adoption of the Parliament Act of 1911, which effectively transferred final decision-making power from the aristocratic House of Lords to the popularly elected House of Commons. One of the most striking (and perhaps most often-mentioned) features of British political development is the feature of political continuity and relatively stable development toward democracy. To a large extent, although Britain has been held up as a model of political democracy, in many ways it is an exception to the rule. Nonetheless, the British pattern of gradual development toward democracy is similar to other European cases (such as the Netherlands and the Scandinavian countries) and hence represents an example of one pattern of democratization.

This degree of continuity in British politics and political development sets it apart from many other European states. Indeed, as Gertrude Himmelfarb (1968, p. 292) wrote, the true "miracle" of modern England was "not that she has been spared revolution, but she has assimilated so many revolutions – industrial, economic, political, cultural – without recourse to revolution." What factors caused the "gradualism" which was so characteristic of the course of English political development? To understand the development of the British political system, we must make reference to the three developments discussed above, all of which occurred prior to the Industrial Revolution: (1) the development of an English national identity; (2) the social transformation of English feudalism; and (3) the development of the principles of accountability and the rule of law which accompanied the ascendance of Parliament over the English Crown.

The trend toward political centralization and the development of an English political national identity

One of the most distinctive characteristics of England in the Middle Ages was its high degree of central government control, even under feudalism. This feature is particularly noteworthy in that the normal tendency at the time on the European continent was for political authority to be quite fragmented, with real power in the hands of the landed nobility. In an age when standing armies were virtually unknown on the Continent, it was commonplace for a king in England to be owed military service and loyalty from nobles whose livelihoods were provided through the possession of land and the serfs or peasants who were bound to the land. On the Continent this practice typically led to the growing independence of the nobility who often warred with one another or with the king in order to increase their territory and enhance their wealth or power.

England largely avoided this fate because of the country's early vulnerability to foreign invasion. In the tenth century, the Anglo-Saxons united under Alfred the Great in order to expel the Danes. In the eleventh century the country was conquered and united first by the Danes (1017) and then by the Normans (1066). Under Norman rule, the trend toward increasing the powers of the Crown continued. Under Henry II (1154–1189), the Crown obtained the power to appoint and dismiss the sheriffs who controlled local government, wrested control of the administration of justice by creating the royal courts, and raised taxes on noble and commoner alike. The expansion of central authority was resisted, however, exemplified by the Magna Carta in which King John was forced by his nobles to curtail the expansion of royal powers.

However, an extended war with France (the Hundred Years War, 1337–1453) again expanded royal prerogatives. It was also in this period that a legislative body, "Parliament," was created. Originally, the body had been convened by the English Crown to act as a consultative body and a forum made up of the nobility from which the Crown sought additional revenues to finance the war with France.

After a period of Civil War in the fifteenth century (the War of the Roses), the Tudor monarchs, Henry VII, Henry VIII and his daughter Elizabeth I, continued this trend toward the strengthening of central authority. The strengthening of central authority fostered national integra- tion. This allowed Henry VIII in 1534 to remove by fiat, and with relatively little serious opposition, the English Church from the control of Rome and place it under the Crown's command. Wars of religion between Catholics and Protestants were to ravage continental Europe for much of the century and a half after Martin Luther first challenged the Vatican in 1517, but England itself was scarcely touched (Erickson and Havran, 1968: 120–174).

Thus, the trend in English political development throughout the period of the Renaissance was toward a greater centralization of political authority. This was largely due to external stimuli where the threat of an invasion and later the threat from imperial continental powers like Spain served to strengthen the Crown, leading to greater national integration and the emer- gence of an English political national identity.

The social transformation of English feudalism and the rise of the democratic impulse

Despite the trend toward the centralization of royal authority, there were developments within English society which counterbalanced the rise of the power of the Crown. Again the impetus for these changes originated from abroad. Of the numerous economic developments in the late Middle Ages in continental Europe, perhaps the most important was the growth of trade with the East, particularly the establishment of trade routes in the four- teenth century with the near East and China, which led to the emergence of the great trading city-states of Venice, Genoa, and commerce centers of the Mediterranean. The rise in commerce around the Mediterranean had an enormous impact economically on England – it gave rise to an increase in the demand for English wool.

One particularly important characteristic of wool production, as opposed to the production of agricultural foodstuffs, is that, wool production requires very little peasant labor. What wool production does require is a

great deal of land for pasturing animals, not a great deal of labor for production. Thus, with the rise in the demand for fine English wool, there
came a greater demand for land and a lesser demand for labor. This provided an incentive for the landed nobility to prohibit peasants from using
valuable pasture lands or "commons" which had historically been open to
them to supplement their crop during hard times and pasture their animals.
The "enclosures" of the commons led to the gradual migration of the peasantry from the countryside to the cities, thus leading to the depopulation
of the English rural areas and the growth of a proto-proletariat in the
English cities (Moore, 1966).

Over time, the enclosures had two significant social effects (ibid.). First,
it led to increases in the population of the cities, thus leading to greater
pressures for colonization, especially of the New World and later Australia.
Moreover, the enclosures effectively "destroyed" the peasantry as a class and
gave rise to the proto-proletariat in the cities. Second, the rise in external
demand for wool and the enclosures also marked the transformation of the
nobility from feudal nobility, to profit-minded commercial landlords.
Thus, although the English nobility did not disappear, their *raison d'être*
had fundamentally transformed, effectively eliminating the English nobility as a feudal class. Thus, long before the coming of the period of industrialization, English feudalism had been fundamentally transformed.
Although the process had begun well before the outbreak of the English
Civil War in 1649 and was completed only after the end of the Napoleonic
Wars, the "enclosures were the final blow that destroyed the whole structure
of English peasant society embodied the traditional village" (ibid., p. 11).

The transformation of English feudalism had important consequences
on English political development as well. The stimulus of trade and commerce led to the growing economic influence of the urban merchant class
and the market-oriented landowners. This growing economic influence, in
turn, led to gradual expansion of their political influence and to increasing
demands from these classes for a say in the political process and the limitation of state intervention into commerce. By the sixteenth century these
interests found greater voice in Parliament, the institution that had been
established in the fourteenth century to act as an advisory council to the
Crown. Throughout the sixteenth century and into the early seventeenth
centuries, tension grew between the Parliament, which was increasingly
under the influence of the commercial classes (both the merchants and the
commercial nobility), and the Crown, which sought to protect the royal
prerogatives so painstakingly built up since the time of Alfred the Great
(Bendix, 1964).

The struggle between Parliament and the Crown came to a head in the seventeenth century when opposition arose to the Stuart monarchy which had sought to continue the trend toward the establishment of absolute authority and the centralization of the power. In particular, two Stuart monarchs, Charles I (1625–1649) and James II (1685–1688) admired the model of absolute monarchy as exemplified by Louis XIV of France, especially his ability to raise taxes, maintain a large standing army, and rule without interference from any national representative institution.

On the other hand, parliamentary forces saw no need for a large standing army, given that England was protected from threatening forces on the Continent by the English Channel. Indeed, it was feared that the purpose for the creation of a large standing army was to suppress all opposition in England itself. Moreover, commercial forces in Parliament voiced open opposition to the policies of the monarch, such as the attempt to curtail the enclosures of the common lands in order to protect the peasantry, as well as its propensity to sell monopoly privileges in manufacturing and trade (Erickson and Havran, 1968).

In 1649, the Stuart monarch Charles I was overthrown, executed, and replaced by a protectorate under Oliver Cromwell. In 1660, the Stuart monarchy was restored under Charles II. In 1689, largely as the result of James II's (Charles II's son) efforts to reimpose absolutism, Parliament deposed James by the "Glorious Revolution," and adopted the English Bill of Rights which effectively limited royal powers and established parliamentary supremacy. So fundamental was the transformation of England that Moore notes that without the triumph of "the capitalist principle and that of parliamentary democracy ... in the seventeenth century, it is hard to imagine how English society could have modernized peacefully ... in the eighteenth and nineteenth centuries" (Moore, 1966, p. 20).

Thus, by the beginning of the eighteenth century, the development of a rudimentary democracy in England had already taken place. The rule of law had already developed earlier, but with the establishment of parliamentary supremacy came the consolidation of the rule of law and the principle of the "popular" accountability of the king. Moreover, with the economic transformation of English society came the rise of a proto "civil society" and sociopolitical groups, made up of various associations of elite groups. Even the practice of electing Members of Parliament had already been established, although the right to vote was extremely limited – only a very small percentage of the male adult population had the right to vote – less than 2 percent of the adult population well into the nineteenth century.

Nonetheless, the basic framework of a minimal democracy had been established prior to the coming of the Industrial Revolution towards the end of the eighteenth century and the beginning of the nineteenth. When industrialization gave rise to new social groups clamoring for a political voice (such as the new industrial bourgeoisie, the middle classes and the working classes), at first governmental authorities responded with repression. Eventually, however, the predominantly aristocratic leaders chose to give way to these demands. This did not require an overhaul of the institutional framework of the existing system, but merely the broadening of participation. The first breakthrough was the Reform Act of 1832 which doubled the size of the electorate (to perhaps 3 percent of the adult population) and redistributed seats to accord better with the population shifts which had taken place. New industrial cities like Manchester, Leeds, and Birmingham gained representation in Parliament for the first time, and many of the "rotten boroughs" (towns whose populations had declined drastically or disappeared altogether) lost representation. This process was carried much farther in 1867, when the Second Reform Act was passed, giving the vote to all men in urban boroughs who paid property taxes. In 1872, the secret ballot was introduced, making it much more difficult for employees or landlords to dictate the votes of their workers or tenant farmers. Reforms in 1884 and 1885 expanded the franchise to those who paid property taxes in rural districts. In 1918, there was the recognition of the idea that every adult male should be able to vote, but only women over the age of 30 were granted the right to vote. In 1948, universal adult suffrage was fully granted.

Thus the deepening and expansion of democracy in England did not require the building of a completely new stadium in which the "game" of politics was to be played, but merely a widening of the entrance ways to allow new participants into the game. This meant that the ship of state did not have to be rebuilt in the rough seas of social and economic transformation, and the passage to full democracy in England was a relatively smooth one.

France

If it has been common to hold up the example of Britain as illustrative of the classic model of capitalist economic and democratic political development in Europe, it is equally common to use France as illustrative of a relatively unstable and checkered path toward political democracy. Indeed,

French political development during the period of economic modernization in the nineteenth century was marred by lurches forward to democracy
(such as the revolutions in 1789, 1836, 1848, 1870) followed by periods of
"thermidor" or the slipping backwards into authoritarian or monarchical
arrangements. What explains this long-term trend of "discontinuity" in the
French case in contrast to the stable trajectory as illustrated by English
democratization?

To illustrate these differences, it is important to consider French historical development in terms of the development of a French national identity,
the timing of the social transformation of French feudalism, and the timing
of the development of proto democratic principles and institutions.

The development of a French political national identity

France can be considered the cradle of modern nationalism (Talmon,
1968). In many ways, the development of a French political national identity proceeded along lines somewhat similar to the process in England, with
the growth of the concentration of political power in the hands of the
Crown in the sixteenth and seventeenth centuries, which promoted a sense
of French political national identity. This notion of "la belle France" was
further developed in intellectual circles in the eighteenth century by scholars like Jean-Jacques Rousseau, who argued that a community of people
stood apart from any particular ruler, that what defined citizenship was not
loyalty to the Crown but an affinity for a national political community in
which sovereignty was invested (Talmon, 1968, pp. 95–96).

Yet, according to Roy Macridis (1990, pp. 66–67), the development of a
French political national identity was only partially accomplished. Unlike
in England where the growth of the state coincided with a growing sense
of English community, the French political culture was marked by a large
degree of dissent as opposed to consensus. For Macridis, there are two
distinct traits of French political culture which set it apart from British
political culture. First of all, the development of individualism or, in other
words, the citizen's distrust of the state and its agency, and a general tendency to seek to be left alone. Individual concerns and aspirations were at
odds with collective and state action. This attitude of distrust of the state
was in part due to the image that the state served the interests of those who
held power rather than the interests of all. The French therefore seemed to
avoid associational activity based on mutual effort and trust. They instead
developed defensive attitudes and defensive mechanisms – the family, the
trade unions, the village, their deputies in Parliament – against state action.

In other words, France, unlike Britain, had not resolved the crisis of integration. The identity of the French remained largely at individual levels rather than an identity with the nation.

A second product of the French Revolution, and more particularly the Napoleonic organization of the state, has been referred to as "statism." Statism refers to the idea that the state (the object of suspicion) is considered the sole instrument to provide a service and to solve problems. In this sense, the French view themselves as "administered." In other words, using Gabriel Almond and Sidney Verba's (1963) terms, as "subjects." Their inclination is to wait for the state, that they distrust, to respond to demands and needs. The result is that if latent demands exist, they continue to build up, ultimately resorting to extra-political means to accomplish political ends.

Macridis argues that the political history of France produced behavioral patterns in French political culture – the French political culture has historically been fragmented rather than consensual, unstable rather than gradualist, and ideological rather than pragmatic, emphasizing violent and abrupt chance as opposed to compromise and agreement. Thus, if anything, the development of a French national identity was less complete than the development of an English national identity prior to the coming of industrialization and economic modernization.

The transformation of French feudalism

In contrast to developments in England, the commercial impulse in France in the sixteenth, seventeenth and eighteenth centuries was considerably weaker. Much of this had to do with the structure and product of French agrarian feudalism, most notably the fact the French estate did not produce wool for market, as was the case in England, but labor-intensive foodstuffs, particularly wine and olives. As international trade expanded, the demand for these products increased.

The increasing demand for French agricultural products had social consequences which were very different than in the case of the transformation of English feudalism. The feudal landlords had much less incentive to rid themselves of surplus labor as was the case with the English lord. Because of the labor-intensive nature of viniculture, the landed gentry were forced to retain peasant labor rather than rid themselves of it. Thus, unlike the case of Britain, the commercial impulse among the French nobility did not result in any significant attempts at enclosure. Rather, profits were made from renting commons lands to peasants rather than hiring their labor to tend the flocks, especially after Louis XIV (1643–1715) required that the lords spend a considerable part of the year at the royal palace at Versailles in order to keep a watchful eye over them. Thus, rather than transforming into a "rural capitalist" class which would promote the limitation of royal authority (as was the case in England), the French nobility turned into a class of absentee landlords, dependent on the Crown for subsidies and support.

These developments also had an impact on the French peasantry. First, this gave the peasantry a measure of autonomy, since nobles became interested only in collecting rents, and set out to rent estate land. On the other hand, the commercialization of agriculture also gave rise to the "differentiations" of the peasantry, into those who succeeded and those who did not, or the emergence of a class of "rich peasants." These developments thus did not weaken or destroy the medieval peasantry, but in fact strengthened it. As Moore (1966, p. 55) notes, "In contrast to England, commercial influences as they penetrated into the French countryside did not undermine and destroy the feudal framework. If anything, they infused new life into old arrangements."

In addition, unlike in the English case where the political struggle between the Crown and the commercialized nobility resulted in the victory of the latter, symbolized by the English Civil War, in the French case the outcome of the struggle did not result in the victory of the aristocracy. Rather, the Crown, especially under the rule of Louis XIV (1643–1715), also called the "Sun King," succeeded in consolidating the power of the Crown and created an absolutist monarchy. One of the principal ways this was accomplished was through the cooptation of the nobility through the sale of high offices in the bureaucracy. Any state requires the institution of some bureaucracy to administer the affairs of a nation. The sale of office accomplished two things for the French absolutist state: First, it accomplished the task of raising capital; second, this practice allowed for the recruitment of bureaucracy which was dependent on royal favors.

Thus, by the beginning of the eighteenth century, the nobility became dependent on the Crown. There were no social forces to speak of, outside a few intellectuals, who clamored for the limitation of royal prerogative and the establishment of the principles of rule of law and political accountability. Further, unlike in England, where the elite groups developed independent of the state, leading to the development of a proto civil society prior to the coming of industrialization, such was not the case in pre-revolutionary France.

The French Revolution (1789–1799) can be viewed within the context of the overall pattern of French political development prior to economic modernization and industrialization. Factors which contributed to the revolution were the weakening of the French state in the eighteenth century as a result of continual wars with England which had effectively bankrupted the royal treasury by the 1780s; the decision in 1786 to normalize relations with England by lowering tariff barriers to English manufactured imports, which caused large-scale unemployment among the urban working class; the disastrous grain harvests of 1787 and 1788; and the inability or unwillingness of the French state to grant tax and rent relief to the rural poor. The storming of the Bastille on July 14, 1789, was the spark which ignited the conflagration which would engulf France for the next five years, and lead to the demise of the French monarchy.

It is not our intention here to go into great detail about the particulars of the French Revolution. Rather, what is important are the consequences of the French Revolution for subsequent political developments. One of the most important socio-political consequences of the revolution was that it effectively destroyed the nobility as a class which acted as an impediment to the development of liberal democratic institutions. However, the revolution itself did not destroy the peasantry but in fact strengthened this class which was decidedly anti-democratic and anti-capitalist in attitude. In turn, this tended to create a degree of intolerance between the masses and the bourgeoisie, as well as lingering distrust between the proletariat and the peasantry. This, in turn, led to the relatively discontinuous and lurching effort toward the institution of French democracy which really did not begin in full until after 1848 and was characterized by a high measure of instability until only very recently. In other words, the institutions of democracy were only partially in place prior to French industrialization and the events of the past had made the lower classes decidedly anti-capitalist in orientation.

The result has been that major class cleavages, when they emerged as an inevitable part of industrialization and economic development, tended to be exacerbated. Indeed, the pressures generated by industrialization tended to create centrifugal tendencies. In other words, as new classes entered the scene, they were not incorporated by a willing elite, but rather were viewed as an enemy who was to be marginalized. The result was that the first 70 years of French political history were marred by lurches between brief periods of a Republic, followed by monarchical restoration and Bonapartism, a pattern which ended only with the establishment of the Third Republic in 1870.

The impetus for large-scale French industrialization resulted from the ashes of the defeat at Sedan at the hands of the newly unified German Empire. French democracy as well was born out of the ruins of the Bonapartist restoration under Napoleon III. The Third Republic (1870–1940) was beset throughout much of its history by internal problems. As new political forces entered the scene in the late nineteenth century, the socially and politically conservative forces sought to defend their prerogatives against the socialist onslaught. In other words, the unwillingness of the Third Republic to allow new social elements into the governing structure led to political paralysis and the emergence of extremist parties, which sought power outside of the governing structure.

The Fourth Republic, established after World War II (1946–1959), was, like the Third Republic, a product of war. As a result of the "victory," French politics had become more fractured than ever. Indeed, the principal resistance to the German occupation had been the Maquis, which was heavily staffed and supported by the French Communist Party. Following the war, the Fourth Republic sought to maximize the representativeness of French politics in order to form some kind of post-war accommodation among the various political forces.

This led to continual legislative deadlock and continual governmental crisis which was exacerbated by the loss of French colonial possessions in Indochina after Diem Bien Phu in 1954 and the continuing Algerian War. The final straw for the Fourth Republic was the military coup by Foreign Legionnaires in Algeria and the revolt of the Pied Noirs (French residents of Algeria) as well the threat of civil war. This crisis led to the appointment of wartime Free French leader Charles de Gaulle as the new French premier. He was invested with emergency powers which included the power to revise the Constitution. However, de Gaulle went far beyond his original mandate and wrote an entirely new constitution, adopted on June 3, 1958. It featured a vastly strengthened presidency and executive. In effect, de Gaulle had staged a bloodless constitutional coup. Yet, since the establishment of the Fifth Republic, France has emerged as a relatively stable democracy (Macridis and Brown, 1960, especially Chapter 10).

The United States

Although in many ways the study of the development of US politics has been outside the subfield of comparative politics, the American case fits our framework quite well. In many ways, like England, the institutions of participatory democracy were already in place (albeit dominated by landed elites). The principle of accountability of those who governed had long been a part of the political tradition in the thirteen colonies (to varying degrees, of course) and was a centerpiece in the justification for the War of Independence against Great Britain. Further, the mechanisms of political participation were already in place with the use of popularly elected assemblies that gradually gained greater power relative to the English-appointed Governors – to such an extent that in Massachusetts and then in New Jersey, North Carolina, and Pennsylvania, the assemblies showed their strength by refusing to pay their governors any salary for several years. Thus, as with the case of England, the democratic institutional framework was already in place prior to the onset of industrial expansion later in the nineteenth century.

The key differences between the American route to modern democracy had to do with the relatively new nature of the United States as a country. First, the United States did not have a well-developed sense of a political *national* identity. Rather, regional or state identities predominated. For instance, a citizen in Virginia was more apt to identify as a Virginian (as Robert E. Lee, the great Confederate General did in 1861) first, and as an American second. Indeed, as some historians have noted this plural American identity (reflected in the statement that the "United States are a great country").

Second, there was also the divided socioeconomic nature of the country in the first half of the eighteenth century, at first, largely a legacy of mercantilist economic relations with England prior to the War of Independence, but later intensified with the expansion westward and the introduction of the agricultural-industrial production of cotton in the South. By 1860, these lines of cleavage had developed into three distinct forms of society in different parts of the country: a cotton-producing South; a food-producing West made of free farmers; and a rapidly industrializing North-east. These national and socioeconomic divisions were to directly affect the rather violent course of the development of American democracy.

An incomplete national identity in the United States
Following the War of Independence from the British Empire, the former colonies emerged largely as a loose collection of allied states. Indeed, the first years of the Republic were focused largely at building a kind of political unity from the very different colonies, with the "Federalist" faction centered in the more trade-oriented North-east, pitted against the "anti-Federalists" centered in the agrarian (and slave-owning) South. Indeed, several scholars

have noted that unlike in England, an American national identity was relatively incomplete at the time of independence (McWilliams, 1980; Murrin, 1987, p. 384; Duncan, 1995). Generally, or so the argument goes, in the early years of the American Republic, localism and local identities predominated. However, to say that an American national identity did not exist at the beginning of the nineteenth century would be inaccurate. Indeed, as Russell Arben Fox notes, it is a mistake to simply treat the debate between the Federalists and the Anti-Federalists in the first years after American independence as a debate between "nationalists" and "localists." Rather, the debate was between different conceptions of "nationhood." On the one hand, the Anti-Federalists like Patrick Henry and Melancton Smith held a "sentimental" vision of nation, speaking of a "national character," "American spirit," and the "necessity of Union." The national vision of the Anti-Federalists was rooted in George Mason's claim that preserving the moral "Attachment of the Citizens to their Laws, to their Freedom, and to their Country would do more to bind America together than any political construct" (Mason, cited in Fox, 1999). In contrast, the Federalist sense of an American nation was more akin to a unified *Staatsnation* with common institutions and a national political system.

Thus the early American sense of national identity as *incomplete* – incomplete in the sense that the process of fusing the collective sense of being American with a political identity and the creation of a centralized unified state was not fully developed. Although there is little doubt that Americans had developed a sense of self, and a common bound (or the idea of *Kulturnation*), and the idea that as a collective they were sovereign, what was missing was the idea that sovereignty was embedded in a unified state, as opposed to a collection of state governments. As Liah Greenfield writes, the affirmation of a specific "American identity" was not originally accompanied by the "sense that Americans constituted a [political] unity" (1992, p. 11). To a great extent, this question of American national identity being consistent with a centralizing and unified national state was not resolved until the American Civil War (1861–1865).

An American feudalism?

Beyond the incomplete nature of the American national identity (at least one that was consonant with a unified political form), there also existed significant social and economic differences between the various regions of the country. As Barrington Moore (1966) argues, the main differences were regional, pitting the cotton-producing South with the industrializing North and the food-producing West. However, to characterize the socioeconomic milieu in the ante-bellum United States as *feudal* would be inaccurate. Indeed, unlike England or France, the battles between a pre-commercial landed aristocracy and a monarchy were not part of American history. Indeed, commercial agricultural production had always been an important part of production in the South, from the time of earliest Virginian tobacco plantations onward. Further, American society has never had a massive class of peasants comparable to the agrarian societies of Europe and Asia.

Nonetheless. a tremendously violent civil war did result from the industrialization of the country. Barrington Moore (1966) convincingly argues that the American Civil War cannot be understood as simply a struggle between a commercial class versus a pre-commercial feudal elite, as was the case elsewhere. Rather, he argues that the American Civil War, one of the bloodiest conflicts in modern human history, was in fact the last capitalist revolution, with industrial capitalism emerging triumphant over the commercial agrarian South. He argues that the Southern plantation owners were just another form of capitalism and that the difference was that although the South had "a capitalist civilization," it was "hardly a bourgeois one." Instead of "challenging the notion of status based on birth, as did the European bourgeoisie when they challenged the right of aristocracies to rule, Southern planters too fought over the defense of hereditary privilege" (1966, p. 121). This privilege was based on a notion of racial superiority and the ownership of slaves. In many ways, this was similar to the commercial impulses of the French nobility, who although became engaged in the market, never abandoned the idea of aristocratic privilege.

Indeed, these differences became more pronounced with the growth of industrial capitalism in the North. Politically these differences were expressed in the ongoing debates over tariff rates from 1820–1861. On the one hand, Senator Henry Clay and his Whig Party, representing Northern industrial interests, argued for high tariffs directed against especially cheap British textile imports which would help protect "infant industries" in the North against their more efficient British competitors. The 1828 and 1832 Tariff Acts reflected this position, which was widely resented in the South. On the other hand, Southern interests favored lower tariffs – higher tariffs meant that Southerners would pay more for imported goods, and be able to sell less cotton abroad (especially to Great Britain) particularly after Britain retaliated by instituting higher tariffs on imported American agricultural products, and sought an expansion of the import of Egyptian and Indian cotton to replace American imports. So intense was the resistance to the 1828 "tariff of abominations" as its detractors called it, that South Carolina, led by Senator John C. Calhoun, attempted to "nullify" the federal tariff and spoke of secession in 1832. The Nullification Crisis forced an abandonment of the Whig position of higher tariffs for over ten years until 1842. When the Whigs won victories in the 1840 and 1842 elections, they re-instituted higher tariffs with the tariff of 1842. The Democrats won in 1844, electing James K. Polk as president. Polk succeeded in passing the Walker Tariff of 1846 by uniting the South with the West in favor of lower taxes and lower tariffs that would pay the cost of government but not show favoritism to one section or economic sector at the expense of another. The United States retained a low-tariff policy that favored the South until the Civil War began in 1861.

While the economic differences between the North and South grew (with the West increasingly aligning with the North as Western food products were exported to the growing populations of an industrializing North), they became increasingly incompatible. For the South to maintain commercial cotton production, they needed, first, access to virgin land as existing land under cultivation became less fertile, and, second, lower tariffs to expand the markets available for Southern cotton. On the other hand, this came into direct conflict with the interests of the North, that sought protection for infant industries through the maintenance of relatively high tariffs. Further, as the western food-producing areas became populated with independent farmers, Southern planters who had "once welcomed Western farmers as allies against the plutocracy of the North came to see the spread of independent farming as a threat to slavery and their own system" (Moore, 1966, p. 129). Southern politicians resisted the various Homestead Acts in the 1850s, objecting to the giving away of "free" land that would effective "abolitionize" these areas. By the election of 1860, a new political alliance had arisen between the North and the West in which northern business would support the farmers' demand for land in return for support for protectionist trade measures. It was this coalition to which the South reacted and was a major catalyst for the American Civil War – ultimately a clash between two different economic systems leading to different civilizations with fundamentally incompatible stands on slavery (ibid.).

These regional divisions have left an indelible mark on the development of the American political system. Nonetheless, it was the Civil War that gave rise to the triumph of the idea of an American *Staatsnation*. To be sure, regional social, economic and political differences pitting North against the South have persisted over time – nonetheless, the political integration of the American state was ultimately a direct consequence of the violence of the middle of the nineteenth century and paved the way for the consolidation of American democracy later.

Germany

Political and national disunity

In contrast to either England, France, and formally the United States, which had established unified states long before industrialization and economic modernization, a key feature of German political development was the fact of disunity and the lack of national integration which persisted well into the modern era. There were several reasons for historical German political disunity. First of all, after the collapse of the Holy Roman Empire, the religious wars of the seventeenth century fractured what little political unity had existed. Indeed, the Treaty of Westphalia (1648), which established the system of states in Europe, formalized this political disunity by recognizing the independence of the various German princes. Even with the consolidation of some of the smaller principalities, in 1800, there were still 314 independent German political units. In 1815, after the end of the Napoleonic Wars, the Congress of Vienna amalgamated these smaller units into larger principalities, and a loose German confederation was established made up of 38 sovereign states (Reinhardt, 1986; Dalton, 1989).

A second reason for political disunity was the struggle between the two strongest German states, Prussia to the East and Austria to the South. Prussian rulers, particularly Frederick the Great (1740–1786) raised Prussia from a weak principality to one of the strongest powers in Europe by combining military build-up with rapid economic modernization. Prussia's dominant position was of immense significance for German political development. Prussia was not a liberal monarchy, but rather a militaristic society. An attempted democratic revolution in 1848 was repressed, driving many in the middle class to emigrate, especially to the United States. Unlike comparable groups in Britain, these Germans could see no hope of liberalizing the political system from within. Thus, political leadership among the middle class, which in many countries played a key role in the movement toward democracy, was weakened greatly (Dalton, 1989).

In addition, there were significant socioeconomic differences between among the various geographic areas of Germany. In the west along the Rhine, Germany is blessed with significant coal and iron ore deposits which later facilitated the growth of industry, a large working class, and stimulated commerce and the growth of a relatively strong bourgeoisie and the weakening of the feudal classes very early on. Indeed, to a large extent, feudalism had already been significantly weakened in this part of Germany prior to the nineteenth century. To the south was Bavaria, which is not endowed with large mineral deposits, and its rolling hills tended to promote small farms and the herding of livestock. In terms of religion, Bavaria also tends to be overwhelmingly Catholic in orientation. To the east was Prussia, which was neither rich in mineral deposits nor the basic stuff of industry and commerce. Rather, in agricultural Prussia, the social and economic landscape was dominated by large estates, and politics was dominated by the landed classes, the *Junkers*. It was from the *Junker* class that the principal political and military leaders of Prussia were recruited.

As a result, in contrast to England where political and national integration had taken place prior to large-scale industrialization, and France, where at least political unification had occurred, by the nineteenth century Germany was neither politically unified nor nationally integrated. Further, these political differences overlapped with strong cultural and socioeconomic differences between the regions, with differences in terms of socioeconomic structure (capitalism in the west, small-scale farming in the south and Feudalism in the east) overlapping with significant cultural and religious differences as well.

Political unification and the transformation of Germany
The political unification of Germany, when it came, was achieved through force. The person who was perhaps most responsible for unification was Otto von Bismarck (1815–1898). At the age of 47, Bismarck was named Minister President (Chancellor) of Prussia by the Prussian Emperor Wilhelm I. From the outset, he made it clear that he was no democrat. In two quick wars, against Denmark in 1864 and against Austria in 1866, he established Prussian dominance over the German confederation. In a war with France in 1870, Germany acquired the cession of the province of Alsace and part of the province of Lorraine. In 1871, the North German Confederation was abolished and a German Empire, consisting of Prussia, the states of the former North German Confederation and Bavaria, was proclaimed (Berghahn, 1982).

Quick political unification, however, did not necessarily lead to national integration. The state forged under Bismarck's tutelage was a delicate balance between the various social and political forces within the "second

Reich." Thus, he forced the alliance between the middle classes – too weak to achieve power on its own – and the military aristocracy in Prussia. Neither the Kaiser nor the military were willing to relinquish any of their powers, and Bismarck certainly did not want to weaken the military might that had unified and guaranteed Germany's international position. So he sought instead concessions for the middle class, such as appointments to important administrative posts and positions in the Prussian Cabinet, as opposed to supplanting the privileges of the quasi-feudal elite in Prussia.

Simultaneously Bismarck tried to convince the Prussian aristocracy that they must learn to live with the liberal, middle-class government ministers and reconcile themselves to the growing wealth and power of the cities. He also attempted to persuade the middle class to be satisfied with the modest concessions he had won for them, arguing that the international situation did not permit weakening the military or the Kaiser. Moreover despite his hostility toward the socialists, Bismarck tried to bring the working classes into the grand balance of social groups through an extensive program of social legislation, which included the first system of national health insurance in the world.

Thus, through the first 30 years of the second Reich, Bismarck had managed to construct an equilibrium, however delicate, between the very disparate social and political forces in the Reich. However, with Bismarck's departure from the political scene in 1890, coupled with the defeat of Germany in World War I (1914–1918), this delicate balance quickly unraveled. It was out of the ashes of World War I, under the most adverse conditions, Germany embarked on its first experience in political democracy with the foundation of the Weimar Republic in January, 1919.

During the Weimar years, the economy fell apart. The war had been funded by loans, not increased taxes and the burden of these loans, the pressure of reparation payments demanded by the victorious allies as a result of the Peace of Versailles, and foreign occupation of the industrial regions of the Ruhr, eroded all confidence in the economy. By 1923, total industrial production was only 55 percent of the pre-war level. By the end of 1923, the inflation rate had reached an incredible 26 billion percent – overnight German currency became worthless, effectively destroying the savings of the German middle class (Childers, 1983, p. 50). The final blow came with the world-wide economic collapse in 1929. By 1932, unemployment in Germany topped 30 percent of the workforce.

The economic collapse during the 1920s translated into ideological polarization and severe political instability. In 14 years there were 20 different Cabinets – such political instability hindered the Weimar government's attempts to deal effectively with the problems facing inter-war Germany. Moreover, extreme left and right movements emerged to challenge the democratic order. Yet the creation of anti-system political movements could not have existed without the existence of latent social and political cleavages. The radicalization of German politics and its polarization and fragmentation were fundamentally exacerbated by the crumbling of the delicate social and economic contract which had been forged in the latter part of the nineteenth century. It was into this political morass that Adolf Hitler and the Nazis were invited to head a coalition government by the then German President Paul von Hindenburg, established on March 24, 1933, with promises of restoring the honor of the German people and righting the wrongs and injustices imposed upon Germany by the Treaty of Versailles. Thus ended the first tentative steps toward German democracy, a democracy which only reemerged via imposition by the victorious allies following World War II.

Japan

The history of Japan was not a history of invasion and conquest, but one of internal civil war and international isolation. After the establishment of a unified Japanese state (the so-called Yamato state) around the third to fifth century CE, Buddhism was introduced, and the semblance of centralized state was established under a monarch, with a political system roughly based on the Chinese model. After the fall of the Korean Baekje kingdom (660 CE) to rival kingdoms on the Korean peninsula, with which the Yamato rulers had maintained close relations, and through which they had contact with Chinese culture and technology, the Yamato government sent envoys directly to the Chinese court. Through these contacts, the early Yamato state imported the Chinese calendar, philosophy and many of the Chinese religious practices, including Confucianism and Taoism.

The Yamato period was followed by successive periods that led to the expansion and consolidation of the early Japanese state during the Nara (710–794), and the Heian (794–1185) eras, with the latter marking the cultural and political highpoint of the early Japanese state. However, within the Heian state there first emerged the warrior (Samurai) class that gained greater and greater influence at court. At the end of the twelfth century CE, a military chief Minamoto no Yoritomo seized power from the emperors and established a *bakufu* (headquarters), the Kamakura Shogunate. From that point until the Meiji Restoration in the middle of the nineteenth century, the Emperor was reduced to largely a figurehead, with little in the way of actual political power. In turn, the Shogunate itself became an object of contention between the great warrior feudal lords of Japan (the *Daimyo*) who fought numerous civil wars down the centuries for control of the Shogunate. By the sixteenth century, Japan had descended into a period of extended and protracted civil war, culminating in the victory of the Eastern Tokugawa clan, and the establishment of the Tokugawa Shogunate at the beginning of the seventeenth century CE.

Thus, in a sense, the process of the centralization of the Japanese state under the Emperor, and later under the Shogunate, was arrested by the disintegration of Japan into warring feudal clans. To large extent, this process of disintegration was assisted by Japan's relative isolation. Although Japan had been invaded by the Mongols in 1274 and again in 1281 (both times repulsed with the assistance of major storms or *Kamikaze*), and the Shogun Hideyoshi had engaged in military adventurism in Korea at the end of the sixteenth century, Japan, for much of its history, remained isolated from the rest of the world. Essentially this meant that without significant external threats, there was less incentive for the development of a powerful and centralized state. To a great extent, this was only changed with the emergence of a foreign perceived threat posed by Portuguese imperial interests at the end of the sixteenth century, which gave rise to the Tokugawa effort to establish a unified (and isolated) Japanese state. Yet even then, the Tokugawa state was hardly centralized, relying heavily on the compliance of the great Daimyo clans to maintain their rule. It was when two of those Daimyo clans (the Choshu and the Satsuma) broke with the Tokugawa, following the appearance of Commodore Matthew Perry's American "Black Fleet" in Edo (now Tokyo) harbor in 1853 and the subsequent arrival of Western foreign missions demanding trade and territorial concessions from Japan, did this spell the end of the Tokugawa Shogunate, and the "restoration" of the Japanese Emperor in 1868.

Japanese national identity

To a great extent, despite isolation and extremely high degrees of ethnic and linguistic homogeneity, the development of a Japanese national identity was incomplete. As Anthony Smith notes, Japan has historically suffered "identity problems, both at the cultural and political levels" (1991, p. 105). Although Japan had evolved into an ethnic state with only a small Ainu minority (in the far north of the country) by the early seventeenth century, and though this identity was "sealed" by Tokugawa isolationist policies, the notion of a political community was notably absent.

The building of a Japanese national political identity was led by the Meiji restorationists of 1868, primarily from the Choshu and Satsuma clans, who replaced the old Shogunate with a modernizing imperial political order. To this end, the Meiji leaders used Confucian and peasant traditions, particularly loyalty to one's lord and one's family (in which the Emperor represented the father of all), and the village community (*mura*), to transform a "politically passive and economically fragmented ethnic community into a more cohesive, economically centralized and mobilized political community and thereby create a Japanese national political identity" (Moore, 1966, p. 105). At the center of this system was the worship of the Emperor (*tennosei*) as the embodiment of all that was Japanese. Thus, membership in the political community (as was the case with the Russian national experience under the Tsars) involved loyalty to the emperor. However, despite Japan's virtual ethnic and linguistic homogeneity, Japanese national identity was incomplete. Indeed, the defeat of Japan by the Allies in World War II shook the foundations of the Japanese national political identity. To be sure, the post-war era saw the rise in interest among intellectual and business circles in Japan in a Japanese distinctiveness and redefining a national cultural identity (Yoshino, 1992). However, as Smith notes, "How far this can prove a durable and comprehensive base for Japanese national identity, cultural or political, remains to be seen" (1991, p. 106).

Japanese feudalism
In many ways, Japanese feudalism was very similar to the development of feudalism in the West. At the top of the social and political order stood the Shogun, not the Emperor, who remained a shadowy and secluded (and generally impoverished) figure. In many ways the Shogun's authority was similar to that of other absolutist monarchs of the time in the West. During the Tokugawa period, the Shogunate controlled about a quarter of the available agricultural lands, deriving enormous revenues in which to pay off vassals (and occasionally other Daimyo). In many ways, however, the Tokugawa Shogunate's control over the fragmented feudal order in Japan was incomplete. Below the Shogun were the 200 or so Daimyo, who were given considerable leeway over the lands they administered. Beneath the Daimyo were the Samurai, who varied considerably in term of wealth and prestige. Generally they were considered retainers of the Daimyo, but there

were also *ronin*, or samurai who were not under obligation to a lord. Generally, however, in order to prevent the instability that had plagued the country in the era of free Samurai, the Tokugawa Shogunate required that Samurai be contracted to the Daimyo and receive a stipend as a retainer. Ultimately the Tokugawa peace deprived the Samurai of any real function in Japanese society, and as the years passed, this warrior class became increasingly impoverished and ultimately a source of opposition to the Tokugawa regime in the nineteenth century (Murdoch, 1925; Sansom, 1963).

As in the West, it was the rise of the merchants (*chonin*) that led to the erosion of the feudal order. In general, the Daimyo and Samurai depended on the merchants to turn agricultural products produced by the peasantry into cash and to supply them with the amenities of life (Sheldon, 1958, p. 32; Sansom, 1963). The merchants in return depended on the warrior aristocrats for protection and security to engage in trade. Over time, as in the West, the aristocracy became increasingly indebted to the chonin, and by the end of the Tokugawa period they had emerged as the dominant partner in the feudal relationship. Indeed, by the end of the period, the growing commercial impulse in Japan had led to the breakdown of the rigid distinctions between Samurai and chonin. Many Samurai families then turned to trade and became merchants. By the beginning of the nine-teenth century no less than 1 in 5 of the major merchant families in Japan could trace their ancestry to the Samurai class (Honjo, 1935, pp. 204–205; Sheldon, 1958, p. 6). Ultimately, as Barrington Moore (1966, p. 245) notes, it was the arrival of the foreign threat, coupled with the "partial erosion of the feudal edifice through the rise of commerce, which was in turn due to the establishment of peace and order" (under the Tokugawa) that led to the overthrow of the Tokugawa and the restoration of the Emperor in 1868.

However, the old order was not entirely swept away. In part, the new Meiji rulers sought to incorporate the Daimyo by first drawing the lines of legal prefectures to correspond with the old feudal domains, appointing Daimyo to important positions in local and national governance, and in the 1870s provided for guaranteed stipends in exchange for the Daimyo's surrender of their fiefdoms (Allen, 1981, pp. 27, 34–37). However, the Meiji government treated the majority of the Samurai quite differently, cutting their stipends to only a fraction of their previous revenues, alienating many and culminating in the Satsuma rebellion (led by the ex-Samurai Saigo Takamori) in 1877. Nonetheless, despite the suppression of the Samurai, the feudal military tradition was maintained, and provides a basis for rapid industrialization and militarization later. In this sense, the survival of feudal traditions coupled with a strong element of a bureaucratized state driven by threats from abroad was a common characteristic of both German and Japanese (and to some extent Russian) history. It distinguishes them from England, France, and the United States, where feudalism was overcome or absent and where industrialization did take place, it took place under democratic auspices.

Russia

The early history of Russia has been a chronicle of foreign invasion and domination. The agricultural Slavic tribes that inhabited the southern steppes of Russia were continually conquered by Asian and other European peoples, which split up the Slavic peoples into western (Czechs, Slovaks and Poles), Eastern (Russians, Byelorussians and Ukrainians) and Southern (Serbs, Croats, Bulgars) branches. The first Eastern Slavic state was established in about 862 by Rurik the Varangian (Viking) who led a band of Norseman and established a settlement around where Moscow is today where he declared himself prince. Later his son moved the capital of the principality southward to the city of Kiev. Later, under Prince Vladimir (980–1015), the Kievan state established relations with the Eastern Roman Empire (Byzantium) and adopted Orthodoxy as the state religion and written Greek as the basis for a written Eastern Slavic language. With the death of Prince Yaroslavl (1054–1236) the unified Kievan state was divided up among various princes who each ruled their own domain. The most famous is perhaps Alexander Nevsky, Prince of Novgorod, who in the period just before the Mongol annexation of Russia in 1242 fought off the Baltic Germanic princes who sought to spread Roman Catholicism into Russia. In that same year the Mongols invaded and destroyed the Kievan state and subjugated the Russian principalities. Under the Mongol "yoke" (1242–1480), individual city-states began to develop under loose Mongol control.

Two of the most noteworthy states were Moscow and Novgorod, the latter was a merchant center governed by an elected council like the city-states in the West. Moscow was ruled by an autocratic Grand Prince. In 1380, the Grand Prince of Moscow Dmitri defeated the Mongols. From that point on, Mongol authority steadily weakened. In 1480, Ivan III declared himself Tsar, the Russian equivalent of Caesar which symbolized the unity of church and state and reflected the Grand Prince's claim that Moscow was the "Third Rome" (after Rome and Constantinople). He sacked Novgorod, and finally expelled the Mongols from Moscow.

The victory of Moscow marked the beginning of the Russian autocracy, or the absolute rule of the Tsar. Yet as in Western Europe there continued to be struggle between the landed nobility and the Crown for dominance. The struggle came to head with the accession to the throne of Ivan IV or "The Terrible" in 1547 at the age of 16. Early on, Ivan relied heavily on a council of landowners (Zemsky Sobor) who guided policy. However, he later destroyed the Council and declared the Russian state to be his personal domain. From 1565–1584, the Tsar led a purge of the nobility, arresting them, exiling them, confiscating their estates, thus neutralizing any threat the nobility posed to his personal power.

After a period of disorder following the death of Ivan's heir Fedor from 1598–1613, a period known as the "Time of Troubles," absolute authority was once again consolidated in the hands of a new dynasty, the Romanovs. One of the most notable of the Romanov Tsars was Peter I (the Great, 1672–1725) who declared himself Emperor, conquered new lands to the west and to south and sought to modernize Russia. Peter introduced several social and political reforms; and established a bureaucracy based on technocratic merit, and introduced the practice of awarding noble status to individuals who had provided service to the state. The latter further undermined the position of the nobility and essentially reduced the nobility to the status of dependence on the Crown. Further, Peter's reforms did not touch all of Russia. Following his death, Peter left a Russia divided between a westernized and often French-speaking elite and a traditionalist peasantry.

The consolidation of the Russian autocracy and the expansion of the Russian Empire also had consequences for the development of a Russian national identity. For instance, Roman Szporluk (1988, p. 206) argues that since Russia was a multinational empire before a modern Russian identity was formed, no distinction between state and society emerged, unlike in the West where nation-building had preceded empire-building. The glue which held the empire together, from Poland in the West to the Caucasus in the South, to Siberia and beyond to the East was loyalty to the Tsar, not loyalty to a particular national community. Tsarism thus denied the Russian nation an identity, through its subjection to autocracy, which was a form of government in which society played no role and was not represented. This was to deny the Russian nation an identity which was separate from the state (Szporluk, 1988, pp. 206–207; see also Torbakov, 1992). Further, for Richard Pipes (1975), this "reversal" of stages left an indelible mark on

Russian political culture. It made it difficult for Russians to distinguish between "Russia proper," that is, their national homeland, and the political boundaries of the state. This confusion not only produced very strong pressure toward statist solutions for both Russian socialists, nationalists and Pan-Slavists, but in turn, made the Russians suspicious of the aspirations of their subject nationalities, which they treated as a threat to the state's integrity and hence a direct threat to the Russian "nation" (Pipes, 1975, p. 1).

In terms of the socioeconomic development of the Russian Empire, by the beginning of the nineteenth century, Russian society resembled the feudal arrangements that were pervasive in Western Europe in the Middle Ages. Nearly 80 percent of the population were peasants, and the majority of those were serfs, or peasants who were legally bound to the land and could be bought and sold with the land. The serfs were not much better off than slaves. Although practiced for some time before, serfdom had been made official by state decree (Ulozhenie) in 1649 which bound peasants to the land in order to prevent the mass migration of peasants eastward to Siberia with the opening up of new lands in the empire.

Thus, by the beginning of the nineteenth century, Russian had not developed a very strong sense of national identity. Moreover, feudalism had hardly been transformed, with the peasantry comprising the bulk of the population. With the subjugation of the nobility by the state, neither a civil society nor checks against the encroachment of autocracy had emerged, and the nature of the state was inimical to notions of popular accountability. In comparative terms, then, Russia represented the polar opposite to the situation that had developed in England.

Nonetheless, modernization did come to Russia. Russian forces were instrumental in the defeat of Napoleon and substantial numbers of Russian troops participated in the occupation of France after Napoleon's defeat. Many young officers were exposed to the principles of the French Revolution and, upon returning to Russia, plotted to overthrow the autocracy. In December 1825, shortly after the death of Alexander I, a group of officers attempted to stage a coup d'état against the new Tsar Nicholas I (1825–1855). The revolt was quickly suppressed and the ringleaders were executed or exiled to Siberia. Nonetheless, despite increased repression following the revolt, revolutionary ideas began to spread.

The outcome of the Crimean War (1853–1856) fought entirely on Russian soil, and the subsequent Russian defeat at the hands of the British, the French and the Turks, accelerated the move toward reform and modernization. For many in the government of Alexander II, who had succeeded Nicholas 1 in 1855, the defeat had resulted from Russian backwardness in economic and military capabilities. In order to facilitate economic modernization, Alexander II issued a decree which emancipated the serfs in 1861 and instituted limited political reforms, although the population remained overwhelmingly made up of peasants. Although Alexander was assassinated in 1881, leading to repression of dissident elements by his successor Alexander III, in the 1880s Russia began a program of rapid industrialization largely financed by state capital. The architect of Russia's industrialization program was Alexander III's Minister of Finance Sergei Witte, who financed the expansion of the railroad network and the construction of heavy industry via foreign loans and increased land taxes which adversely affected the agrarian classes, both nobles and peasants alike. Industrialization also created new social classes by the end of the nineteenth century, an industrial bourgeoisie and a proletariat, although their numbers were quite limited.

Industrialization served to weaken the social bases of the Russian autocracy and create greater stresses in Russian society. Burdensome taxation on the peasantry created greater resentment against the existing order in the countryside. The proletariat lived and worked in squalid and unsanitary conditions in the cities. The situation came to a head when on January 9, 1905 (Bloody Sunday), soldiers fired on a procession of striking workers bringing a list of grievances to Tsar Nicholas II in St Petersburg. Hundreds were killed. This event started a revolt, which the Tsar was able to put down only with great difficulty. The 1905 Revolution forced Nicholas II to grant token reform, including establishment of a parliament (the Duma) and a promise of a constitution, free elections, and protection of civil liberties. Nonetheless, the Tsar kept the power of absolute veto over the Duma and the power to dismiss the Duma at will, and once the furor of the revolution died down, he also reneged on promises of a constitution and guarantees for the protection of civil liberties.

Arguing that there were too many revolutionaries represented in the First Duma (1906), the Tsar dissolved this body in July. The second Duma which was elected in March 1907 was even more radical than the first and was dissolved shortly after the election. In 1907, the Tsarist government changed voter registration laws to benefit the wealthier and propertied classes. The third Duma, which was elected at the end of 1907, and served its full term until 1912, was predictably made up of more conservative political elements.

The outbreak of World War I in 1914 proved to be disastrous for the Russian Empire. Russian forces suffered a series of catastrophic defeats on the battlefield, and by the end of 1916 the economy had virtually collapsed from the strain of the war. In February 1917, the Tsar was forced to abdicate and he was replaced briefly (for a few hours) by his brother Mikhail. Mikhail in turn abdicated and was replaced by a provisional government made up of a coalition of centrist democratic parties in the State Duma. The provisional government in turn was overthrown in a coup led by the Bolshevik leader Vladimir Ilych Lenin in November, whereupon Lenin proclaimed a dictatorship of peasants and workers. After an extended Civil War (1917–1922), the Communist Party leadership declared the establishment of the Union of Soviet Socialist Republics. The period of communist rule had begun.

Patterns of Political Development

The above six cases were analyzed in light of three questions: (1) To what extent had a *political* national identity been established prior to the Industrial Revolution?; (2) To what extent had the principle of accountability and the rule of law been established prior to the coming of industrialization?; (3) To what extent had the old social order been swept away prior to the coming of industrialization? Each of the four cases represents very different patterns of historical development. These patterns are illustrated in Table 2.1.

The English case illustrates the pattern where prior to industrialization a political national identity (or *Staatsnation*) had been developed which tied people together. Although the development of a strong central authority early on had contributed to the development of this identity, by the end of seventeenth century, English national identity was not equivalent merely to loyalty to the monarch, but identity with the political national community. This meant that the disruptive and centrifugal forces unleashed by industrialization were somewhat buffered by the sense of community and common political destiny that bound the English together. Second, the feudal social structure had been fundamentally changed prior to industrialization; the peasantry as a class was destroyed by the enclosures and the nobility transformed into a commercially minded rural bourgeoisie. This meant that the social classes most inimical to modernization had been effectively neutralized. Third, the development of the principles

Table 2.1 Comparison of six cases on three dimensions of pre-industrial transformation.

	England	*France*	*The United States*
National identity	National identity tied to country, not king Development of a strong national identity	Ruler preeminent, loyalty to ruler demanded (absolutist monarchy) Development of a partial national identity	Historical political divisions between regions of the country. Late development of national identity after Civil War
Transformation of feudalism/ society	Bourgeoisification of the nobility Disappearance of feudalism (peasants disappear as result of enclosures)	Nobility dependent on king (especially Louis XIV and after) Labor-intensive agriculture (viniculture; wheat); need for large workforce on the land, i.e. peasants remain Feudalism only partially dismantled by French Revolution	Feudalism maintained in South Labor-intensive agriculture and cotton production Quasi-feudal legacy maintained in South
Institutionalization	Commitment to some form of representation and accountability of ruler in place before the Industrial Revolution	Move to absolutism means: NO accountability and NO rule of law	Commitment to some form of representation and accountability in place prior to industrialization

of accountability and participation led to the development of a semblance of the rule of law and the civil society prior to industrial transformation. Further, the institutions of participation (a parliament and elections) were already in place. Thus, when demands for increased participation took place in the nineteenth century, all that was required was the

Germany	Japan	Russia
Historical political disunity; strong regional differences Weakly developed sense of national identity	Historical political disunity, strong feudal differences However , national identity as an island develops fairly early	Empire built prior to concept of nation; loyalty to Tsar preeminent National identity questionable even now
Limited transformation Nobility remains influential in military and in feudal East (Prussia)	Limited transformation Nobility remains powerful.	Nobility upheld the old, feudal order Feudalism did not disappear prior to industrialization; government-led industrialization
Resistance by Crown to popular mandate; strong tradition of obedience toward established authority, NO principle of accountability and rule of law	Feudalism and some limited form of accountability of the Shogun and Emperor. However, popular representation not in place prior to industrialization	No institutionalization under Tsars; NO principle of accountability and rule of law

expansion of the "openings" in the political arena – not the reconstruction or construction of the arena itself. In a sense, this meant that in the English case a ship capable of making the passage through the rough seas of industrial transformation had already been built prior to the coming of stormy seas.

The French case represents the pattern where incomplete pre-industrial transformation contributed to a checkered unstable path toward democracy. On the one hand, France had developed some sense of political national identity, at least among intellectuals. However, as Macridis points out, this identity was somewhat fractured, with French political culture marked by a large degree of dissent as opposed to consensus. Further, although the French Revolution partially swept away feudalism with the destruction of the monarchy and the nobility, the peasantry remained a largely anti-modern and at times anti-democratic force in French politics. Finally, although a tradition of limited government and accountability did ultimately develop later in the nineteenth century, these traditions were not longstanding. The subordination of society to the Crown earlier on meant that the principles of accountability and representative government were only very weakly developed by the time economic modernization took place in the latter part of the nineteenth century. This meant that the French ship was only partially constructed prior to the passage to democracy.

The case of the United States represents another example of the ship being partially constructed – especially the incomplete nature of an American political national identity prior to the Civil War. The Civil War, violent as it was, brought about the beginnings of the creation of a more "complete union" and political national identity paving the way for the expansion of the democratic polity. On the other hand, as with other older democracies, the vestiges of feudalism and the institution of a political order that instituted accountability, were already in place prior to the economic expansion and social upheaval that accompanied industrialization.

Unlike Britain, France and the United States, Germany, Russia and Japan did not have the institutions of democracy in place prior to economic expansion and social upheaval that accompanied industrialization. In the German case, the three pre-industrial transformations were even less developed than in the French case. There was only a weakly developed sense of political national identity, given the degree of political disunity and regional differences that existed among the major regions of Germany. Second, although a limited transformation of the feudal order had taken place in the western areas of the German lands, particularly along the Rhine, feudalism remained ensconced in the East in Prussia. Finally, there had been no tradition of accountability and participation in pre-unification Prussia, at least under Bismarck some of the features of participatory government were in place (if only for appearances) and an opposition in the form of the Catholic Center Party and the Social Democrats was tolerated.

Japan also had an incomplete national identity at least in the sense of a *Staatsnation* concept, had remained feudal quite late into the modern era, although there had been some sense of the accountability of the emperor and the relative autonomy of the Daimyo nobility even during the Tokugawa period. Again using the ship analogy, this suggests that in the German and Japanese cases the ship was only partially built and very rickety.

The Russian case represents the polar opposite from that of the English case. In the Russian case, no discernible Russian national identity was possible under Tsarist rule. Further, unlike even in Germany, virtually no transformation of the feudal order had taken place by the middle of the nineteenth century, and arguably not until the beginning of the twentieth. Finally, given the nature of the Russian autocracy, no principles of accountability, rule of law or participation were developed under a system which concentrated all power into the hands of a single autocrat. When such principles began to develop at the beginning of the twentieth century, they were granted only very grudgingly by the autocracy and were undermined later. But it was far too late for such hesitant actions. The social forces which would ultimately destroy the autocracy were far greater than the feeble efforts to contain them. In a sense, the Russian case represents the attempt to make the passage to democracy in a rowboat.

The historical approach to the development of democracy is quite useful to an understanding of the macro social, economic, and political forces that helped shape dictatorship and democracy. However, as mentioned above, it is largely based on the experience of a limited number of Western cases, and hence may not adequately explain developmental processes elsewhere. Nonetheless as noted above, whether one likes it or not, our current understanding of comparative politics is rooted in such Western cases, and hence an understanding of the principles of comparative politics requires some idea of where these general principles originated.

Second, one should not think of these macro historical processes as deterministic of democracy or dictatorship. As we noted earlier, they represent constraints in which real human choices can be made, regarding rules, procedures and other arrangements that may promote or detract from the development of political democracy.

Before we address these "menu of choices," however, we need first to examine other sets of constraints that affect the development of political democracy. In Chapter 3, we examine another factor that affects the political development of a country – economic development and modernization.

References

Allen, G.C. (1981) *A Short Economic History of Modern Japan, 1867–1937*, New York: St. Martin's Press.

Almond, Gabriel and Powell, G. Bingham (1996) *Comparative Politics Today*, 6th edn., New York: HarperCollins.

Almond, Gabriel and Verba, Sidney (1963) *The Civic Culture*, Princeton, NJ: Princeton University Press.

Barry, Brian (1975) "Review Article: Political Accommodation and Consociational Democracy," *British Journal of Political Science*, 5: 57–67.

Bendix, Reinhard (1964) *Nation-Building and Citizenship*, New York: John Wiley & Sons.

Berghahn, V.R. (1982) *Modern Germany*, Cambridge: Cambridge University Press.

Childers, Thomas (1983) *The Nazi Voter*, Chapel Hill, NC: University of North Carolina Press.

Covell, Maureen (1985) "Ethnic Conflict, Representation and the State in Belgium," in Paul Brass (ed.) *Ethnic Groups and the State*, Totowa, NJ: Barnes and Noble Books, pp. 230–235.

Daalder, Hans (1974) "The Consociational Democracy Theme," *World Politics*, 26: 604–621.

Dahl, Robert (1971) *Polyarchy: Participation and Opposition*, New Haven, CT: Yale University Press.

Dahl, Robert (1989) *On Democracy*, New Haven, CT: Yale University Press.

Dalton, Russell (1989) *Politics in West Germany*, New York: Scott Foresman/Little Brown.

Deutsch, Karl W. (1953) *Nationalism and Social Communication*, New York: John Wiley & Sons, Inc.

Deutsch, Karl W. (1961) "Social Mobilization and Political Development," *American Political Science Review*, 55: 493–514.

Diamond, Larry (1994) "Rethinking Civil Society: Toward Democratic Consolidation," *Journal of Democracy*, 5: 5–17.

Duncan, Christopher M. (1995) *The Anti-Federalists and Early American Political Thought*, DeKalb, IL: Northern Illinois University Press.

Duverger, Maurice (1986) "Duverger's Law: Forty Years Later," in Bernard Grofman and Arend Lijphart (eds.) *Electoral Laws and Their Political Consequences*, New York: Agathon Press, pp. 69–84.

Erickson, Arvel and Havran, Martin (1968) *England: Prehistory to the Present*, Garden City, NY: Anchor Books/Doubleday.

Fine, Robert and Rai, Shirin (eds.) (1997) *Civil Society: Democratic Perspectives*, London: Frank Cass.

Fox, Russell Arben (1999) "'Tending' and 'Intending' a Nation: Conflicting Visions of American National Identity," *Polity*, 31: 561–586.

Freeman, John and Snidal, Duncan (1982) "Diffusion, Development and Democratization in. Western Europe," *Canadian Journal of Political Science*, 15: 299–329.

Gerschenkron, Alexander (1979) *Economic Backwardness in Historical Perspective*, Cambridge, MA: Harvard University Press.

Greenfield, Liah (1992) *Nationalism: Five Roads to Modernity*, Cambridge, MA: Harvard University Press.

Held, David (1996) *Models of Democracy*, 2nd edn., Stanford, CA: Stanford University Press.

Himmelfarb, Gertrude (1968) *Victorian Minds*, New York: Knopf.

Honjo, Eijiro (1935) *Social and Economic History of Japan*, Kyoto: Maruzen.

Huntington, Samuel (1968) *Political Order in Changing Societies*, New Haven, CT: Yale University Press.

Linz, Juan J. and Stepan, Alfred (1996) *Problems of Democratic Transition and Consolidation: Southern Europe, South America and Post-Communist Europe*, Baltimore, MD: Johns Hopkins University Press.

Macridis, Roy (1990) *Modern Political Systems: Europe*, 7th edn., Englewood Cliffs, NJ: Prentice Hall.

Macridis, Roy and Brown, Bernard (1960) *The de Gaulle Republic: Quest for Unity*, Homewood IL: Dorsey.

McWilliams, Wilson Carey (1980) "Democracy and the Citizen: Community, Dignity and the Crisis of Contemporary Politics in America," in Robert A. Goldwin and William A. Schambra (eds.) *How Democratic Is the Constitution?* Washington, DC: American Enterprise Institute, pp. 79–101.

Moore, Barrington (1966) *Social Origins of Dictatorship and Democracy: Lord and Peasant in the Making of the Modern World*, Boston, MA: Beacon Press.

Murdoch, James (1925) *A History of Modern Japan*, London: Kegan Paul, Trench Trubner and Co.

Murrin, John M. (1987) "A Roof Without Walls: The Dilemma of American National Identity," in Richard Beeman, *et al.* (eds.) *Beyond Confederation: Origins of the Constitution and American National Identity*, Chapel Hill, NC: University of North Carolina Press.

Pipes, Richard (1975) "Introduction: The Nationality Problem," in Z. Katz (ed.) *The Handbook of Major Soviet Nationalities*, New York: Free Press.

Reinhardt, Kurt (1986) *Germany: 2000 Years*, New York: Ungar.

Rose, Richard, Mishler, William, and Haerpfer, Christian (1998) *Democracy and Its Alternatives: Understanding Post-Communist Societies*, Baltimore, MD: Johns Hopkins University Press.

Sansom, Sir George (1963) *A History of Japan*, Vol. 3, Stanford, CA: Stanford University Press.

Sartori, Giovanni (1968) "Political Development and Political Engineering," in J.D. Montgomery and A.O. Hirschman (eds.) *Public Policy*, Vol. 17, Cambridge, MA: Harvard University Press, pp. 261–298.

Sartori, Giovanni (1987) *The Theory of Democracy Revisited: Part One*, Chatham, NJ: Chatham House.

Schumpeter, Joseph (1950) *Capitalism, Socialism and Democracy*, New York: Harper and Row.

Sheldon, Charles D. (1958) *The Rise of the Merchant Class in Tokugawa Japan, 1600–1868*, New York: Augustin.

Smith, Anthony D. (1991) *National Identity*, Las Vegas, NV: University of Nevada Press.

Sørenson, Georg (1993) *Democracy and Democratization*, Boulder, CO: Westview Press.

Szporluk, Roman (1988) *Communism and Nationalism: Karl Marx Versus Friedrich List*, New York: Oxford University Press.

Talmon, J.L. (1968) *Romanticism and Revolt*, London: Harcourt Brace.

Tilly, Charles (ed.) (1975) *The Formation of National States in Europe*, Princeton, NJ: Princeton University Press.

Torbakov, Igor (1992) "The 'Statists' and Ideology of Russian Imperial Nationalists," *RFE/RL Research Report*, 1 (49): 10–16.

Yoshino, Kosaku (1992) *Cultural Nationalism in Contemporary Japan*, London: Routledge.

3

Economics and Political Development

A singularly important contextual factor that affects political development is the economic environment. In particular, it is generally argued that changes in the economic environment, particularly through industrialization, technological innovation, and economic globalization, have a profound effect on the type of political system that emerges. Nonetheless, there has been considerable debate over the nature of that relationship, whether it is direct, or indirect, whether economic changes actually affect political changes, or vice versa.

Since the behavioral revolution, three general approaches have examined the relationship between economic development and political development. These include "modernization theory," "dependency theory," and "statism." In this chapter we review the contributions of each approach, and how each has contributed to our understanding of the relationship between economic transformation and political development.

Modernization Theory

What is the relationship between economic development and "modernization," on the one hand, and the emergence of political democracy, on the other? This is a central question addressed by what many now refer to as "modernization theory." Modernization theory is less a coherent theory than an approach to how economic modernization is related to political development. Although rooted in a longstanding literature in sociology,

Comparative Politics: Principles of Democracy and Democratization, First Edition.
John T. Ishiyama.
© 2012 John T. Ishiyama. Published 2012 by Blackwell Publishing Ltd.

modernization theory in political science grew out of the behavioral revolution's desire to focus on factors outside of institutions to explain political development (as discussed in Chapter 1). It is rooted in many of the older sociological approaches associated with socialist thought (in particular, Karl Marx) but also the classic works of Emile Durkheim and Talcott Parsons.

The idea that economic development has a direct effect on political development is not new. Many scholars historically have noted the profound social changes that resulted from industrialization. Indeed, basic principles associated with modernization theory are derived from the Age of Enlightenment, particularly the "human-centric" notion that people can control and change their environment. The eighteenth-century French philosopher Marquis de Condorcet was one of the first to argue that the rise of technology and economic transformation would enable humankind to make changes in their moral and cultural values and that economic development would make enormous improvements in the state of human affairs and that technological progress would allow for the promotion of social progress. Early socialist thinkers at the beginning of the industrial era in the nineteenth century, such as Henri de Saint-Simon (1760–1825), also emphasized the positive power of economic development and technology in enabling humanity to better its social conditions. Saint-Simon's student, Auguste Comte (1798–1857) thought of modernization and technology as empowering humans in a new scientific or "positive" era where science and technology would fundamentally alter the human condition. Such was also the perspective of Karl Marx in his critique of capitalism, when he noted that industrialization of the economic base had fundamentally changed the social and political superstructure, that is, that economic changes created the conditions for social and political change.

One of the earliest scholars to systematically examine the impact of economic transformation on the evolution of social structures and societal development was the French scholar Emile Durkheim. Durkheim is considered one of the founders of modern sociology and a pioneer in comparative social science. He is one of the first to develop the idea of "functionalism," an idea later incorporated into theories of structural functionalism (as discussed in Chapter 1). Essentially Durkheim thought of all societies as having functions that needed to be performed (such as security, political leadership, spiritual leadership, etc.) and what differentiated societies was the degree of complexity in the division of labor in how these functions were performed. Durkheim thought that societies evolved in ways similar to biological organisms, in stages from simple to complex. These changes were necessitated by changes in the surrounding environment, and in the modern era the primary environments were the economic and cultural environments. In "primitive" societies, he argued, relatively little complexity was needed to maintain social order. However, with industrialization and the development of capitalism, societies became more complex, and more functional differentiation and a more complex division labor were needed to maintain social order. He stressed that the major transition from a primitive social order to a more advanced industrial society could bring about crisis and disorder. Durkheim is associated with the concept of *social anomie*, which is generally a sense of rootlessness produced by the disorder resulting from capitalist industrialization. Essentially, older justifications for society and certainties (such as God) were increasingly called into question by the rise of science and technology, thus producing a sense of widespread social rootlessness. In turn, this sense of anomie produced criminality and social violence (Durkheim, [1893] 1964; Giddens, 1972).

Another giant in sociology who contributed greatly to the understanding of the relationship between economic transformation (primarily via industrialization) is Talcott Parsons. Parsons (1951; 1971) identified the primary characteristics of what he referred to as "traditional" versus "modern" societies. These "systems of patterns" were "ideal" types which anchored the ends of a continuum. No society was purely traditional; further, no society was purely modern. Rather, contemporary societies in the world possessed elements of both. Table 3.1 illustrates the different characteristics of traditional versus modern societies.

Essentially, Parsons contended that in traditional societies, one's place in the social hierarchy was determined more by social and demographic characteristics (such as race, ethnicity, birthright, bloodline, etc.) or "ascriptive" status. In other words, one's status was more dependent on "who one is" as opposed to "what one does." However, in modern societies, social status is affected more by what one achieves, rather than determined by "who one is." This would suggest far greater opportunities for upward social mobility than would exist in traditional societies. This is not to suggest that status is purely determined by achievement in modern societies. Indeed, it is clearly the case that many racial and ethnic groups face significant limitations on status even in the most modern societies, as is the case for women as well. Further, this is not to suggest that status is purely determined by ascription in less developed societies, and that there are no opportunities

Table 3.1 Traditional vs. modern societies.

	Traditional societies	Modern societies
How is social status determined?	Ascriptive status	Achievement status
What are the social roles that people play?	Diffuse roles	Specific roles
Are values universal or dependent on individual cases?	Particularistic values	Universalistic values
Which is more important, the group or the individual?	Collectivity orientation	Self-orientation
Do people act based on current circumstance, or do they postpone immediate rewards for future benefit?	Affectivity	Affective neutrality

for upward social mobility. Rather, Parsons thought of these ideal types anchoring a continuum along which were arranged a variety of different contemporary societies.

In terms of social roles, traditional societies are characterized by individuals playing multiple roles. For instance, a chief of the village would act not only as a political leader, but also as military leader (as well as religious leader). On the other hand, in modern societies, there is an increased division of labor and a specialization of roles as societies become more complex, as the result of industrialization and economic modernization.

Particularistic values versus universalistic values refer to the application of rules. In traditional societies, social rules and laws are applied depending on the situation. The law is applied differently for "paupers" as opposed to "princes." *Collectivity orientation versus self-orientation* refers to the relative importance of individual versus collective interests. In traditional societies, the interests of the collective unit (the community, the village, etc.) supersede the interests of individuals. On the other hand, in modern societies, the protection of individual rights and liberties often hold sway when in conflict with collective interests. As far as *affectivity vs affective neutrality* is concerned, in traditional societies individuals act in order to meet immediate needs (such as food, drink, procreation, etc.) whereas in modern societies, because these basic needs are met, individuals often forgo immediate satisfaction to attain future gain. In a sense, this is much like what John Stuart Mill, the famous nineteenth-century English philosopher, referred to as "enlightened rationality" where individuals would make short-term sacrifices (and hence not behave rationally in the short run) in order to attain greater benefits later.

With the coming of the behavioral revolution, and the search for explanatory variables to account for the emergence of different kinds of political systems, one of the first variables that political scientists began to examine was economic development, especially its effects on the emergence of political democracy. A most noteworthy figure in the development of modernization theory was Seymour Martin Lipset. In his classic work on the emergence of political democracy entitled *Political Man* (1959), he argued that there was a direct relationship between economic modernization (industrialization) and the development of political democracy. Essentially, he contended that economic modernization created the social requisites for the emergence of political democracy (a large vibrant and literate middle class, and wealth). Further, he noted that in the modern era there was a direct correlation between a number of measures of modernization (including higher urbanization, higher literacy, and greater per capita income) and political democracy. From this, he concluded that economic development had a direct causal relationship with political democracy.

Others, however, were more nuanced in assessing the relationship between economic modernization and political development and democracy. Karl Deutsch (1961) argued that industrialization and economic modernization do not necessarily lead to the development of political democracy (as Lipset had argued in 1959) but rather produced something Deutsch referred to as *social mobilization*. For Deutsch (1961, p. 494), social mobilization is: the process in which the major cluster of old social, economic and psychological commitments are eroded or broken and people become available for new patterns of socialization and behavior. Thus, for example, as industrialization occurred in the West, there was a massive shift in population from rural areas to urban areas. People who used to identify with localities were now thrust into a position of making new acquaintances, learning new things, and ultimately questioning their own sense of identity. It was because of this massive shift that there emerged a sense of national identities, as local rural identities were undermined to be replaced by a new sense of national community (Deutsch, 1953).

According to Deutsch, social mobilization is also a politically important process because it expands "the politically relevant strata of the population," by which is meant "those persons who must be taken into account in politics" (Deutsch, 1961, pp. 497–498). These changes produces pressures that present themselves to existing political systems, and the extent to which the existing political system deals with these pressure will affect the political consequences of social mobilization (violence and social disorder, or political stability).

Similarly, in their landmark study, Gabriel Almond and James Coleman (1966) in *The Politics of the Developing Areas* argued that economic modernization creates "crises" that systems must resolve. What results from modernization and social mobilization depends heavily upon how the existing political system deals with these crises. These include:

- the identity crisis
- the legitimacy crisis
- the participation crisis
- the penetration crisis
- the distribution crisis.

The *identity crisis* refers to the process by which traditional social ties are broken under the weight of social and economic transformation that results from economic modernization. Prior to modernization and the social upheavals it causes (for instance, the uprooting of people from rural areas to the industrializing cities with the rise in demand for labor), identities were often local, tied to villages, local communities, or regions. Modernization leads to the breakdown of these identities, as people realize they have much in common with other people whom they meet as they move to the cities (in terms of language, religion and cultural practices, etc.) but also realize there are people who are not like them. Modernization thus creates the basis for national communities and new national identities. Thus, what results is an identity crisis in which there is a rising need for a new sense of community identity, one presumably part of the process of building a new national identity.

The *legitimacy crisis* deals with the uprooting of old institutions and the tearing away of the quasi-religious basis of authority that existed (presumably) in traditional agrarian societies. Prior to modernization and the social transformation that accompanies it, authority patterns were based on "divine right" or the idea that rulers and elite derived their right to rule from God. Modernization (along with the rise of secularism and the growing importance of science and reason) gave rise to the "revolutionary" idea that the right to rule should be based on the consent of the governed, not a right provide solely by God.

The *participation crisis* deals with the generation of new demands for participation, thus putting considerable pressure on existing institutions. As the population becomes generally increasingly educated and literate, there is a "revolution in rising expectations" not only for material rewards, but for political aspirations as well. Gradually, the notion that people should merely be subjects of a monarch or a state erodes, to be replaced with the revolutionary idea that people should participate in the act of governance. Existing political systems must either accommodate (on on occasion suppress) such demands in order to survive the "storm" of modernization.

The *penetration crisis*, deals with the problem of creating new institutions to link the rulers with the governed. For example, before the onset of the modernization of the Western world, kings and other national rulers ruled indirectly, usually relying on local nobles to swear allegiance to them as national leaders, while they were charged with local administration and tax collection (giving them very considerable autonomy, including warring with neighboring nobles). However, as modernization undermined the old feudal order, the need arose to create new more direct links between rulers and ruled (largely for the purposes of subordinating the population and extracting taxes).

Finally, there is the *distribution crisis*. Economic development and social mobilization not only raise greater demands for goods and services but also produce new social groups who make new demands. New social groups, mobilized by industrialization (like workers organizations and businessmen, as well as "traditional groups" like farmers and landlords) demand from the political system their material share of the economic pie. The existing political system must find a way to accommodate such demands if it is to survive.

From the perspective of modernization theory, political development results from the social transformations that emerge from economic development. Indeed, a key feature of modernization theory is the idea that political development is caused (in some fundamental way) by economic development. But what does one mean by "political development"?

There have been several ways to conceptualize political development. Lipset (1959) in his classic work *Political Man*, thought of a politically developed state as one that was democratic. Others have thought of political development in non-democratic terms. For instance, Samuel Beer (1973) argues that political development is equivalent to the expansion of the bureaucratic state. From his perspective, he argues that economic development leads to social complexity and the need for specialization and division of labor (which he calls *patterns of interests*). In turn, the emergence of these patterns of interests creates demands for the political modernization of the state – which becomes more specialized, more bureaucratized, or what he calls *patterns of power*. The creation of these new patterns of power (bureaucratic agencies, and groups aligned with them) leads to them developing their own interests – or new patterns of interests. These new patterns of interests make new demands for access and representation, creating new patterns of power *ad infinitum*. Thus, political modernization ultimately leads to the differentiation and expansion, inevitably, of the realm of the state's activities.

However, perhaps one of the best known ways in which to conceptualize political development was offered by Samuel Huntington (1965, 1968). Huntington thought of political development as equivalent to "political institutionalization" or "the process by which organizations and procedures acquire value and stability" (Huntington, 1968, p. 12). Institutions are stable valued recurring sets of behavior – different organizations and procedures (and political systems for that matter) vary in the degree to which they are institutionalized, or stable. The extent to which a political system is institutionalized is a crucial variable explaining whether that system survives the "storm" of social mobilization. Indeed, Huntington contends that social mobilization does not always breed stable development or participation – in fact, social mobilization can breed something else – *political decay*, which he thought was characterized by political instability and violence (Huntington, 1965).

So how does one determine whether a political system is institutionalized? Huntington offered four key dimensions of political institutionalization: (1) adaptability/rigidity; (2) complexity/simplicity; (3) autonomy/subordination; and (4) coherence/disunity.

Adaptability/rigidity refers to the extent to which an organization can adapt to changing circumstance. Adaptable organizations are better able to survive changes in the environment (such as the changes wrought by rapid socioeconomic transformation) than are rigid organizations. Adaptability can be measured in several ways, but the three that Huntington suggests are: the chronological age, the generational age, and the functional age of the organization.

Generally organizations that are older are more likely to have faced many challenges, and hence by definition are more institutionalized than younger organizations. Yet many political systems may be chronologically old, but dominated by single leaders. Thus, Huntington also suggests *generational age* or the extent to which there have been leadership transitions. The more leadership transitions there have been, the more institutionalized is the political system. Finally, there is *functional age* or the number of times that organizations have switched functions. A case in point is the distinction between the YMCA (the Young Men's Christian Association) and the Women's Christian Temperance Union. Both organizations started as religious organizations dedicated to promoting the morals of young Christian men. Over time, the YMCA took on other roles – providing recreational activities not only to young Christian men, but later to young Christian women (YWCA) and still later to everyone. Now the YMCA is known more for the recreational activities (such as swimming lessons for children) than the original function it performed. On the other hand, the WCTU dedicated itself to promoting forced sobriety via the national prohibition of the production of alcoholic beverages. However, once that was achieved in 1919 in the United States, the organization could not adapt to perform other functions, and subsequently disappeared. Thus, the YMCA represents an example of an "institution" because of its functional adaptability.

Generally, as in the case of biological organisms, *complex* organizations are more adaptable than simple ones. Complex organizations are characterized by a division of labor into specialized tasks, as well as the replication and redundancies of structures (such as two kidneys in human beings) that promote survivability. Complex political systems (such as modern bureaucratic ones) are better able to accommodate and adapt to new challenges and changes in the social, economic and international environments than are simple political systems (such as traditional monarchies). *Autonomous* organizations, as well as autonomous political systems, are not dominated by some social group and have a degree of independence to adjust to new circumstances. Further, *coherent* organizations, or those that have a unity of purpose and unifying ideology that helps hold the organization (or the political system) together, are more likely to be institutionalized than organizations and systems that are fundamentally divided.

It is the combined effect of social mobilization and the political institutionalization that explains what results in terms of political development. For Huntington, like other modernization theorists, social mobilization created greater demands for goods and services (as the result of a revolution of rising expectations) and greater demands for political participation. If

Table 3.2   Huntington's classification of different regime types.

	Institutionalization high	*Institutionalization low*
Social mobilization high	Civic	Corrupt (Praetorian)
Social mobilization low	Contained	Primitive

Table 3.3   Country examples of regime types.

	Institutionalization high	*Institutionalization low*
Social mobilization high	The United States Great Britain Soviet Union	Most of the developing world
Social mobilization low	Contained? (Perhaps colonial societies)	Traditional agrarian monarchies (Imperial Ethiopia)

the existing political system cannot accommodate these demands, then this leads to political instability and ultimately, political decay.

In Table 3.2, Huntington's basic types of regime outcomes are outlined. Each type is the product of the interaction between the level of social mobilization and the extent to which the existing political system is institutionalized. In the case where social mobilization is high, which generates greater demands for material rewards and political participation (among other things) and the political system is able to adapt, accommodate, and channel these demands, this results in what Huntington referred to as a "civic" regime. On the other hand, where social mobilization was low (such as in pre-industrial or pre-modern societies) and where the level of institutionalization is low (as in the case of simple political systems), Huntington referred to this as a "primitive" regime.

In countries where social mobilization was low, but a "modern" bureaucratic system "sat" upon society (as in the case of twentieth-century colonies in Africa and Asia), Huntington referred to this as "contained" regimes. The final and most problematic situation was the "corrupt" or "praetorian" regime where social mobilization essentially overwhelms the political system, leading to instability, political violence, corruption, and decay. He thought of systems that were plagued by instability, with frequent coups and counter-coups, as prime examples of such regimes. Table 3.3 illustrates the kinds of country examples that fit these regime types.

What is perhaps most noteworthy regarding this table is that not only are the old democracies included as "civic" but so is the Soviet Union. This is because the USSR had undergone a massive and rapid modernization program during the 1930s, with extensive social mobilization pressures. However, the Soviet system, which was highly complex, autonomous, and armed with a legitimizing ideology (Marxism-Leninism) generally met these demands (or contained them via repression and violence) which allowed the Soviet system to survive. Thus, although it accomplished the development of a "stable" system, it did so in a fundamentally different way than what occurred in the West. As discussed in Chapter 2, the fact that both the United States and Britain developed fairly institutionalized political systems prior to industrialization and social mobilization was more a historical accident. In the Soviet Union, building the state occurred simultaneously with the rapid economic expansion and social transformation of society – rather like building a ship in a stormy sea.

Thus, for Huntington, the models of development represented by the old democracies (the US, the UK) were perhaps, inapplicable to the developing world. Unlike the challenges currently facing most developing countries, the old democracies did not have to contend with the overwhelming (and simultaneous) crises produced by social mobilization, along with the necessity of building of political institutions. A more appropriate model, albeit perhaps in a softer form, is represented by the Soviet Union (particularly after the death of the totalitarian dictator Josef Stalin in 1953) where a one-party state was able to contain and channel the pressures generated by social mobilization. Indeed, Huntington (at least in his classic works of the 1960s) appeared to favor the adoption of a one-party state solution for the developing countries of the world.

There are many advantages of a one-party state solution to social mobilization. Unlike personalist dictatorships, or the rule of the military, one-party states are more complex organizations than single-person dictatorships, and allow for the articulation of multiple interests (albeit internal to the governing party). Further, they are autonomous organizations in that they are not subordinated to the will of other groups (such as the military) and do not rule simply via the barrel of a gun. Indeed, one-party states (or at least dominant one-party regimes) are more likely to cultivate the institutionalization of the state, by relying on rules and procedures, rather than on individual leaders. Potentially such states can evolve into competitive democracies, and perhaps the one-party configuration is a transitional phase to a more democratic outcome. Certainly one can make that argument regarding more recent (and frequently cited examples) of the development of democracy outside of the West. In cases like India and Japan, a single party dominated politics (although via the electoral process) for much of the histories of these countries in the twentieth century. In India, the Congress Party dominated national government from independence in 1947 to well into the 1990s. The Liberal Democratic Party of Japan has governed the country almost continuously since the 1950s (shortly after the end of the American occupation) with only brief interludes in the 1990s. In Mexico, the Institutional Revolutionary Party dominated Mexican politics for over 70 years before the opposition came to power. Thus, perhaps the single party solution proffers the best chance for the emergence of institutionalized political systems in the developing world.

To summarize, then, what are the fundamental characteristics of modernization theory? To be sure there are many different approaches – some equate political development with democracy, others with the expansion of a modern complex bureaucratic (but not necessarily a democratic state). However, there are some common characteristics that modernization theorists share. First, all see political development primarily as a consequence or a function of economic development. In other words, the political system largely evolves as the result of stimuli posed by changes in the economic environment. Second, most all of these approaches are at their cores based upon historical observations of the processes of development in the Western, particularly the European experience. Finally (and this is the focus of Chapter 4), an often cited key intervening variable in modernization theory is the role played by political culture. In other words, economic development led to the embrace of certain values associated with the Western (and in particular Protestant) experience that helped explain the course of political development in Europe and North America.

Dependency

At about the same time that modernization theory was developing among North American political scientists, a very different approach to political development emerged in the post-war era – in Latin America. This approach, which later became known as "dependency theory" was rooted in the neo-Marxist approaches of Latin American scholars who were dissatisfied with the international economic status quo. In particular, they rejected the liberal free trade theories in the 1950s as the best solution to promoting economic development in the developing world. Raúl Prebisch (1950), whose research with the Economic Commission on Latin America (ECLA) suggested that decreases in the wealth of poor countries correlated with the increasing wealth of rich industrial countries, helped spark the emergence of an approach that would challenge modernization theory. Several scholars like Paul A. Baran (1957) and André Gunder Frank (1966), used neo-Marxian analyses to demonstrate the development of international capitalism had led to the "de-development" of the developing world. Theotonio dos Santos (1970) described a "new dependency," which focused on how the external relations of less developed countries were reflected or "articulated" in the internal relationships between center and periphery within countries. Similarly, the past President of Brazil, Fernando Henrique Cardoso, trained as an economist and while in exile before becoming president, wrote extensively on the growing disparities between center and periphery, both in the world system and internal to developing countries. The American sociologist Immanuel Wallerstein (2004) focused on what he called the "World System" and traced the historical development of international capitalism.

It was André Gunder Frank (1966, 1967) who first introduced an American audience to the concept of dependency theory, with the publication in 1966 of a short essay in the *Monthly Review* entitled "The development of underdevelopment." This was followed by a more substantial work in 1967, entitled *Capitalism and Underdevelopment in Latin America*. At the heart of his argument was the notion that underdevelopment and poverty in the developing world were a direct result of the expansion of world capitalism. In other words, modernization in the industrial world had led to the "de-development" of the periphery. A case in point he uses is the example of the Indian textile industry prior to the establishment of British imperial domination. Prior to the arrival of British East India Company, textile production (largely based in household industries) employed a large number of people and was quite extensive. However, with the arrival of the British came later a flood of cheap manufactured textiles that quickly destroyed the indigenous textile industry, thus creating massive unemployment and poverty.

Beyond the development of underdevelopment, there are a number of other features of dependency theory that stand in stark contrast to modernization theory. First, dependency theory contends that modernization theory does not take into account the impact of the international system on internal development. Indeed, modernizationists generally tend to focus on internal structural factors to explain economic and political development, without reference to the international environment. Second, there seems to be the assumption embedded in modernization theory that economic and hence political development occurs, and that importantly the pattern of development as exemplified in the industrial West should be applicable to the developing world as well. This of course, has been a long-held theme in economic and political theories, that the Western experience is replicable elsewhere. Karl Marx also shared this point of view when he once remarked (in the 1867 Preface to Volume 1 of *Das Kapital*) that "the country that is more developed industrially only shows, to the less developed, the image of its own future."

For dependency theorists, there are fundamental differences between the earlier experiences of the industrialized countries, and the experiences of the developing world in the twentieth century. Indeed, whereas in the West, the bourgeoisie had been the engine for economic modernization, the overthrow of feudalism, and the onset of political democracy, in the developing world the bourgeoisie has been less of a progressive force and has in fact reinforced the persistence of quasi-feudal social and economic relations, as well as a social form in support of political authoritarianism.

The reason for the different trajectories followed by the countries of the developing world in contrast to the industrialized West was the current existence of a world capitalist system. Unlike the West, which had developed before the world capitalist system had consolidated (indeed the countries of the industrial West were the ones who created the world capitalist order), the developing world is faced with the impediments presented by the world capitalist order on their ability to "catch up" with the counties of the "core." Taking as their point of departure the theories of imperialism offered by Vladimir Lenin, Karl Kautsky, and Rosa Luxemburg, dependency theory contends that the rise of imperialism fundamentally transformed the countries of the periphery (McLellan, 2007).

Figure 3.1 illustrates the relationship between the countries of the economic core of the industrial world in the latter part of the nineteenth century into the first half of the twentieth century. What motivated the industrialized, capitalist countries of the world to seek empires, by establishing colonies and dependencies (countries that were technically politically independent, but economically dependent upon the core imperial states) was the desire to establish markets for their surplus production of manufactured goods, and sources of supply for raw materials. Essentially, by compelling their colonies and dependencies to trade only with them, the imperial state could extract enormous amounts of wealth. Consumers in the peripheral countries were compelled to purchase relatively expensive

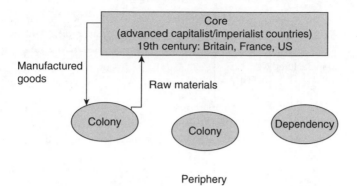

Figure 3.1   Imperialism, nineteenth century.

manufactured goods in exchange for the core's purchase of cheap raw materials. This system of "unequal exchange" helped the core to stave off revolution, by using the extracted surplus value to institute such "reforms" in the core to raise the wages of the working class, and to engage in changes that improved their working and living conditions. Essentially off the back of the poor in the developing world, the capitalists have been able to "buy off" their own workers.

According to "classical" Marxist theory (espoused by Lenin, Luxemburg and Kautsky) over time, as wages (the cost of labor) are reduced in the periphery, there is a greater incentive for capitalists to relocate industry and capital to the latter areas, especially as labor costs increase in the core. Eventually, from the classical Marxist approach, these peripheral countries begin to resemble the capitalist core, including the emergence of their own bourgeoisie and proletariat, thus creating the conditions for the international proletarian revolution.

Neo-Marxist dependency theory, on the other hand, denies that the peripheral countries will develop along the same lines as the capitalist core (as classical Marxists might argue). Indeed, although political imperialism died after World War II with the coming of the post-war period of decolonization, economic imperialism remained, and was subsequently strengthened in the new liberal post-war economic order. In particular, as is illustrated in Figure 3.2, the ties that bound the peripheral countries with the capitalist core grew, and became more complex. Foreign direct investment (FDI), often held as a solution to the economic ills of the developing world, only served to further shackle poor countries. This is because FDI

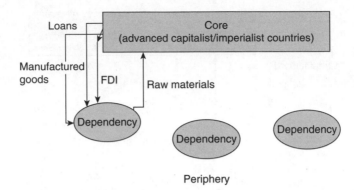

Figure 3.2 Neo-imperialism, twentieth century. FDI, foreign direct investment.

often comes in the form of "farming out" manufacturing parts as opposed to finished projects. Thus, auto parts are made, for example, in the "maquiladoras" (or duty-free factories on the Mexican-US border) rather than finished automobiles. Although there may be some marginal material benefits for Mexico, the bulk of the profit is accrued to the finished product, which is invariably assembled in the United States. Thus, profits from FDI are repatriated back to the capitalist core. Further, loans provide capital, but also shackle the developing world to the international financial system (especially via interest payments) that is controlled by the capitalist core. Thus, economic imperialism had not disappeared, but from the perspective of dependency theory, had become more complex and insidious.

According to dependency theory, the establishment, maintenance and deepening of dependent economic relations between core and periphery had a strong distorting effect on the course of social and political development in dependent countries. First, as mentioned above, the penetration of international capital led to the destruction of infant industries and the creation of widespread poverty. However, it also created a strong incentive for the maintenance of quasi-feudal social relations in rural areas. Indeed, as Frank (1967) noted, the maintenance and strengthening of the hacienda/plantation system were a direct result of the rise in demand for industrial crops in Latin America, especially since the hacienda system was very good at extracting and collecting products for export, and also for maintaining social control over the countryside.

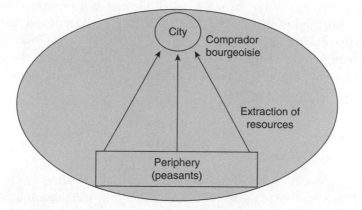

Figure 3.3 International articulation of imperialism and maintenance of quasi-feudalism.

The social effect of all this was the replication of systems of unequal exchange internally within the dependent countries, or what Samir Amin (1974, 1976) called the internal "articulation" of world capitalism. With the establishment of connections with world capitalism, "enclaves of modernity" were created, generally in cities near the coast where import/export activities could be pursued (see Figure 3.3). In these enclaves one can find many of the amenities one finds in the industrial West. Within these enclaves there also emerged a bourgeoisie of sorts, although not quite like the industrial bourgeoisie that had led the transformation of Europe. Unlike the Western bourgeoisie, who were a progressive class that dismantled feudalism and paved the way for the emergence of political democracy, the "comprador bourgeoisie" are neither socially progressive nor champions of political democracy. Rather, given that their wealth is generated from trade rather than industrial production, they have little incentive to change a system from which they benefit. Thus, in alliance with the feudal landlords (with whom they have common economic interest), they maintain the existing system of internal unequal exchange, which feeds into the international system of unequal exchange. Further, they have little incentive to "empower" the masses, and hence prefer the maintenance of conservative authoritarianism.

However, even if by some chance a populist leader emerged from the masses that declare a "revolution" (usually having risen themselves through the ranks of the military as was so often the case in Latin American and elsewhere), they were likely to eschew something as Western and "corrupt" as bourgeois democracy. Thus, from the dependency perspective, there is little hope for the emergence of political democracy as long as the system of dependent economic relations is maintained between the international core and the world periphery.

Statism

A core argument of the advocates of the "classical" dependency approach is that the structure of the world capitalist economy will prevent the countries of the periphery from ever catching up with the countries of the capitalist core. However, there were numerous examples of formerly peripheral countries "catching up" with the core – such as Japan, Russia, Turkey, and more recently the so-called "Asian Tigers" – Taiwan, Singapore, and South Korea. What could possibly explain this?

Many former scholars who had been influenced by the dependency approach began to offer alternative explanations for "dependent development" (Evans, 1979). Scholars such as Peter Evans, Dieter Reuschmeyer, and Theda Skocpol (Skocpol, 1979; Evans, Reuschmeyer, and Skocpol, 1985; Evans, 1995) and others who were trained in dependency literature and the terminology of neo-Marxism, began to question the applicability of dependency outside of Latin America (see Evans, Reuschmeyer, and Skocpol, 1985) – clearly there were countries in the periphery that were catching up, primarily via state-led industrialization.

Essentially, the scholars who formed the "statist" school viewed both modernization theory and dependency theory as incapable of explaining why states in the periphery had been able to develop in the way they did. In particular, they were critical of what they called the "society-centered" approaches to development, approaches that ignored the important role the state had played in terms of capital accumulation and investment. This allowed many dependent economies to break the bonds of economic dependency, and move from the periphery to (at least in the case of Japan) the capitalist core.

At the heart of the statist approach to politics is the Weberian conception of the state (as opposed to the Marxist or liberal conception of the state). In the "liberal" conception of the state, the state (or the political system) is considered an arena in which various interests compete. For Marxists, the state is merely a tool used by the dominant class to remain dominant. In both cases, the state is an object, devoid of interests of its own. Max Weber, on the other hand, thought of the state as "a human community which claims the monopoly of the legitimate use of physical force within a given territory" (Weber, 1946, p. 78). Like other human communities, the state therefore has interests of its own – paramount among these interests, the need to survive. What compels states to pursue modernization strategies is the threat posed by external enemies. Rapid industrialization is seen as a way to increase the military capacity of the state, and hence provide greater security against external enemies. Thus, for the statist approach, rather than politics being a reflection of changes in the economic environment (either internally as in the case of modernization theory, or externally as in the case of dependency theory), "politics" is a cause for economic transformation.

Modernization, Dependency, and Statism Compared

In summary, how do modernization theory, dependency theory and statism compare with one another? J. Samuel Valenzuela and Arturo Valenzuela (1978) offered a systematic way in which to compare the different approaches. They argued that both modernization theory and dependency theory are very different in terms of fundamental assumptions. For instance, modernization theory assumes a tradition–modernity distinction and that the cultural and social values which are characteristic of "tradition" are the reasons for underdevelopment. Further, there is extensive agreement that the best way for the developing world to progress is to replicate the models that have been offered by the early modernizers. Dependency theory, on the other hand, argues that underdevelopment is the product of dependent relations between the world periphery and the capitalist core – in other words, the "fault" of the developed world, not the underdeveloped. Generally, earlier models cannot be replicated, given the unique circumstances facing the countries of the periphery in the era of economic imperialism.

Table 3.4 illustrates several dimensions by which the three approaches that relate political development and economic development can be compared. Along the rows are a variety of dimensions that help distinguish each approach. The first is the unit of analysis – for modernization theory (as well as statism), the unit of analysis is the state, in as much as development

Table 3.4 Modernization, dependency, statism, compared.

	Modernization theory	Dependency	Statism
Unit of analysis	State	Global System	State
Can earlier models be replicated?	Earlier models can be replicated	Earlier models cannot be replicated	Earlier models can be replicated
Economic development	Possible when modern values are adopted	Possible only when international economic order changes	Possible as the result of the voluntaristic action of the state.

is largely a function of the internal characteristics of countries. For dependency theory, the unit of analysis is the global system, which is at the root of all economic and political change. In terms of earlier models, both modernization theory and statism hold that earlier models can be replicated in the developing world (although for modernization theory, these are the developed countries of the West, and for the statists, the state-led industrializers like Japan and Turkey represents promising models for emulation). On the other hand, for dependency theory, earlier models are inapplicable, given the unique circumstances the periphery currently faces in the form of the world capitalist economy. Further, economic development is possible for modernizers when the developing world adopts the values and attitudes of individualism that underpinned the industrial transformation of the West. For dependency theory, real development is only possible if the fundamental structure of the world capitalist system were to be changed. For the statists, development and "catching up" are possible when the state pursues policies of fundamental transformation, motivated by the desire for self-preservation.

Although there has been considerable debate over the relationship between economic and political development, there is a general consensus that the economic environment in which political development occurs (whether it originates from internal sources – either social, cultural or political – or from external sources) is a crucial explanatory factor for the emergence of a variety of political forms, including political democracy. In Chapter 4, we investigate another widely cited variable that is often held as having an independent effect on political development – political culture.

References

Almond, Gabriel A. and Coleman, James S. (1960) *The Politics of the Developing Areas*, Princeton, NJ: Princeton University Press.

Amin, Samir (1974) *Accumulation on a World Scale: A Critique of the Theory of Underdevelopment*, New York: Monthly Review Press.

Amin, Samir (1976) *Unequal Development: An Essay on the Social Formations of Peripheral Capitalism*, New York: Monthly Review Press.

Baran, Paul A. (1957) *The Political Economy of Growth*, New York: Monthly Review Press.

Beer, Samuel H. (1973) "The Modernization of American Federalism," *Publius*, 3 (1): 49–95.

Deutsch, Karl (1953) *Nationalism and Social Communication: An Inquiry into the Foundations of Nationality*, Cambridge, MA: MIT Press.

Deutsch, Karl W. (1961) "Social Mobilization and Political Development," *American Political Science Review*, 55 (4): 634–647.

Dos Santos, Theotonio (1970) "The Structure of Dependence," *American Economic Review*, 60 (2): 231–236.

Durkheim, Emile ([1893] 1964) *The Division of Labor in Society*, trans. George Simpson, New York: Free Press.

Evans, Peter (1979) *Dependent Development: The Alliance of Multinational, State, and Local Capital in Brazil*, Princeton, NJ: Princeton University Press.

Evans, Peter (1995) *Embedded Autonomy: States and Industrial Transformation*, Princeton, NJ: Princeton University Press.

Evans, Peter, Reuschmeyer, Dietrich, and Skocpol, Theda (1985) *Bringing the State Back In*, Cambridge: Cambridge University Press.

Frank, Andre G. (1966) "The Development of Underdevelopment," *Monthly Review*, 18 (4): 17–31.

Frank, Andre G. (1967) *Capitalism and Underdevelopment in Latin America: Historical Studies of Chile and Brazil*, New York: Monthly Review Press.

Giddens, Anthony (ed.) (1972) *Emile Durkheim: Selected Writings*, Cambridge: Cambridge University Press.

Huntington, Samuel (1965) "Political Development and Political Decay," *World Politics*, 17 (3): 386–430.

Huntington, Samuel (1968) *Political Order in Changing Societies*, New Haven, CT: Yale University Press

Lipset, Seymour Martin (1959) *Political Man: The Social Bases of Politics*, Garden City, NY: Doubleday.

McLellan, David (2007) *Marxism After Marx*, 4th edn., London: Palgrave Macmillan.

Parsons, Talcott (1951) *The Social System*, Glencoe, IL: Free Press.

Parsons, Talcott (1971) *The System of Modern Societies*, Englewood Cliffs, NJ: Prentice Hall.

Prebisch, Raúl (1950) *The Economic Development of Latin America and Its Principal Problems*, New York: United Nations.

Skocpol, Theda (1979) *States and Social Revolutions*, Cambridge: Cambridge University Press.

Valenzuala, J. Samuel and Valenzuela, Arturo (1978) "Modernization and Dependency: Alternative Perspectives in the Study of Latin American Politics," *Comparative Politics*, 10 (4): 535–552.

Wallerstein, Immanuel (2004) *World-Systems Analysis: An Introduction*, Durham, NC: Duke University Press.

Weber, Max (1946) *From Max Weber: Essays in Sociology*, trans. and eds. H. H. Gerth and C. W. Mills, New York: Oxford University Press.

4

Political Culture and Ethnopolitics

A longstanding argument in the literature on comparative politics is that political culture has an important effect on the emergence of political democracy. In part, the focus on political culture is rather a natural extension of the behavioral revolution in political science (which was discussed in Chapter 1) and a product of economic modernization (as was discussed in Chapter 3). With modernization came changes in values regarding the role of the individual in the political system. No longer was it considered acceptable by the masses to defer to the authority of a monarch claiming to represent a heavenly deity. These values in turn led to the emergence of demands for political participation, and in turn, the emergence of a set of values that catalyzed the development of political democracy in the West.

In the extant literature in political science, political culture has been defined in many ways but essentially it involves the basic values, ideas, beliefs, attitudes, and orientations about politics. This involves issues of right and wrong, good and bad, what is acceptable in politics and what is not. The notion of a "political culture," and that it had an impact on political development is not a new idea. Indeed, the argument that an underlying set of values regarding political relationships promoted market capitalism and democracy has been a longstanding theme in sociological studies. The notable German sociologist Max Weber argued, for instance, argued that the values associated with Protestantism contributed to the capitalist revolution and rapid economic expansion from the eighteenth to the twentieth centuries, which in turn ultimately led to the emergence of political democracy. In his massive comparative study that compared the values embedded

Comparative Politics: Principles of Democracy and Democratization, First Edition.
John T. Ishiyama.
© 2012 John T. Ishiyama. Published 2012 by Blackwell Publishing Ltd.

in Buddhism, Catholicism, Confucianism, and Islam, he argued that the values of hard work, honesty, seriousness, and monetary thrift and efficiency were especially conducive to the accumulation of capital and the development of business skills. Especially important was the recognition that the accumulation of wealth through commerce (and usury, which had been frowned upon before by the Catholic Church) signified that one was viewed favorably in the eyes of God. The other societies he studied may have had some of these values, but none had all of them save Protestantism. More recent scholars like David Landes (1998) have pointed out other cultural factors that explain why industrialization emerged first in Northern Europe (particularly in England, Germany, the Netherlands and the Scandinavian countries). In particular, he points to the cultural factors that supported the emergence of a valuing of science, the respect of autonomous intellectual inquiry and an emphasis on empiricism (which arose from the Protestant emphasis on the observable as proof that one was viewed favorably by God). These values are what prompted the expansion of science and technological innovation during the Renaissance and into the early modern era, laying the intellectual groundwork for the Industrial Revolution later.

As Wiarda (1999) notes, political culture studies were boosted by World War II. In particular, the work of cultural anthropologists like Ruth Benedict (1934, 1954) and Margaret Mead (1964), as well as sociologists like Nathan Leites (1951), contributed greatly to the expansion of scholarly understanding of political culture, particularly through providing explanations for Japanese and Soviet behavior during World War II. In many of these cases these works were commissioned by the US government to be utilized in the struggle against Japan during World War II and then the Soviet Union during the Cold War (Leites, 1951; Benedict, 1954). Although these studies did focus on Japanese and Soviet attitudes to power, hierarchy, duty, etc. (that is, the political aspects of power) they were essentially non-comparative, single-country studies. Indeed, these cultural anthropological studies, in keeping with the tradition in that field, tended to emphasize what was unique to these political cultures, which did little in providing a more general (and more systematic) approach by which political scientists could study political culture.

A major breakthrough occurred with the publication of Gabriel A. Almond's and Sydney Verba's seminal work *The Civic Culture: Political Attitudes and Democracy in Five Nations* (1963). Unlike previous cultural anthropological studies that were resistant to imposing categories on the cases that they examined (preferring to have such patterns "emerge"),

Almond and Verba sought to establish a framework by which different political cultures across different countries could be systematically compared. Further, although they acknowledged that political culture involved beliefs, values, attitudes, and orientations, they addressed directly the question of: beliefs, values, attitudes about *what*?

In keeping with the behavioral tradition that gave rise to the idea of a "political system" (which was discussed in Chapter 1), Almond and Verba defined a political culture as "a set of specifically political orientations – attitudes toward the political system and its part and attitudes towards the role of the self in the system" (Almond and Verba, 1963, p. 12). The two principal components of this definition are "orientations" and "objects." The objects of the system include those parties of the political system as identified by the structural-functionalist approach described in Chapter 1 (input processes, output processes, structures of system, etc.).

Orientations, on the other hand, refer to psychological dimensions, particularly citizens' attitude and values and how these affect politics. For Almond and Verba, there are three sets of different kinds of psychological orientations. These include:

- *cognitive orientations* – the knowledge of and belief about the political system, its roles, and the incumbents of these roles, inputs and outputs;
- *affective orientations* – that is, feelings about the political system, its roles, personnel, and performance;
- *evaluational orientations* – the judgments and opinions about political objects that typically involve combining value judgments or feelings with information.

The three sets of orientations can then be translated into four different systems dimensions:

1 The cognitive, affective and evaluational orientations vis-à-vis the system as a whole, such as its constitutional characteristics, political structures, etc.
2 The cognitive, affective and evaluational orientations vis-à-vis the policy process (input objects, for example, interest groups, parties).
3 What knowledge, feelings, opinions does an individual have about policy enforcement or how policy is implemented, etc. (output objects)?
4 How does the individual perceive him or herself as a member of the political system? Do they believe they have a positive impact on the system or what?

Table 4.1 Political culture types.

	System	Input objects	Output objects	Role of self
Parochial	−	−	−	−
Subject	+	−	+	−
Participant	+	+	+	+

These four dimensions can be combined to identify particular types of political cultures as indicated in Table 4.1.

The three types of political cultures that Almond and Verba identify are: parochial, subject, and participant. Generally, in parochial political culture, citizens are only remotely aware of the presence of central government, and live their lives regardless of the decisions taken by the state. Parochials know very little or nothing about the political system, its parts and its processes, and hence are not "positively" oriented to the input or output functions, nor have a positive role for the "self" in the political system. In other words, "parochials" do not believe they should participate, nor that they should be the beneficiaries of policy, nor do they see themselves as having any role in the political system. In a way, these sentiments are consistent with the old Russian peasant proverb "God is high above and the Tsar is far away." In general, for Almond and Verba, a parochial political culture predominates in relatively poor, underdeveloped, and agrarian societies, where social orientations are local as opposed to national. However, they are also very careful to note that parochial individuals can be found virtually in any society.

Subject political culture is characterized by people who are aware of the political system, and know something about how it operates, but primarily see themselves as subjects to authority. Hence they are positively oriented towards the output processes of the political system (that is, what is produced by the system as "benefits" such as employment, education, health-care, etc.) which they are quite willing to "consume." However, they are not positively oriented to the input side of the system, nor do they believe they have a positive role to play in the operation of the system itself. They do not believe that they can (nor should) articulate interests, participate in the aggregation of those interests, nor play a role in the policy process. In short, they do not see themselves as "participants" in the political system.

Generally a subject political culture tends to dominate in modern authoritarian states (such as the Soviet Union or in Nazi Germany) where citizen activities are defined as "duties" as opposed to "rights" and authority emanates from the top down. Such societies often base their right to rule on some ubiquitous "law of history" (which only the political elite can interpret) and reinforce their legitimacy through system performance (*performance legitimacy*), that is, as long as the outputs are produced, people will remain loyal to the system. As with parochials, Almond and Verba thought that all societies, to some extent, had their share of "subjects."

The third type of political culture is what Almond and Verba refer to as "participant" political culture. Participant political culture is characterized by individuals who not only know a great deal about the political system, but also are positively oriented towards *both* input and output processes (that is, they both want to participate AND receive the benefits of policy) and believe they have a positive role to play in the political system. Such political cultures are often found in modern, developed, wealthy societies, with high levels of mass literacy and education. Indeed, participant political culture was closely related to development, and as Almond and Verba noted in 1963, as the result of modernization the world could be expected to become *more participant*.

It is important to note that Almond and Verba considered these three types of political cultures as *ideal types* (or types that may not exist perfectly in nature, but are idealized characterizations of what might exist). Second, they believed that these attitudes were held at the individual level (given the emphasis on the psychological dimensions of culture – attitudes, beliefs, orientations, etc.) and that in the aggregate they form national political cultures. When aggregated to the national level, a country's political culture is in fact a mix of all three types. In other words, one could find parochials, subjects, and participants in any country. What differentiated different types of national cultures was the relative mix of all three. In some, the parochial impulse predominated, in others, the participant.

The particular research question that Almond and Verba addressed was which mix best supported the development of stable political democracy. They argued that that cultural mix or the *civic culture* comprised of a majority of participants, tempered by a significant minority of subjects and some parochials. They argued that such a civic cultural mix could be found in the older democracies (such as the United States and Great Britain) where more subject- and parochial-dominated mixes could be found in societies that had a recent experience with totalitarianism (Germany and Italy) and in developing societies (such as Mexico). Using data from interviews from over 5000 people across five countries (conducted over five years) they found evidence that appeared to confirm their suppositions. Great Britain and the United States had the highest proportion of participants of the five cases (although Almond and Verba did express some concerns that the proportion of participants in the United States was too high, and presented a destabilizing element in American politics). Germany and Italy had a higher proportion of subjects than any other case (consistent with the recent history of those two countries as they emerged from totalitarianism),with Mexico being the least democratic, and with the greatest number or subjects and parochials.

The Almond and Verba study had an enormous impact on the development of political cultural studies. Numerous studies began to examine the impact of political culture on political development in Africa, Asia, Latin America, and elsewhere (see Pye and Verba, 1966; Rudolph and Rudolph, 1967; Dealy, 1977; Dawson, Prewitt, and Dawson, 1977; Smith, 1979). Indeed, it also had a significant impact on the understanding of politics in the United States as well. Daniel Elazar (1994), in a way similar to Almond and Verba, argued that the political culture refers to what people believe and feel about government, and how they think people should act towards it or "the particular pattern of orientation to political action in which each political system is imbedded." However, its focus is largely on how people perceive the role of government. In this regard he identifies three types of political cultures that exist in the United States. A *moral political culture*, where social concerns are held up to be more important than the individual. Individualism is not submerged in any way, but the group recognizes the need of individuals to assign value to the group. Government tends to be seen as a positive force. This emphasizes the commonwealth conception as the basis for democratic government. Politics is considered one of the great activities of man in the search for the "good society." Good government is measured by the degree to which it promotes the public good. Issues have an important place in the moralistic style of politics. Politicians are expected not to profit from political activity. Serving the community is the core of the political relationship even at the expense of individual loyalties and political friendships. In practice, this often results in more amateur participation in politics than in the other political cultures.

Another type of political culture that Elazar identifies is the *individual political culture*. Government is seen largely as an impediment and something to be restricted so as not to interfere with private activities. Government does have a role, but it should be largely restricted to those areas which encourage private initiative. Unlike in a moral political culture, private concerns are more important than public concerns. Finally, there is the *traditional political culture*. In such a political culture, according to Elazar, social and family ties are prominent where this type of political culture is found, and the emphasis is on traditional hierarchies. Government is seen as an actor with a positive role in the community, but the role is largely limited to securing the maintenance of the existing social order. Political leaders play a largely conservative and custodial role rather than being innovative. Otherwise, limited government is viewed as best because that is all that is required to meet the needs of those in power (Elazar, 1994, pp. 230–235).

Yet this approach that emphasized the explanatory importance of political culture on political behavior and political systems development was not without its critics. These criticisms generally fell primarily along three lines: questions regarding the definition and conception of political culture and the explanatory power of political culture apart from other factors; and finally, what can explain the emergence of different political cultures?

Defining political culture

Arend Lijphart (1980), a leading figure in comparative studies of political culture and ethnicity, was very sympathetic to the idea that political culture is powerful explanatory variable in accounting for the emergence of political systems, particularly democracy versus autocracy. However, he argued that Almond and Verba "stretched" the concept beyond orientations about the political system, and to include general social and personal relations, such as the notion of the role of the self in the system. Rather, the focus should be entirely on how politics is conducted, rather than "feelings" regarding the role of the self and how the self interacts with others. This produced an unnecessary "vagueness" in the concept and he argued that what was necessary was focusing specifically on the political.

Rather than conceiving of political culture as an individual set of attitudes, Lijphart (1999) focused on the way in which political decisions were made, either via a consensual approach (or the idea that political decisions should be based on maximizing the number of points of view represented, and that consensus among these points of view should be achieved and a tolerance of societal differences) or the conflictual/adversarial approach (which paints politics in terms of stark contrasts (right and wrong) and an emphasis on the triumph of one side over the other). For Lijphart, consensual political culture leads to a "kinder and gentler" policies in contrast to majoritarian political cultures (ibid., p. 305). In a somewhat similar vein, Bradley Richardson (1984) describes, in his work on Japanese political culture, the difference between the consensual Japanese tendency to view politics in terms of "fair share" (that is, what is important in the political game is that all share equally in the outcome) as opposed to "fair play" (that is, no matter the outcome, as long as the game was played fairly, then the results are legitimate) in the more adversarial political cultures of the West.

What Lijphart and Richardson have in common (along with Almond and Verba) was the idea that political culture had an independent and unique effect on the development of democracy and political systems. For Lijphart consensual political culture is associated with consensual political institutions and adversarial political culture is linked to majoritarian political institutions. A more significant criticism is that the concept of political culture, as portrayed by Almond and Verba, cannot be neatly separated from other factors, to act as an independent variable in explaining the emergence of political system and political behavior. For instance, Carole Pateman (1971) argues that if political orientations are an integral part of the political system, then attitudes can exist only in relation to a specific set of institutions. If this is true, then it is impossible for Almond and Verba to retain the view that political culture constitutes an independent variable, because it cannot be separated from the institutional context in which it exists.

In part, in response to these criticisms, more recently scholars have tried to separate political culture from an attachment to particular sets of institutional arrangements. David Elkins and Richard Simeon (1979, p. 128) think of political culture in much broader terms than Almond and Verba. Rather than as a set of "orientations" regarding politics, they contend that political culture really is about a set of assumptions about politics These assumptions about the political world "focus attention on certain features of events, institutions, and behavior, define the realm of the possible, identify the problems deemed pertinent, and set the range of alternatives among which members of the population make decisions." Thus, they see political culture as a "mind set" which has the "effect of limiting attention to less than the full range of alternative behaviors, problems, and solutions which are logically possible." Therefore, political culture limits to only a few alternatives those choices that are considered credible or legitimate, and most people who "choose from a restricted set will, for most of them, remain below the threshold of consciousness, because they seldom encounter individuals who take for granted quite different assumptions" (Elkins and Simeon, 1979, p. 128).

The idea that political culture involved something much more fundamental than attitudes and orientations about particular political systems was particularly appealing to many European scholars, working at about the same time as Elkins and Simeon. These scholars took a much broader view of political culture, rather than attitudes associated with particular kinds of political systems (as had Almond and Verba and Lijphart). David Robertson (1985, p. 263) defines political culture as "the totality of ideas and attitudes towards authority, discipline, governmental responsibilities and entitlements." Richard Rose (1980, pp. 116–117) thinks of political culture as sets of "values, beliefs and emotions," that are "taken for granted" by individuals and essentially "give meaning to politics." Dennis Kavanagh (1985) thinks of political culture in a similar way, arguing that it "disposes its members to regard certain forms of political behaviour and institutions as 'normal' and others as 'abnormal.'" Richard Topf (1989) thinks of political culture as comprised of attitudes and stances that people adopt to make sense of politics. Topf proposes that political attitudes are viewed as "expressions of 'values,' or better, of positions in the moral order, constitutive of the political culture." Stephen Welch (1993, p. 34) provides yet another way to think of political culture, not so much as a set of assumptions, but as a set of "resources." According to this approach, political culture supplies images, symbols, myths, traditions, which enable people to make sense of their situation or predicament which generates certain needs that influence the selection and interpretation of the available cultural resources. Thus, the original notion that political culture was associated with attitudes about particular political systems has increasingly been replaced with the idea that political culture is a set of attitudes and orientations that help people make sense of politics.

The Explanatory Power of Political Culture

In addition to questioning the way in which political culture was defined, many other scholars have criticized Almond and Verba's assertion that political culture can be used to explain such phenomena as political democracy. Indeed, scholars like Carol Pateman (1971) and Brian Barry contend that it is better to think of political culture as a product of political and socioeconomic processes as opposed to as a reason for such processes.

Barry suggests that "political culture" is merely composed of "reasonable expectations founded on common experience" of the existing system. "Obviously, if this interpretation is correct," he argues, "there are no grounds for saying that the correlation arises from the conduciveness of the 'civic culture' to 'democracy', but rather for the unexciting conclusion that 'democracy' produces the 'civic culture'" (Barry, 1978, pp. 51–52). Marxist critics such as Jerzy Wiatr (1980) point to the causal influence of social and economic realities on political culture. Similarly, Carol Pateman contends that the Almond and Verba argument "neglects the association between class and participation and implies that social status is irrelevant to which side of the balance a citizen occupies, or to the citizen's view of the rationality of action or inaction" (1980, p. 84).

Arend Lijphart, however, defends Almond and Verba from these criticisms by arguing that the e question of political culture's explanatory power has been incorrectly conceived, especially the idea that structure and culture should be thought of in separable terms. Lijphart (1980) contends that it is a mistake to think the relationship between culture and structure in either/or terms. In fact, he contends they are inherently linked and occur simultaneously – political and social and economic structures clearly affect political culture, but culture clearly impacts the kinds of political structures that emerge. Although Lijphart's defense of the political culture concept seeks to retain a place for political culture in explaining such phenomena as political democracy, his answer raises more questions regarding how political culture contributes to the emergence of political forms.

Perhaps an answer to the proper place political culture has in explaining political phenomenon (such as the emergence of democracy) can be found in Elkins and Simeon (1979). They do not deny the importance of political culture in explaining political behavior and political development, but they contend that most efforts have failed to control for other factors when attributing causal properties to political culture. Elkins and Simeon contend that it is difficult to separate political culture from other "structural" explanations (such as the level of education at the individual level, or political institutions at the systems level). For them, political culture should not be the explanation of the "first resort" but only after other explanations have been ruled out (or the explanation of "last resort"). In other words, what cannot be explained by social, economic, and political structures, can be attributed to political culture. In a sense, political culture is the variation in the dependent variable that cannot be explained by structural factors.

Explaining Political Culture

Another question that has emerged regarding the theory of Almond and Verba is the question of the "production" of political culture. Indeed, by demonstrating empirically correlations between attitudes and educational attainment, Almond and Verba suggest the possibility that political culture is "produced" by the combined action of individuals and institutions. However, they never really explain how this process actually occurs beyond referring to "political socialization." Nonetheless, as Carol Pateman (1980) points out, socialization only takes an active role if there are tensions between the (independently generated) orientations of people and the way the system actually works. The inability to explain the evolution of political culture and its development, along with criticisms regarding definitions and the independent explanatory power of political culture, led to a decline in interest in the concept in the comparative politics literature.

Renaissance of Political Culture

At the end of the 1980s, there occurred a renewed interest in political culture in the United States (although as we noted earlier, there had been a continuing interest in the concept in Europe throughout the 1970s and 1980s). In particular, the work of Ronald Inglehart (1971; 1977) was most important in leading this renewed interest in the political culture concept. For Inglehart, culture was a system of common basic values that help shape the behavior of the people in a given society (1997, p. 217). Political culture is those fundamental political values that help guide the behavior of people. In keeping with the shift away from defining political culture as attitudes and orientations with reference to a particular political system, Inglehart thinks of political culture as a set of values and attitudes independent of particular political structures.

As a result of his work (as well as the continuing work of Almond and Verba themselves), the concept experienced a remarkable revival (Inglehart, 1988; Laitin and Wildavsky, 1988; Diamond, 1993; Reisinger, 1995). There are several reasons for this revival. First, developments in the real world that could not be explained without making reference to cultural factors – phenomena such as the emergence of radical Islamic fundamentalism and the extraordinary modernization of the several East Asian countries. Second, the collapse of the Soviet Union and the demise of communist systems in Central and Eastern Europe raised again the issue of how the changing political cultures in the communist world had led to the demise of communism itself. Further, scholarship again focused on the congruence of political culture with institutional structures as a prerequisite for the consolidation of new democracies in the region (Linz and Stepan, 1996; Rose, Mishler, and Haerpfer, 1998; Diamond, 1999). In particular, scholars like Robert Putnam (1993) in his *Making Democracy Work*, pointed to the importance of such republican virtues of civic community, tolerance, cooperation, and solidarity, in promoting the development of political democracy.

The importance of Ronald Inglehart's work in helping to revive the political culture concept cannot be overestimated. One of his major contributions to the study of political culture was the idea of post-materialism. As with the well-known Maslow's hierarchy of human needs, Inglehart argues that individuals pursue goals in hierarchical order, with the satisfaction of material needs like food and sustenance coming first, gradually shifting to non-material need as material needs are satisfied. Using this logic, Inglehart argues that in the past in the West (and still characteristic of most of the world) material scarcities and lack of economic development led to a popular emphasis on economic growth and security (via a strong national defense and "law and order," for example). Over time, however, as societies develop economically and acquire greater wealth, material affluence leads to changing values, away from material needs to "post-material" values, such as personal freedom and political participation, and quality of life issues such as maintaining a clean environment. Inglehart, however, did not see this as a temporary phenomenon. As a result of the process of socialization, these post-material orientations would be transferred to subsequent generations, and will emerge as a rather stable value-system in contrast to more volatile political attitudes. In this way, post-material values have been incorporated into the fundamental political value system (that is, political culture) of many countries in the West.

Although most of the world remains largely in a "materialist" state, many countries in the West have witnessed a shift away from materialism to post-material politics. This shift was largely due to the rapid economic expansion following the end of World War II in Europe and the West. The period was characterized by an unprecedented period of positive economic growth (albeit with slowdowns in the 1980s, 1990s and early twenty-first centuries). Incomes and material benefits grew rapidly – for instance, between 1945 and 1970 income per capita grew at an average rate of 6.69 percent per year in Austria, 6.62 percent in Germany, 5.64 percent in Italy, 4.61 percent in France, and 4.12 percent in the Netherlands.

This unprecedented period of economic growth and rise in per capita incomes (along with the creation of the extensive "welfare state") provided for unprecedented levels of economic security. As a result, there has been a shift in political values as well. To measure this shift, Inglehart, relying on survey data from the American National Election Studies (NES), constructed a simple index base that essentially asked respondents to choose two values out of range of four that were most important to them. Respondents were asked:

> For a nation, it is not always possible to obtain everything one might wish … several different goals are listed. If you had to choose among them, which one seems most desirable to you?

1   Maintaining order in the nation.
2   Giving the people more say in important political decisions.
3   Fighting rising prices.
4   Protecting freedom of speech.

Respondents were then asked "Which one [goal for our nation] would be your second choice?" and were given the three remaining choices. Following Inglehart (1971), those respondents who chose both (1) and (3) were coded as "pure materialists" and those responding with (2) and (4) as post-materialists (Inglehart, 1971, p. 94). There have been subsequent variations of the index used in studies (most notably the General Social Survey, the World Values Survey and others). Data from the World Values Survey (2000) have indicated that the highest proportion of the population that could be classified as post-materialist were highest in Australia (35 percent), Austria (30 percent), Canada (29 percent), with the United States at 25 percent (Inglehart *et al.*, 2004, p. 384).

By the 1990s, this shift had resulted in the emergence of a new set of political values, in particular:

- The diminishing effectiveness and acceptability of bureaucratic authority (small is better).
- A growing emphasis on individual freedom and emotional experience and questioning all forms of authority.
- The diminishing prestige of science technology and rationality, and a re-embrace of religion.

Table 4.2   Material versus post-material values by authority type.

	Traditional values (materialist)	Postmodern values (post-materialist)
Rational/legal/ secular (emphasis on state authority)	Post-communist Eastern Europe, China, Japan (somewhat)	Northern Europe Canada (increasingly Japan)
Traditional authority (e.g. religion)	Poland, most of the developing world	Italy, Spain, Mexico, Argentina, the US (is a borderline case), Ireland,

The growing rediscovery of religion (in part as a response to the rapidly changing modern world) added another dimension to the materialist/post-materialist distinction between different national cultures. Using Max Weber's (1947) understanding of different patterns of authority (particularly his distinction between traditional and rational legal bases for the political authority of the state), Inglehart distinguished between post-materialist and materialist political cultures by whether or not the state authority was based on rational legal (or secular) power (that is, people obey because it is in their self-interest to do so) or on tradition (that is, people follow state authority because that is the way it has always been, often because authority is based on religious values). In Table 4.2 we summarize the primary distinctions between different countries.

In the columns of Table 4.2 are the traditional versus the post-materialist values; in the rows are the different types of authority patterns. Generally, countries that are based on some secular non-religious basis of authority (but where materialist values predominate) include most all of the post-communist states (except for Poland where Catholicism represents a powerful legitimizing force for the state). This pattern derives from the secular legacy of communism (which is also true of China) coupled with relatively lower level of economic development of these states when compared to the West. Japan is rather a borderline case (secular but increasingly imbued with post-materialist values as compared to materialist values). Secular and post-materialist countries include most all of northern Europe, as well as Canada and to some extent the United States (which is a borderline case with traditional authority, given the particularly strongly influence of religion on politics in that country). Countries that are both traditional in authority patterns and materialist in cultural values include most of the developing world (some examples are illustrated). Countries where traditional authority patterns predominated but where post-material concerns for the quality of life, freedom and the environment predominate, include many Catholic countries of southern Europe, Latin America, and, to some extent (as mentioned above) the United States.

Generally speaking, different cultural combinations will affect the politics (and in many ways the development of democracy) in particular countries. In countries where traditional authority patterns predominate, one can expect a less participatory impulse on the part of the population (which is somewhat akin to Almond and Verba's "Subject" political culture discussed above). Further, this coupled with materialist values (including both political and economic security concerns) invites something less than participatory democracy. Although economic development and the emergence of post-material values may lead to democracy, the quality of that democracy, or its type, is powerfully affected by the legacy of past authority patterns.

More recently, Inglehart (1997) has sought to generalize beyond post-materialism to argue that western industrial democracies have moved into a new period of "postmodernization" politics. The term "postmodernization" refers to a new historical phase in which the processes of economic, cultural, and political change shape values and behavior: "In the postmodernization phase of development, emphasis shifts from maximizing economic gains to maximizing subjective well-being" (ibid., p. 86). Postmodern values include not only post-material values, but political values such as tolerance and permissiveness. Inglehart thus argues that the post-materialist shift is "only one part of a broader shift toward postmodern values, involving changing orientations towards politics, work, family life, religion, and sexual behavior" (ibid., p. 132). As a result, new priorities emerge and are expressed in the emphases on issues such as environmental protection, abortion, ethnic diversity, women's issues, and gay rights (ibid., p. 247).

What have been some of the specific posited micro-political effects of this rise in post-material values and postmodernization? Over the past two decades, some of Inglehart's predictions for the West such as the rise of post-materialism have come to fruition in the United States (Inglehart and Abramson, 1994). For instance, class-based political cleavages have weakened (Huckfeldt and Kohfeld, 1989; Ladd and Hadley, 1975), and social and cultural concerns such as abortion, homosexual rights, women's rights, and prayer in the public schools have moved to the forefront of American politics as opposed to bread and butter economic issues. Further, the rise in post-material political issues has changed the ways in which political actors behave. A case in point is the experience of the European Social Democratic/Labor Left in Europe during the post-war period. Prior to World War II, the Social Democratic Left was concerned with basic materialist issues, such as wages, the economic rights of the working classes, and the struggle with ownership. To a large extent this was in keeping with the Marxist roots of the "revisionist" Social Democratic Left (with its lingering emphasis on class warfare and the struggle for the ownership over the means of production). Thus Socialist, Social Democratic, and Labor Parties prior to World War II primarily viewed themselves as champions of the working classes, seeking material benefits for their mass constituencies.

However, following the economic boom in the post-war period, there also occurred a "greening" of the European Left. This accelerated in the 1990s with the collapse of the communist systems of Central and Eastern Europe, where the materialist demands for ownership of the means of production and nationalization of industry (which had been a call of the British Labor Party in the 1970s, for instance) gave way to calls for greater openness and accountability of government, and the emphasis on private and public partnerships. It also led to calls for smaller government, and the protection of individual rights. Indeed, the post-material shift, can, to some extent, be used to explain the rise of Blairism in the British Labour Party, and the merger of the Dutch Green Party and the Dutch Communist Party in the 1990s (and the creation of *Groenlinks* or the Green-Left Party).

Inglehart's post-materialist/postmodernization thesis has not been without its critics (Flanagan, 1982a; 1982b). Chief among these has been the argument concerning the inadequacy of the four-item index first employed to measure the extent to which post-materialism exists (Clarke and Dutt, 1991, Duch and Taylor, 1993; 1994). For instance, Clarke *et al.* (1999, p. 637) argue that simply changing the item asked has a significant impact on who is counted as a "post-materialist." Indeed, by "substituting an unemployment statement for the standard inflation statement in the battery has major consequences for the classification of respondents as materialist or postmaterialist." This would suggest also that respondents' answers are dependent upon current economic conditions – indeed,

> When inflation is not a salient economic problem, respondents eschew the
> rising prices item but are forced by the format to choose one of the remaining

three, none of which deals with other economic concerns they may have. Respondents who do not select the prices item have a zero probability of being classified as materialist. (ibid., p. 637)

However, this also suggests a more serious potential problem with Inglehart's notion of a post-material politics. Indeed, the issue is not simply related to the measurement validity of the Inglehart index. It may also be the case that post-materialism as a stable set of values, is not so stable after all, and is subject to changes in the economic environment, that is, people respond in a "post-materialist" way when economic times are good, and in a "materialist" way in periods of economic downturn (or for that matter. an international crisis when threats to security occur). This is reminiscent of the criticisms of the earlier Almond and Verba work that "political culture" does not truly have an independent effect on politics beyond economic and material conditions.

Ethnic Politics and Nationalism

As the conception of political culture moved towards the idea that it was a set of values through which politics is interpreted, it made it closer to other "shortcuts" by which people make sense of their political world. In the era of "multiculturalism" culture has become equated with ethnicity. Indeed, multiculturalism often is used interchangeably (particularly in the United States) with inter-ethnic or inter-racial relations. This is because there is a close relationship between cultural and ethnic identities.

Ethnicity and the political effects of diversity

What is meant by "ethnicity"? Although Nathan Glazer and Daniel Patrick Moynihan (1975, p. 1) remarked in their landmark study that "ethnicity seems to be a new term," the root word "ethnic" is really a very old concept. The term is derived from the Greek "ethnos" which originally meant "heathen" or "pagan." In scholarship, the term was largely ignored by social science (with notable exception in the work of the famous German sociologist Max Weber, discussed below).

Although there have been many different approaches to understanding ethnicity as a concept over the years in the social sciences, more recently there have been two basically different ways to think of ethnicity and politics – the primordial and the constructivist. On the one hand, there are advocates of the "primordial" or "essentialist" approach which generally holds that ethnicity is a "natural phenomenon, existing at all times in human history and that modern ethnic groups have roots that extend far into the past. For primordialists, ethnic groups are defined by kinship and bloodlines. The "essentialist" school in the primordialist approach is most extreme, contending that ethnic groups are not simply historical but also naturally occurring – this view is consistent with the scientific racialist approaches of the early twentieth century – approaches that gave rise to the eugenics movement and National Socialism (for a review of such approaches, see the work of Anthony Smith, 1999, pp. 4–7). Another school of thought in the primordialist approach is the historical – that ethnic groups are historical entities that are extensions of kinship units but more than kinship. They are, however, defined by cultural signs (language, religion, traditions) which symbolize biological unity. However, ethnicity itself may not be a biological condition, but as Clifford Geertz (1973) argues, what matters is that humans perceive ethnicity as such. Thus, ethnicity, he argues, is an objective condition and just as real if it were a physical condition.

On the other hand, there is the constructivist or "subjective" conception of ethnicity. Although, there are variations on the idea that ethnicity and ethnic identity are more malleable and flexible than the primordialists would argue, essentially the subjectivist point of view is consistent with the Germans sociologist Max Weber's definition of ethnicity as a "subjective belief" in "common descent. Whether or not an objective blood relationship exists" (Weber 1978, 389: cited by Guibernau and Rex, 1997, p. 3; see also Horowitz, 1985; Smith, 1986). Similarly, Enid Schildkrout (1979, p. 184) argues that "the minimal definition of an ethnic unit ... Is the idea of common provenance, recruitment primarily through kinship, and a notion of distinctiveness, whether or not this consists of a unique inventory of cultural traits" (see also Schildkrout, 1974). Benedict Anderson (1991), writing about "nations," thinks of such structures as ethnicity as "imagined communities" and social constructed products of human social interaction which are maintained for instrumental reasons – they are used to validate governance, to bind a community together, etc. Related to this subjective notion of ethnicity is the "modernist" perspective that contends that ethnicity is purely a modern invention only appearing in the modern period of world history. This was certainly an argument made by Karl Marx and Friedrich Engels, who thought of "nations" as primarily a "bourgeois" construct that would wither away after the collapse of capitalism. Others, such as Eric Hobsbawm (1990), argue that prior to the modern industrial era there was no ideal of politicized ethnic identities – these were created by modernization (on this point, see also Karl Deutsch, 1953).

Although ethnicity can express itself politically in many ways (see Ishiyama and Breuning, 1998), in the modern era many ethnically based conflicts are often couched as "nationalist" struggles. Although nationalism is often based on ethnicity, not all ethnopolitics, as John Ishiyama and Marijke Breuning note, is nationalistic. Indeed, nationalism as a concept is a type of socio-political ideology whose core principles are popular sovereignty (a people must have a state) and the glorification of the community. Nationalists see the establishment of and protection of the nation state as the highest political goal.

Based upon this notion that nationalism is a political ideology like any other ideology, there can be different types of nationalisms. Some nationalisms are based on ethnicity, whereas others are not. Greenfield (1992) identifies two different dimensions by which one can classify different kinds of nationalisms (which will importantly affect not only the emergence of democracy, but the form democracy takes if it does emerge). These two dimensions are:

1 What is the nation? A collection of individuals (individualism) or is the nation a collective entity (collectivism)?
2 Who belongs to the nation? Does citizenship alone qualify for membership (civic) or is membership defined by blood (ethnicity)?

Using these two dimensions, Greenfield classified three different types of nationalisms, some of which were based on an "ethnic" community whereas others were based on a "civic" notion of community. Table 4.3 illustrates the types of nationalism that can be identified when taking into consideration these two dimensions.

Table 4.3 Types of nationalism.

	Civic	*Ethnic*
Individualism	Individualist/civic (US)	Not possible
Collectivism	Collectivist/civic (France)	Collectivist/ethnic (most of Eastern Europe)

As illustrated in Table 4.3, there are three logical types of nationalism rising from the combination of dimensions of the conception of community (whether the nation is defined as a collection of individuals, or as a collective unit that is more than the sum of its parts) and who is eligible for membership in the national community (whether this is based on allegiance to a set of principles – or civic – versus communities based on blood and kinship – or ethnic). The first type, exemplified best perhaps by the United States, is characterized by an individualist conception of "nation" coupled with membership in the national community defined by allegiance (in theory) to a set of principles as enshrined in the US Constitution. In this type of nation, individual rights are often held as more important than the interests of the collective unit. Another type of nationalism is found in France, where the nation is conceived as something more than a collection of individuals (or the idea of "La Belle France") although *who* can be part of the national community is based on allegiance and (at least in principle) not on blood.

More problematic (and also most common), at least from the perspective of building consolidated democracies, is the third type of nation – one in which the nation is thought of as a collective unit and where membership is defined primarily by blood and kinship ties. In Europe this type of nation is found in much of Central and Eastern Europe. This type of national community does not generally favor the development of political democracy, particularly given that collective interests are often valued more that individual rights. Further, blood connections defining a nation provides little opportunity for outgroups to enter the national community – in periods of social and economic stress, this can also lead to growing intolerance, incivility and unwillingness to compromise with "outsiders" which is inimical to political democracy.

Another theme that is common in the literature on ethnic politics is the relationship between ethnic diversity and political democracy. Indeed, does ethnic diversity endanger democracy? Although most scholars would not argue that ethnic heterogeneity precludes the development of democracy, many scholars, like David Welch, note that "establishing and sustaining democratic institutions in ethnically divided societies is a difficult task" (Welch, 1993, p. 55). The idea that ethnic heterogeneity and diversity are inimical to democratic development has been a longstanding theme in Western scholarship. John Stuart Mill, for instance, argued that "free institutions are next to impossible in a country made up of different nationalities" and thought that multinational societies would pose a continuous threat to social peace and hence be inimical to the development of political democracy (Mill, 1958, p. 230).

The idea that ethnically diverse societies are relatively more prone to violent conflict is at the heart of the argument that ethnic heterogeneity is a bad thing for political democracy. Gabriel Almond made this argument in the 1950s when he noted that probability of violent conflict rose as a function of ethnic heterogeneity (Almond, 1956). Later, G. Bingham Powell (1982) found a negative relationship between ethnic fractionalization, on the one hand, and governmental stability, civil peace, and the prospects for democracy, on the other. Alvin Rabushka and Kenneth Shepsle (1972), in their path-breaking work on ethnic politics argue that ethnic divisions are inimical to democracy – in fact, democratization and democratic competition help to exacerbate ethnic conflict. In the Rabushka and Shepsle model, a key role is played by ethnic elites and the organizations that they lead. Indeed, these organizations engage in the politics of ethnic outbidding that ultimately undermines multiethnic cooperation and inevitably leads to nondemocratic, ethnically-exclusive states. Other authors have similarly argued that because ethnic parties make their political appeal specifically on ethnicity, their emergence often has a centrifugal effect on politics (Reilly, 2003). This is *especially* harmful to new democracies, where democratic institutions are quite fragile. Indeed, under such conditions, ethnic competition can easily turn into ethnic conflict. This is because the competition for votes for the ethnic party involves mobilizing the ethnic group – and the best way to do that is to use inflammatory and confrontational rhetoric, distinguishing between "us" versus "them." Donald Horowitz (1993, p. 19) once observed:

> Democracy has progressed furthest in those East European countries that have the fewest serious ethnic cleavages (Hungary, the Czech Republic, and Poland) and progressed more slowly or not at all in those that are deeply divided (Slovakia, Bulgaria, Romania, and of course the former Yugoslavia).

Although the contention that ethnic diversity is inimical to political stability and democracy is a longstanding theme, more recently several scholars have offered a more contingent view of the relationship between ethnicity and democracy. James Fearon and David Laitin (1996) argue strongly that ethnic heterogeneity does not predispose such societies to political conflict, civil war, and the collapse of incipient democracies. In fact, they argue that factors such as the size of the population and the proportion of the country that is mountainous have a far greater impact on the incidence of civil conflict than does ethnic fractionalization. Others have argued that the relationship between ethnic fractionalization and conflict and democracy is more complex than was portrayed by the earlier literature. Donald Horowitz (1985, 1993) has made precisely that point – conflict may result from ethnic diversity only under conditions of very high fractionalization or very low fractionalization. The probability of conflict, however, is perhaps highest when societies are divided, where a majority group faces a very sizeable minority group – (as in Sri Lanka between Sinhalese and Tamils, or in Fiji between Fijians and ethnic Indians). Paul Collier and Anke Hoeffler (1998) have also argued that what is important is the extent to which groups are polarized (that is, when there are two groups posed against one another): "Highly fractionalized societies are no more prone to war than highly homogeneous ones. The danger of civil war arises when the society is polarized into two groups." José Montalvo and Marta Reynal-Querol (2005) found that polarization rather than fractionalization explained conflict. Some writers argue that ethnic heterogeneity may be good for controlling conflict and promoting democracy. Ben Reilly (2000), for instance, contends that in Papua New Guinea the fact that there were so many groups thus guaranteed that no one group could monopolize power and dominate others. The ethnic diversity has thus promoted toler-ance and the politics of ethnic coalitions. A similar argument has been made regarding the emergence of peace and democracy in India (Hardgrave, 1993).

More recent literature in the field offers a more contingent view of the link between ethnic cleavages and conflict, and stresses the importance of ethnicity and ethnic cleavages as cost-effective strategic resources for group formation, interest definition and collective action (Fearon and Laitin, 2003; Birnir, 2007; Chandra, 2004; Posner, 2004). Most of these authors argue that whether ethnicity becomes destructive of democracy depends on several intervening variables, such as the extent to which ethnic interests are represented in a democratic polity, and the behavior of politi-cal elites.

For instance, advocates of the *consociational* school have long argued that by promoting the emergence of ethnic politics and then representing groups broadly, this will facilitate the integration of as many subcultures as possible into the political game, thus creating the conditions for interethnic cooperation (Lorwin, 1971; Nordlinger, 1972; Daalder, 1974; McRae, 1974; Lijphart, 1977). Further, by securing representation for minority groups, openness serves to facilitate the integration of disaffected groups into the political system, which ultimately leads them to moderate their demands. Frank Cohen (1997, p. 613) argues that the broader the representation, the more likely the ethnic group feels bound to the existing system – as he puts it, "by making institutions more accessible and making ethnic cleavages more explicit, ethnic groups will engage in more frequent but less intense conflict. They will use moderate means of resistance to effect change in the status quo."

Perhaps one of the strongest and most articulate proponents of the notion that ethnicity can have a positive effect on the stabilization of new democracies is Kanchan Chandra (2004). Chandra directly attacks the notion of ethnic outbidding, which is so central to the argument that the mere appearance of ethnic parties sets off a chain reaction leading to a spiral of extremism that destroys democratic politics altogether. Rather, she argues that ethnic parties can help sustain democracy if these parties are institutionally encouraged to compete on multiple dimensions rather than on just the unidimensional axis of ethnicity. Indeed, political institutions that restrict "ethnic politics to a single dimension destabilize democracy, whereas institutions that foster multiple dimensions of ethnic identity can sustain it" (Chandra, 2005, p. 236).

In a similar vein, Johanna Birnir (2007), in examining patterns of ethnic politics in a broadly comparative way, contends that the ethnification of politics does not necessarily translate to violence. Indeed, like Chandra, she argues that ethnic identity serves as a stable but flexible information shortcut for political choices, and assists in stabilizing party formations and hence the development of democracy. If violence occurs, it is largely the result of political institutional factors, particularly restrictions on access to the executive. This exclusion is what leads to violence, not the political mobilization of ethnicity.

Birnir argues that, *ceteris paribus*, ethnic parties (which she refers to as ethnic "attractors") are predisposed to seek peaceful means to gain access to political power. This is because, as with all parties, ethnic attractors seek to act on the behalf of a constituency and seek leverage for that constituency. In turn, voters who use ethnic identity as a shortcut to sort through candidate preferences, prefer parties that act on behalf of the ethnic constituency (this could be a non-ethnic party as well). This provides a strong incentive for the ethnic attractor to gain access to the political executive, and this is best achieved through peaceful means.

Why is it the case, then, that members of some ethnic groups appear to peacefully support their group in electoral politics, while others do not support their groups, exit electoral politics and even engage in protest and violence? Her answer is that if political intransigence and violence result, it is not because of the ethnification of politics but rather the denial of political access to an ethnic group. It is the shutting out from the core of power that produces the kinds of violence and instability that are commonly associated with ethnic politics in the existing literature.

Thus, there remains considerable debate on the effects ethnic diversity has on the development of political democracy. Nonetheless, what is clear, is that the development of democracy is generally more difficult in ethnically heterogeneous societies than in ethnically homogeneous ones. However, the construction of democracy is not impossible in even deeply ethnically divided societies. What is key is that careful attention must be paid to *how* democratic institutions are designed, and whether or not they fit a particular ethnic and cultural context.

The Effects of Culture and Ethnicity on Democracy

In this chapter, we outlined some of the posited effects of the cultural and ethnopolitcal context on the development of democracy. Indeed, although there is considerable debate over whether culture has a truly independent effect on the development of democracy, or whether ethnic diversity leads to conflict and the demise of incipient democratic experiments, there is little question that culture and ethnopolitics have *some* kind of effect. Further, there is little question that in countries that have political cultures that value tolerance, moderation, compromise and civility, democracy is easier to develop than in countries that do not have such political cultures. In addition, although ethnic diversity may not necessarily lead to conflict and the demise of democracy, incipient democracies face greater challenges in societies that are deeply divided than those that are more ethnically or culturally homogeneous. Although these cultural and ethnopolitical factors may not determine whether democracy succeeds, they certainly are important variables to consider when assessing the probability of success of democracy in places with these cultural characteristics and as divided as Iraq, for example.

References

Almond, Gabriel A. (1956) "Comparative Political Systems," *Journal of Politics*, 18: 381–409.

Almond, Gabriel and Verba, Sidney (1963) *The Civic Culture: Political Attitudes and Democracy in Five Nations*, Boston, MA: Little, Brown and Company.

Almond, Gabriel and Verba, Sidney (eds.) (1980) *The Civic Culture Revisited*, Boston, MA: Little, Brown and Company.

Anderson, Benedict (1991) *Imagined Communities: Reflections on the Origin and Spread of Nationalism*, London: Verso.

Barry, Brian (1978) *Sociologists, Economists, and Democracy*, Chicago: University of Chicago Press.

Benedict, Ruth (1934) *Patterns of Culture*, New York: Houghton Mifflin.

Benedict, Ruth (1954) *The Chrysanthemum and the Sword: Patterns of Japanese Culture*, Rutland, VT and Tokyo: Charles E. Tuttle Co.

Birnir, Johanna K. (2007) *Ethnicity and Electoral Politics*, New York: Cambridge University Press.

Chandra, Kanchan (2004) *Why Ethnic Parties Succeed: Patronage and Ethnic Headcounts in India*, Cambridge: Cambridge University Press.

Chandra, Kanchan (2005) "Ethnic Parties and Democratic Stability," *Perspectives on Politics*, 3: 235–252.

Clarke, Harold D. and Dutt, Nitish (1991) "Measuring Value Change in Western Industrialized Societies: The Impact of Unemployment," *American Political Science Review*, 85: 905–920.

Clarke, Harold D., Kornberg, Allan, McIntyre Chris, Bauer-Kaase, Perta and Kaase, Max (1999) "The Effect of Economic Priorities on the Measurement of Value Change: New Experimental Evidence," *American Political Science Review* 93: 637–647.

Cohen, Frank S. (1997) "Proportional Versus Majoritarian Ethnic Conflict Management in Democracies," *Comparative Political Studies*, 30: 607–630.

Collier, Paul and Hoeffler, Anke (1998) "On Economic Causes of Civil War," *Oxford Economic Papers*, 50.

Daalder, Hans (1974) "The Consociational Democracy Theme," *World Politics*, 26: 604–621.

Dawson, Richard E., Prewitt, Kenneth, and Dawson, Karen S. (1977) *Political Socialization*, Boston, MA: Little, Brown and Company.

Dealy, Glen Caudill (1977) *The Public Man: An Interpretation of Latin American and Other Catholic Countries*, Amherst, MA: The University of Massachusetts Press.

Deutsch, Karl (1953) *Nationalism and Social Communication: An Inquiry into the Foundations of Nationality*, Cambridge, MA: MIT Press.

Diamond, Larry J. (1993) *Political Culture and Democracy in Developing Countries*, Boulder, CO: Lynne Rienner.

Diamond, Larry (1999) *Developing Democracy: Toward Consolidation*, Baltimore, MD: Johns Hopkins University Press.

Duch, Raymond M. and Taylor, Michaell A. (1993) "Postmaterialism and the Economic Condition," *American Journal of Political Science* 37: 747–779.

Duch, Raymond M. and Taylor, Michaell A. (1994) "A Reply to Abramson and Inglehart's 'Education, Security, and Postmaterialism,'" *American Journal of Political Science*, 38: 815–824.

Elazar, Daniel J. (1972) *American Federalism: A View from the States*, New York: Thomas Y. Crowell.

Elazar, Daniel (1994) *The American Mosaic*, Boulder, CO: Westview Press.

Elkins, David and Simeon, Richard (1979) "A Cause in Search of Its Effect, or What Does Political Culture Explain?" *Comparative Politics*, 11: 1–31.

Fearon, James D. and Laitin, David D. (1996) "Explaining Interethnic Cooperation," *American Political Science Review*, 90: 715–735.

Fearon, James D. and Laitin, David D. (2003) "Ethnicity, Insurgency, and Civil War," *American Political Science Review*, 97: 75–90.

Flanagan, Scott (1982a) "Changing Values in Advanced Industrial Societies," *Comparative Political Studies*, 14: 403–444.

Flanagan, Scott (1982b) "Measuring Value Change in Advanced Industrial Societies: A Rejoinder to Inglehart," *Comparative Political Studies* 15: 99–128.

Geertz, Clifford (1973) *The Interpretations of Culture*, New York: Basic Books.

Glazer, Nathan, and Moyniha, Daniel P. (1975) *Ethnicity: Theory and Experience*, Cambridge, MA: Harvard University Press.

Greenfield, Leah (1992) *Nationalism: Five Roads to Modern Identity*, Cambridge: Cambridge University Press.

Guibernau, Montserrat and Rex, John (eds.) (1997) *The Ethnicity Reader: Nationalism, Multiculturalism and Migration*, Cambridge: Polity Press.

Hardgrave, Robert L. (1993) "India: Dilemmas of Diversity," *Journal of Democracy* 4: 71–85.

Hobsbawm, Eric J. (1990) *Nations and Nationalism Since 1780*, Cambridge: Cambridge University Press.

Horowitz, Donald (1985) *Ethnic Groups in Conflict*, Berkeley, CA: University of California Press.

Horowitz, Donald L. (1993) "Democracy in Divided Societies," *Journal of Democracy*, 4: 1–25.

Huckfeldt, Robert and Kohfeld, Carol W. (1989) *Race and the Decline of Class in American Politics*, Urbana, IL: University of Illinois Press

Inglehart, Ronald (1971) "The Silent Revolution in Post-Industrial Societies," *American Political Science Review*, 65: 991–1017.

Inglehart, Ronald (1977) *The Silent Revolution: Changing Values and Political Styles Among Western Publics*, Princeton, NJ: Princeton University Press.

Inglehart, Ronald (1988) "The Renaissance of Political Culture," *American Political Science Review*, 82: 1203–1230.

Inglehart, Ronald (1997) *Modernization and Postmodernization: Cultural, Economic, and Political Change in 43 Societies*, Princeton, NJ: Princeton University Press.

Inglehart, Ronald and Abramson, Paul (1994) "Economic Security and Value Change," *American Political Science Review*, 88: 336–354.

Inglehart, Ronald, Basánez, Miguel, Díez-Medrano, Jaime, Halmann, Loek, and Luijkx, Ruud (eds.) (2004) *Human Beliefs and Values: A Cross-Cultural Sourcebook Based on the 1999–2002 Values Surveys*, Coyoacan: siglo veintiuno editores.

Ishiyama, John and Breuning, Marijke (1998) *Ethnopolitics in the New Europe*, Boulder, CO: Lynne Rienner.

Kavanagh, Dennis (1985) *British Politics: Continuities and Change*, Oxford: Oxford University Press.

Ladd, Jr. Everett C. and Hadley, Charles D. (1975) *Transformations of the Party System: Political Coalitions from the New Deal to the 1970's*, New York: Norton.

Laitin, David W. and Wildavsky, Aaron (1988) "Political Culture and Political Preferences," *American Political Science Review*, 82: 589–596.

Landes, David (1998) *The Wealth and Poverty of Nations: Why Some Are So Rich and Some So Poor*, New York: W.W. Norton.

Leites, Nathan (1951) *The Operational Code of the Politburo*, New York: McGraw-Hill.

Lijphart, Arend (1974) *The Politics of Accommodation: Pluralism and Democracy in the Netherlands*, 2nd edn., Berkeley, CA: University of California Press.

Lijphart, Arend (1977) *Democracy in Plural Societies: A Comparative Exploration*. New Haven, CT: Yale University Press.

Lijphart, Arend (1980) "The Structure of Inference," in G. Almond and S. Verba (eds.) *The Civic Culture Revisited*, Boston, MA: Little, Brown and Company.

Lijphart, Arend (1999) *Patterns of Democracy: Government Forms and Performance in Thirty-Six Countries*, New Haven, CT: Yale University Press.

Linz, Juan and Stepan, Alfred (1996) *Problems of Democratic Transition and Consolidation: Southern Europe, South America and Post-Communist Europe*, Baltimore, MD: Johns Hopkins University Press.

Lorwin, Val (1971) "Segmented Pluralism," *Comparative Politics*, 3: 141–175.

McCrae, Kenneth D. (1974) *Consociational Democracy: Political Accommodation in Segmented Societies*, Toronto: McClelland and Stewart.

Mead, Margaret (1964) *Continuities in Cultural Evolution*, New Haven, CT: Yale University Press.

Mill, John Stuart (1958) *Considerations on Representative Government*, New York: Liberal Arts Press (first published in 1859).

Montalvo, José and Reynal-Querol, Marta (2005) "Ethnic Polarization, Potential Conflict, and Civil Wars," *American Economic Review*, 95: 796–816.

Nordlinger, Eric A. (1972) *Conflict Regulation in Divided Societies*, Cambridge, MA: Center for International Affairs, Harvard University.

Pateman, Carole (1971) "Political Culture, Political Structure and Political Change," *British Journal of Political Science*, 1: 291–305.

Pateman, Carol (1980) "The Civic Culture: A Philosophic Critique," in G. Almond and S. Verba (eds.), *The Civic Culture Revisited*, Boston, MA: Little, Brown and Company.

Posner, Daniel N. (2004) "Measuring Ethnic Fractionalization in Africa," *American Journal of Political Science*, 48: 849–863.

Powell, G. Bingham (1982) *Contemporary Democracies: Participation, Stability, and Violence*, Cambridge, MA: Harvard University Press.

Putnam, Robert (1993) *Making Democracy Work: Civic Traditions in Modern Italy*, Princeton, NJ: Princeton University Press.

Pye, Lucien and Verba, Sydney (eds.) (1966) *Political Culture and Political Development*, Princeton, NJ: Princeton University Press.

Rabushka, Alvin and Shepsle, Kenneth A. (1972) *Politics in Plural Societies*, Columbus, OH: Merrill.

Reilly, Benjamin (2000) "Democracy, Ethnic Fragmentation, and Internal Conflict: Confused Theories, Faulty Data, and the 'Crucial Case' of Papua New Guinea," *International Security*, 25.

Reilly, Benjamin (2003) "Political Engineering of Parties and Party Systems," paper presented at the Annual Meeting of the American Political Science Association, Philadelphia, PA.

Reisinger, William M. (1995) "The Renaissance of a Rubric: Political Culture as Concept and Theory," *International Journal of Public Opinion Research*, 7: 328–352.

Richardson, Bradley (1984) *Politics in Japan*, New York: Longman.

Robertson, David (1985) *The Penguin Dictionary of Politics*, Harmondsworth: Penguin.

Rose, Richard (1980) *Politics in England: An Interpretation for the 1980s*, London: Faber.

Rose, Richard, Mishler, William and Haerpfer, Christian (1998) *Democracy and Its Alternatives*, Baltimore, MD: Johns Hopkins University Press.

Rudolph, Lloyd and Rudolph, Susan (1967) *The Modernity of Tradition: Political Development in India*, Chicago, IL: University of Chicago Press.

Schildkrout, Enid (1974) "Ethnicity and Generational Differences among Urban Immigrants in Ghana," in A. Cohen (ed.) *Urban Ethnicity*, London: Tavistock.

Schildkrout, Enid (1979) "The Ideology of Regionalism in Ghana," in William A. Shack and Elliott P. Skinner (eds.) *Strangers in African Societies*, Berkeley, CA: University of California Press.

Smith, Anthony D. (1979) *Nationalism in the Twentieth Century*, Oxford: Martin Robertson.

Smith, Anthony D. (1986) *The Ethnic Origins of Nations*, Oxford: Basil Blackwell.

Smith, Anthony D. (1999) *Myths and Memories of the Nation*, Oxford: Oxford University Press.

Topf, Richard (1989) "Political Change and Political Culture in Britain, 1959–87," in John. R. Gibbins (ed.) *Contemporary Political Culture*, London: Sage.

Weber, Max (1947) *The Theory of Social and Economic Organization*, trans. A. M. Henderson and Talcott Parsons, New York: The Free Press.

Welch, David (1993) "Domestic Politics and Ethnic Conflict," in Michael E. Brown (ed.) *Ethnic Conflict and International Security*, Princeton, NJ: Princeton University Press.

Welch, Stephen (1993) *The Concept of Political Culture*, New York: Macmillan and St Martin's Press.

Wiarda, Howard (1999) *Introduction to Comparative.Politics*, Fort Worth, TX: Harcourt Brace.

Wiatr, Jerzy (1980) "The Civic Culture from a Marxist Sociological Perspective," in G. Almond and S. Verba (eds.) *The Civic Culture Revisited*, Boston, MA: Little, Brown and Company.

5

Social Structure and Politics

In previous chapters we identified the "background" factors that help shape the development of political systems – historical processes, economic development, and political culture. However, what also shapes the emergence of democracy or dictatorship is the social structure. By social structure, I mean the way in which society is organized. Societies may be organized hierarchically (such as in caste systems) where there are layers of groups, one higher than another. Other types of societies can be more egalitarian, with little distinction between different types of groups in terms of superordinate or subordinate status.

A longstanding theme in the existing literature is the idea that the structure of societies shapes the kinds of political systems that emerge, independent of political culture and economics. Karl Marx in particular argued that conflict between groups (especially classes) was the prime determinant of the political systems that emerges (although those conflicts were primarily economic in nature). More recently, scholars have argued the extent to which societies are "plural" impacts upon the likelihood of democracy. In particular, several scholars (for instance, Huntington, 1984) have argued that the development of democracy is facilitated by the existence of a widely differentiated and articulated social structure with relatively autonomous social classes, regional groups, occupational groups, and ethnic and religious groups. Some scholars have argued that "pluralism" or the existence of a large number of relatively autonomous associational groups best promotes democracy. These "associational" groups are independent of the state, and provide a way for citizens to articulate their interests. Examples

Comparative Politics: Principles of Democracy and Democratization, First Edition.
John T. Ishiyama.
© 2012 John T. Ishiyama. Published 2012 by Blackwell Publishing Ltd.

of such groups include trade unions, gun clubs, professional associations, athletic groupings, etc. (see Almond, 1958). Such groups perform several functions in terms of the promotion of political democracy. First, they promote the development of "cross-cutting" social cleavages that build ties between erstwhile different social, ethnic, or religious groups. For instance, people of different racial or ethnic groups or from different social classes may find themselves sharing common recreational interests, or bound together in a labor union. This provides ties that cross-cut social, ethnic, racial, or religious differences that ultimately promote tolerance and acceptance, things that are considered "good" for democracy. Further, such groups also provide the basis for the limitation of state power, promoting the control of the state by society, and hence leading to the emergence of democratic political institutions as the most effective means of exercising that control. On the other hand, societies that do not have such autonomous groups are much more likely to be dominated by a centralized state, or an authoritarian or totalitarian dictatorship.

Although there are many different approaches that suggest a relationship between the structure of societies and the rise of different types of political systems, in this chapter we limit ourselves to three issues: (1) the relationship between the legacy of feudalism and democracy; (2) the relationship between inequality and democracy; and (3) the relationship between civil society and democracy.

Feudalism and Democracy

As was pointed out in Chapter 2, the historical development and transformation of feudal societies had a direct impact on the evolution of dictatorship or democracy. However, the relationship between feudalism and democracy is not as straightforward. On the one hand, feudalism can be seen as an early form of pluralism that led to the limitation of the development of centralized state power and hence such systems are more likely to evolve into democracies than those that lack such social pluralism. The record of Western Europe versus Russia and of Japan versus China suggests that there may well be something to this theory (certainly this was the point made by Barrington Moore, as discussed in Chapter 2). On the other hand, some have pointed to the absence of feudalism as contributing to democracy. For instance, Alexis de Tocqueville noted that the absence of feudalism contributed to the emergence of democracy in the United States, because there were no embedded hierarchies that prevented the social and political mobility of the population. The persistence of feudalism in Latin America has been held up as an example of how feudalism is inimical to the development of political democracy.

The key perhaps is not so much whether feudalism existed or not, but what kind of feudal system existed. Indeed, Barrington Moore (1966) argued that a key factor in the development of English democracy was the transformation, or commercialization, of the English feudal lords, who later became the basis for the bourgeoisie. This was not the case elsewhere, and certainly not in Latin America. Indeed, as Moore has restated the proposition succinctly in a more limited formulation: "No bourgeois, no democracy."

For many scholars, it is the connection between economic transformation (discussed in Chapter 3) and the social structure that helps promote democracy. Thus, for Barrington Moore, the development of a large indigenous bourgeoisie is the key to democracy. The seemingly central role played by the bourgeoisie in the development of democracy highlights the relationship between the economic system, the social structure, and the political system. Scholars have long noted the connection between the development of a market economy and the social bases for democracy (Lipset, 1961). At least two reasons suggest themselves. A market economy requires a dispersion of economic power and invariably the emergence of some form of private property. This dispersion of economic power creates alternative centers of political power that help check the powers of the states. Further, economically, market economies are more likely to lead to sustained periods of economic growth, more so than command economies (although centrally planned economies are often able to promote rapid growth over short periods of time), thus providing the desire for wealth protection that gives rise to social organizations.

Socioeconomic Inequality and Democracy

There has been a longstanding argument in the literature concerning the relationship between socioeconomic inequality (or gaps between rich and poor) and democracy. At least since Aristotle, scholars have argued that by reducing inequalities in the distribution of political power, democracy helps to reduce inequalities of wealth and status (see also John Stuart Mill, 1862). In terms of the causal relationship between socioeconomic inequality and democracy, it also has been argued that extreme inequalities in wealth undermine democratic political structures.

Indeed, scholars have long explained that socioeconomic inequality inhibits the development of political democracy. Aristotle pointed to the importance of a large middle class in promoting political democracy (a sentiment echoed much later by Lipset, 1959). Robert Dahl (1971, Chapter 6) has suggested that extreme inequalities in the distribution of material goods in fact produce dictatorship, for two reasons. First of all, the concentration of economic resources in the hands of the "haves" make the haves unwilling to accept political reforms and extend rights to the "have nots," given they believe that the "have nots" will deprive the haves of their wealth and resources. Essentially, concentrated wealth in the hands of a few undermines meaningful political democracy. A second way that economic inequalities may undermine democracies is that they produce high levels of resentments among the "have nots" (Dahl, 1971, Chapter 6). This resentment is likely to translate into violence, or at the very least, undermine the legitimacy of the political system upon which democracies depend. An authoritarian government can repress reactions against these inequalities, while a democracy cannot indefinitely repress and remain democratic. As Bollen and Jackman (1985, p. 440) point out, "The effect of inequality on democracy is anticipated because concentrated economic rewards lead to similarly concentrated political resources, undermining political equality. And economic inequality generates frustrations that undermine allegiance to democratic procedures."

Civil Society and Democracy

A key part of the relationship between social structure and the rise of democracy is the idea that "civil society" is directly related to the rise of political democracy. Thus, in this section, we focus on the literature that suggests that a key factor explaining the emergence of political democracy is the existence of *civil society*.

What is civil society? There are a myriad definitions of civil society. For instance, the London School of Economic Centre for Civil Society defines it as:

[An]arena of uncoerced collective action around shared interests, purposes and values. In theory, its institutional forms are distinct from those of the state, family and market, though in practice, the boundaries between state, civil society, family and market are often complex, blurred and negotiated ... Civil societies are often populated by organizations such as registered charities, development non-governmental organizations, community groups, women's organizations, faith-based organizations, professional associations, trade unions, self-help groups, social movements, business associations, coalitions and advocacy groups.

Larry Diamond (1994) defines civil society as:

The realm of organised social life that is voluntary, self generating, self supporting, autonomous from the state, and bound by the legal order or set of shared rules ... it involves citizens acting collectively in a public sphere to express their interests, passions, and ideas, exchange ideas, exchange information, achieve mutual goals, make demands on the state, and hold state officials accountable. It is an intermediary entity, standing between the private sphere and the state.

Generally speaking, scholars who point to the importance of civil society make a distinction between civil society and society at large – civil society focuses on expressly public/political goods, not private goods. The concept thus excludes family life, inward-looking group activity, or the profit-making enterprise of individual business firms (which are organizations that pursue private gain). Civil society groups pursue public goods, such as promoting particular policies or particular goals that have a broader impact on a public at large. Civil society is also different from political society, or those groups directly tied to the state, such as institutional bodies (like Congress, or the bureaucracy, and political parties). Although civil society affects and shapes political society, civil society is conceptually distinct from political society.

Although there has been great deal of current interest in the concept of a civil society in recent years, the concept itself is quite old. Indeed, the ancient Greeks and Romans used the term to describe the "good society." For instance, Socrates taught that truth could be discovered via open public argument using the dialectic, a form of rational dialogue. For Socrates, public argument was the key to ensure civility in the body politic and the goodness of the people. Plato, too, argued that a just society was one in which people worked for the common good and practiced civic virtues such as wisdom, moderation, and justice (or the occupational roles for which they were best suited). For Aristotle (circa 335 BC), in order for individuals to make the correct decision in choosing leaders, citizens had to know about each other. Lacking this knowledge, it was impossible to make proper political decisions for the community. In this way, Aristotle viewed the city as a group in which individuals interacted to gain knowledge of each other's character and preferences. This interaction was necessary where politics required the participation of citizens. He believed that the "polis" was an "association of associations" that enables citizens to share in the virtuous task of ruling and being ruled. For the Romans, the concept of *societas civilis*, introduced by the philosopher Cicero, involved the idea of a good society that ensured the existence of peace and order among in the population. However, this classical notion of civil society did not distinguish between society and the state. Rather, civic virtues were held out as the best way to the proper functioning of a body politic.

It was only later, particularly after the recognition of the sovereign state after the Treaty of Westphalia in 1648, which ended the Thirty Years War in Europe, that society was thought of as different from the state. The Treaty allowed for the development of monarchs who sought to establish central state control over their dominion. They established national armies and a professional bureaucracy to exert direct control and supreme authority over their subjects. Outside of England, there emerged a number of absolutist states in Europe, which dominated the political landscape well into the eighteenth century. The rise of absolutism led many political thinkers of the "Enlightenment" to consider alternatives to absolutism. These Enlightenment thinkers opposed the alliance between the State and the Church as the enemy of human progress, and championed human liberty.

Although a champion of absolutism, the political philosopher Thomas Hobbes sought to establish a rational basis for absolutism, that citizens in a society provided their consent via a social contract in forming political authority. For Hobbes, human beings are motivated by self-interests. In a situation where there is no government (which Hobbes referred to as the "state of nature"), individuals defended their interests on their own, which meant constant struggle and violence with other individuals in order to survive. Thus, for Hobbes, the state of nature was a condition of a war of all against all and life was "solitary, poor, nasty, brutish and short" (Hobbes, 1982, p. 25). Compelled by reason, human beings became aware of the need of a better mechanism to protect them from these dangers. As far as Hobbes was concerned, rationality and self-interest persuaded human beings to agree to surrender sovereignty to a common power – the state (Kaviraj and Khilnani, 2001, p. 289). Thus, he distinguished between something akin to a civil society that existed prior to and apart from the state. In Hobbes's paradigm, the formation of the civil society led to the formation of government, state, and laws. In turn, the state promoted and sustained civility among humans. For Hobbes, there was an inherent connection between civil society and the state.

John Locke also thought of civil society giving life to the state. In general, Locke's work sought to justify the replacement of the King during the Glorious Revolution of 1688, when the English Parliament removed King James II, in alliance with the Dutch. James had sought to assert the Crown's divine right to rule (that is, that the right to rule came from God, not the people) and to limit the political rights of Parliament. Locke forged a social contract theory of a limited state and a powerful society. Like, Hobbes, Locke also viewed the state of nature as generally an unpleasant life, but not inevitably the "state of war" that Hobbes described. Rather, for Locke, humans had the ability to protect their natural inalienable rights themselves, and would only contract to leave the state of nature if they could find a better way to protect their right to life, liberty, and property. Submitting to an absolute monarch as recommended by Hobbes would not be a "better" way to protect one's liberty and property. Thus, Locke argued, we would only leave the state of nature as long as there were reliable restrictions placed on government to prevent it from turning into an autocracy (Kaviraj and Khilnani, 2001, p. 291). Therefore, Locke set out two treatises on government which outlined reciprocal obligations. In the first treaty, people submit themselves to the common public authority. This authority has the power to enact and maintain laws. The second treaty contains the limitations of authority, that is, the state has no power to threaten the basic rights of human beings. Thus, society gave life to the state, and the state was charged with protecting civil society.

The literature on relations between civil society and democratic political society has its roots in early liberal writings such as those of Alexis de Tocqueville (1840). It was Alexis de Tocqueville who wrote at length on the prevalence and necessity of civil associations for the development of democracy. Americans, he noted, tended to join voluntary organizations of all kinds, from social clubs to service organizations. He argued that the rich associational life that characterized the United States in the first part of the nineteenth century had led to the blossoming of democracy in the new republic. De Tocqueville viewed these associations as important to the type of participatory society that had blossomed in the country. In the United States, he noted, involvement in associations allowed American citizens to overcome their lack of influence as separate individuals. As the associations grew, the state and other political actors were forced to take notice of the associations and recognize their preferences. In this way, associations empowered individuals in the political context and forced recognition of these interests by policy-makers.

Following the observations of Tocqueville, Emile Durkheim ([1893] 1984) explored the interactions of individuals within society and observed that connections between individuals remain after the initial interaction. These remaining social ties contribute to the functioning of the community in a manner that is broader than the initial interaction by shaping the condition of social capital that results from the interaction. In this way, associations persistently affect one another through the lasting impact that individuals make on each other.

In the twentieth century, political scientists identified civil societies as made up of interest groups, particularly "associational" interest groups. These groups act as the organizational vehicles by which individuals can collectively express their interests. For instance, Gabriel Almond (1958) identified several types of interest groups, in particular, the anomic, non-associational, institutional, and associational. Anomic groups are generally spontaneous groups with a collective response to a particular frustration, such as organized protest or riots. However, these groups have little in the way of an organizational infrastructure to sustain the activities of the group, and generally dissipate quickly once the fury of the mob is spent. Second are the non-associational groups which are generally not organized and their activity is dependent upon the issue at hand. They differ from anomic groups in that individuals are usually held together by some common kinship or identity ties (such as race or ethnicity). Institutional groups are mostly formal and have some other political or social function in addition to the particular interest. These would include "groups" made up of individuals with common sets of interests, such as caucus groups in the US Congress, or the interests of various bureaucratic agencies. Finally, there are the associational groups which are formed explicitly to represent a particular set of issues and interests. Examples include free trade unions, organizations that advocate gun or animal rights, professional organizations, etc. The key features of such groups are that: (1) they are often highly organized, with an internal hierarchy and access to a steady stream of funds that allow them to sustain efforts on behalf of the particular interests they purport to represent (which are also characteristic of institutional interest groups; and (2) they are independent of the state in as much as they are not merely organizations that are a party of the state (which make them different from institutional interest groups). This does not mean that they do not impact the actions of the state, only that they are not part of it.

At the core of a developed civil society is the existence of many associational groups, and a citizenry who actively seek to participate in such groups. These groups do not seek to win formal office but rather seek to influence those in office. In a civil society there is a good deal of tolerance for a pluralism of different ideas and attitudes. Although these groups often form alliances with political parties and organizations in "political society," these alliances are rarely permanent. The United States and the Western European democracies are held out as the best examples of older civil societies.

What are the benefits of civil society for democracy?

The idea that civil society was an important contributing factor to the development of democracy was put forward by twentieth-century political scientists like Gabriel Almond and Sidney Verba (1963), who argued that voluntary associations were the most important mediating factor between individuals and the state. Associating with other individuals in a voluntary association gives a person increased political resources that can be used to achieve his or her desired political goals. Also, membership in associations affects an individual's political attitudes. They argued that the political element of many voluntary organizations facilitates better awareness and a more informed citizenry, who make better voting choices, participate in politics, and hold government more accountable as a result.

Beyond having an important impact on cultivating better citizens, civil society is held out as a check on political authority. Associational interest groups continually monitor the activities of the state, and as a result, they hold leaders in authority accountable by subjecting state leaders to popular scrutiny. Further, the existence of "dense networks" of associational interest groups stimulates political participation by providing multiple channels for citizens to voice opinions, attitudes, and articulate citizen interests. This gives individuals a reason to become politically engaged.

In addition to stimulating political participation, civil society groups also provide a crucial arena for development of attitudes that promote democratic development such as tolerance, moderation, and willingness to compromise. For instance, by working together for a common purpose in organizations such as the Boy Scouts, or the Young Pioneers, or a labor union, or a professional organization, individuals learn important skills such as cooperation, teamwork and compromise. Further, these organizations also provide the primary channels for leadership training and political recruitment. In a sense, civil society becomes a "school for democracy" that prepares citizens and political leaders.

More recently, Robert D. Putnam (1993, 1995) has argued that even non-political organizations in civil society are vital for democracy. Activities conducted by social organizations like bowling leagues or sporting clubs are important because such groups build social capital, trust, and shared values, which are transferred into the political sphere and help to hold society together, facilitating an understanding of the interconnectedness of society and interests within it (Coleman, 1988; Uslaner, 2002). "Social capital" is analogous to other forms of "capital" such as physical capital or human capital. Indeed, as with any firm (or for that matter, any social system), physical capital (the machines, the economic inputs, etc.) helps productivity. Similarly human capital (such as having an educated workforce) assists in promoting the productivity of a firm (or a society for that matter). However, a third form of "capital," that is, social capital, refers to the way societies are organized – this also impacts the productivity of a society. For Putnam (1995), what made the American economy and American state strong was the existence of a strong civil society with "dense social networks." These social networks created the "social capital" which promoted norms as social trust that facilitated coordination and cooperation among Americans that was for their mutual benefit. This echoed the observations made by de Tocqueville almost a century and a half earlier.

For Putnam, this was not merely a characteristic of the development of democracy in the United States, but also in many European democracies. For instance, in his landmark study of internal difference in the development of democracy in Italy, he notes that the development of self-help organizations, and community policing mechanisms in the northern part of the country, led not only to a stronger democratic impulse in the country, but also the emergence of Northern Italy as an economic and industrial powerhouse, in contrast to the more impoverished (and historically state-dominated) south of the country (Putnam, 1993).

Although Putnam argued that the development of civil society has led to the development of democracy (not only in the United States but elsewhere as well, such as in Italy), in the latter part of the twentieth century there has been a notable change. Civil society has become less important and vibrant as participation in group activity (such as bowling leagues) has declined – as a result, groups have become less important in social and political life. Using the metaphor of the decline of organized bowling leagues in the United States, Putnam notes that Americans are much less likely to join groups than in de Tocqueville's time. As a result, Americans are becoming less trusting and more disengaged from politics.

Why has civil society declined? For Putnam, there are a number of reasons, which include:

1 *Movement of women into the labor force.* In the past, women comprised the bulk of the membership of voluntary social organizations. As more and more women entered the workforce in the latter half of the twentieth century, this led to the decline in women's civic participation and also family participation overall.
2 *Greater mobility.* As the transportation infrastructure improved in the post-World War II period, this provided greater mobility opportunities. People no longer are born, live and die in the same neighborhood, which had once been the case. This has led to the downfall of traditional neighborhoods and hence the decline of social bonds that held people together in identifiable communities.
3 *Other demographic changes.* There have been fewer marriages, and more divorces in the latter part of the twentieth century than ever before. Further, movement from urban neighborhoods to more impersonal suburbia has led to less connectivity among people, and hence the decline of civil society.
4 *The technological transformation and privatization of leisure.* In the past, people would engage in face-to-face activities for entertainment and enjoyment – such as bowling leagues. However, with the rise of television, video games, DVDs, the internet, and virtual reality, there is no need to interact in a face-to-face way to entertain oneself. One can be completely alone to be entertained.

The negative implication of this, of course, is that the decline of civil society in Western democracies has had serious negative consequences for civic engagement and ultimately the health of democracy in the developed world.

The critique of civil society–democracy nexus

Although the idea that pre-existence of civil society led to the development of democracy (as in Italy) or continues to support the maintenance of democracy emerged as quite a popular argument in the 1990s, the thesis was not without its detractors. Indeed, one might argue whether these "dense networks" of numerous interest groups are a "good" thing for democracy. For instance, E.E. Schattschneider (1960) argued some time ago that interest groups are elite groups and motivated primarily by private interest (as opposed to promoting the public good). Mancur Olson (1965) argued because of the logic of collective action, that small well-organized interest groups dominate the political process leaving many voices unheard. Similarly, Theodore Lowi (1969) contends that "interest group liberalism" or the emergence of interest groups that seek some progressive goals, in fact has led to status quo conservatism – interest groups seek to protect what they have once they achieve their goal. Thus, interest group pluralism came under fire as being "undemocratic" and it was claimed that the special interests they represent detracted from democracy.

There is also no reason in principle why these dense networks of special interests should create a more efficient operation of the democratic state. Indeed, it is quite possible that "the counterweight of civil society" emerges as a burden to a democratic state. These "dense webs of association" in fact leach off resources and represent an enduring threat to the smooth and equitable function of the modern state.

There has also been considerable debate over the utility of the civil society concept in explaining the development of political democracy. For instance, Foley and Edwards (1996) argue that there are at least two (and potentially contradictory) conceptions of civil society that can be found in the literature. The first (or what they call Civil Society I) puts special emphasis on the ability of associational life in general and the habits of association in particular to foster patterns of civility in the actions of citizens of a democratic polity. Thus, civil society is seen as a socializing and educating force that promotes values for tolerance and cooperation. The second conception (or Civil Society II) places special emphasis on civil society as a counterweight to the state, claiming that it is by definition independent from the state, helping to promote state accountability and hence checking tyranny. The contradiction, according to Foley and Edwards, is that Civil Society I focuses on the positive effects of association with governance (and hence is related to the state serving a positive socializing function in creating a "good citizenry") whereas Civil Society II emphasizes civil association as a counterweight (and hence separate) from the state. Booth and Richard (1998) further extend the discussion of civil society to include Civil Society III. Basically, Civil Society III includes that part of civil society that does not promote democracy but often includes voluntary associations that are revolutionary in nature. These dense civic networks may in fact lead to separatist, centrifugal and divisive forces in weak or unstable systems (especially deeply ethnically divided ones). Whether they do or not would depend on the kinds of state that already existed. Indeed, for civil society to work, there must be political peace and some degree of openness. So what is the relationship between the state and civil society? Are they independent from one another or not? As Foley and Edwards (1996, p. 281) note:

> The strength and responsiveness of a democracy may depend on the character of civil society, as Putnam argues, reinforcing both the democratic functioning and strength of the state. But such effects depend on the prior achievement of both democracy and a strong state.

This is more than just an academic question. Understanding the nature of the relationship between state and civil society helps us understand which caused which. In other words, did civil society "cause" the emergence of democracy in the West (as suggested by de Tocqueville and Putnam) or did the existence of a democratic (or democratizing) state give rise to the emergence of civil society? Unless one understands the nature of the relationship, it is difficult to contend that civil society causes anything at all (calling into question all of the civil society building programs advocated by policy organizations such as USAID, the US Agency for International Development).

Another prominent criticism of the social capital and civil society literature is that the importance of attachment to voluntary associations is overstated. While many researchers contend that social capital directly impacts aspects of individual and societal life, others disagree, saying that it is only a part of the puzzle. For instance, Dietlind Stolle and Marc Hooghe (2003) question the importance of associational life for individuals. They conclude that the impact of social capital outside of the group setting is weak, if at all. While they do not desire to remove associational life from its prominent position of study, they encourage a distinct focus on the internal workings of groups (and the subsequent social capital movement) rather than on pronouncements of the importance of civil society as a whole. Foley and Edwards (1996) argue that a focus on voluntary non-political organizations as the core of civil society underestimates the impact of participation in explicitly political organizations. Indeed, one might wonder if participation in a bowling league is necessarily and inevitably connected to increases in political participation. In other words, there is no necessary connection between civic engagement and political engagement which is crucial for the development of democracy.

Another criticism that often arises in studies of social capital, social networks, and civil society is that of its measurement. How does someone accurately measure an idea like social capital? Approaches to measurement abound. Some individuals prefer surveys to identify social capital. Not without problems, surveys can often make cross-country comparisons impossible due to a lack of transferability of ideas. For civil society, many researchers employ the number of groups in a society or the number of groups to which an individual belongs on average. Again, problems of measurement emerge pertaining to what groups to include, distinguishing between group types, and whether or not to include a time element in the measure. Social networks also pose difficulties in measurement due to the intrinsically weak nature of the connections between individuals. Although these issues are not insurmountable, they must be considered in evaluating the conclusions about the concepts that are drawn by researchers.

Conclusion

In this chapter we outlined some of the posited effects of certain features that characterize a country's social structure, in particular, the historical effects of feudalism, the existence of socioeconomic inequality and the impact of civil society. Although as with most factors discussed thus far, there is little consensus over the effects of civil society on the development of democracy, there is considerable agreement that it has *some* effect. Further, as we noted in Chapter 4, there is little question that in countries that have political cultures that value tolerance, moderation, compromise, and civility, democracy is easier to develop than in countries that do not have such features. To a large extent, civil society helps promote these cultural values that are conducive to the development of democracy. Although it is not always clear whether civil society helps promote democracy or whether democracy helps promote civil society, there is consensus in the literature that civil society helps maintain democracy. Ultimately, the relationship between social structure and the development of democracy must be subject to further empirical investigation, but that is beyond the scope of this chapter.

References

Almond, Gabriel (1958) "Interest Groups in the Political Process," *American Political Science Review*, 52 (1).

Almond, Gabriel and Verba, Sidney (1963) *Civic Culture*, Boston, MA: Little, Brown and Company.

Bollen, Kenneth and Jackman, Robert (1985) "Political Democracy and the Size Distribution of Income," *American Sociological Review*, 50: 438–457.

Booth, John A. and Richard, Patricia B. (1998). "Civil Society, Political Capital, and Democratization in Central America," *Journal of Politics*, 60: 780–800.

Coleman, James S. (1988) "Social Capital in the Creation of Human Capital," *American Journal of Sociology*, 94 (Supplement), S95–S120.

Dahl, Robert A. (1971) *Polyarchy*, New Haven, CT: Yale University Press.

de Tocqueville, Alexis (1840) *Democracy in America*, New York: Schocken.

Diamond, Larry (1994) "Rethinking Civil Society: Toward Democratic Consolidation," *Journal of Democracy*, 5: 4–17.

Durkheim, Emile ([1893] 1984) *The Division of Labor in Society*, trans. W.D. Halls, New York: The Free Press.

Foley, Michael. W. and Edwards, B. (1996) "The Paradox of Civil Society," *Journal of Democracy*, 7: 38–52.

Hobbes, Thomas (1982) *The Leviathan*, New York: Penguin Classics.

Huntington, Samuel (1984) "Will More Countries Become Democratic?" *Political Science Quarterly*, 99: 193–218.

Kaviraj, Sudipta and Khilnani, Sunil (2001) *Civil Society: History and Possibilities*, Cambridge: Cambridge University Press.

Lipset, Seymour M. (1959) *Political Man*, New York: Doubleday.

Lowi, Theodore (1969) *The End of Liberalism*, New York: Norton.

Mill, John Stuart (1862) "The Contest in America," *Harper's New Monthly Magazine*, 24(143): 683–684.

Moore, Barrington (1966) *Social Origins of Dictatorship and Democracy: Lord and Peasant in the Making of the Modern World*, Boston, MA: Beacon Press.

Olson, Mancur (1965) *The Logic of Collective Action*, Cambridge, MA: Harvard University Press.

Putnam, Robert D. (1993) *Making Democracy Work: Civic Traditions in Modern Italy*, Princeton, NJ: Princeton University Press.

Putnam, Robert D. (1995) "Bowling Alone: America's Declining Social Capital," *Journal of Democracy*, 4: 65–78.

Schattschneider, E.E. (1960) *The Semisovereign People.* New York: Holt, Rinehart and Winston.

Stolle, D. and Hooghe, Marc (2003) "Conclusion: The Sources of Social Capital Reconsidered," in M. Hooghe and D. Stolle, *Generating Social Capital: Civil Society and Institutions in Comparative Perspective*, New York: Palgrave Macmillan.

Uslaner, Erik M. (2002) *The Moral Foundations of Trust*, New York: Cambridge University Press.

6

Democratization and the Global Environment

Thus far in previous chapters we have focused almost entirely on internal (that is internal to a country) factors to explain the development of political systems (with the exception of our discussion of neo-Marxist dependency theory and the effects of the world economic system in Chapter 3). However, external influences are of great importance in affecting whether a country moves in a democratic or non-democratic direction. In this chapter we examine the effects that external forces have on the development of democracy, particularly democratic diffusion and "waves of democratization," the effects of the legacies of colonialism, globalization, and "imposed" democracy.

Democratic Diffusion and Waves of Democratization

During the most recent wave of democratization, several scholars have argued that global pressures sweep across the globe leading to transitions from authoritarianism. For instance, Samuel Huntington, in his 1991 book *The Third Wave*, argues that democratization has historically been a global phenomenon, occurring in global waves in the modern era. Using the metaphor of increasing concentric waves emanating outward after throwing a stone in a pond, Huntington argues that these waves of democratization were, in part, a result of war and the spread of democratic ideals

Comparative Politics: Principles of Democracy and Democratization, First Edition.
John T. Ishiyama.
© 2012 John T. Ishiyama. Published 2012 by Blackwell Publishing Ltd.

that were often carried at the barrel of a gun – be it by the armies of Napoleon or by the occupation forces of the United States and the West.

In the history of the modern world, Huntington identifies three distinct waves. The first wave began shortly after the end of the Napoleonic Wars in 1815 and spread outward, particularly in Europe. In part, this wave was inspired by the ideals of the French Revolution of 1789, with its emphasis on human rights and governance by the people (although Napoleon himself undermined many of those ideals). The cry of liberty, equality, and brotherhood spread throughout Europe, and these ideals had repercussions in Europe long after the defeat of Napoleon's armies. Indeed, the revolutionary upheavals that swept across Europe in 1836 and 1848 to a large extent were inspired by the ideals of the French Revolution. This outward wave of democratization, and especially the notion of self-determination of peoples, contributed to the nationalistic tensions that ultimately undermined the great empires of central and eastern Europe, particularly the Austro-Hungarian, Ottoman, and Russian Empires, ultimately precipitating World War I.

The first wave began roughly in the 1820s and expanded outward by the end of World War I to include 29 democracies. It is important to note that, for Huntington, democracy merely meant the conduct of competitive elections, akin to the minimalist definition offered by Joseph Schumpeter that we discussed in Chapter 1 (that is, that elections alone define what is and what is not a democracy) as opposed to "consolidated" democracies. However, with the rise of Fascism in Italy, and later Germany, and the series of coups that installed military or royal dictatorships throughout the central and eastern European states (such as Hungary, Romania, Bulgaria, Yugoslavia, the Baltic States, etc.) by the 1930s, the number of democracies had been reduced to 12.

The end of World War II in 1945 marked the beginning of the end of the formal global empires, particularly the British and the French Empires, but also the Japanese, Belgian, and ultimately the Portuguese ones. This marked the period of rapid decolonization throughout Asia and Africa, a period in which the number of democracies expanded to include 36 countries by 1962 (by Huntington's count). However, as with the previous first wave, this second wave was also followed by a period of authoritarian contraction. This second reverse wave (1960–1975) significantly reduced the number of electoral democracies in the world. In this period, incipient young democracies were undermined by persistent poverty, political instability, and the machinations of both the United States and the Soviet Union during the Cold War.

However, beginning in about 1974–1975, this contraction halted, and a third wave of democratization emerged. This wave began with the re-democratization of three European states in the 1970s: Portugal, Spain, and Greece. The beginning of the wave was marked by the collapse of the long-standing military dictatorship in Portugal and the death of Francisco Franco, the longtime dictator of Spain, as well as the collapse of the military regime in Greece following the Greco-Turkish war over Cyprus in 1974. This was followed by the extension of the wave to Latin America (Brazil and then throughout the Spanish-speaking South and Central America) in the late 1970s and 1980s, and East Asia (Korea and Taiwan) in the late 1980s and into the 1990s. This was in turn followed by the liberalization of the Soviet Union after 1985 with the ascendency to the Soviet leadership of Mikhail Gorbachev and the subsequent collapse of the Soviet Union in 1991, which catalyzed the expansion of democracy into Central and Eastern Europe. By the end of the 1990s and into the twenty-first century, this expansion had spread to Africa, and to some extent, the Middle East.

What caused this third wave? For Huntington, there were several catalyzing factors that promoted the democratic expansion featured in the third wave. First, for many authoritarian countries in the 1960s, there had been a period of economic boom (particularly in places like Portugal, Spain, and many Latin American countries) that accompanied the global economic expansion of the 1950s and 1960s. However, after the oil crisis of 1973, with the rapid rise in the price of fuel that resulted from the Organization of Petroleum Exporting Countries' (OPEC) boycott of the West for their support of Israel in the Yom Kippur War of 1973, there was a major global economic slowdown.

According to Bergesen (1992), developing states are more constrained than core states in their responses to this global recession. With state legitimacy already low in developing countries, the strains of economic recession, brought on by the rapid rise in the price of oil, can topple governments. Such economic crises thus spur political changes, especially political changes that are designed to accommodate the opposition, as well as to show a more democratic face to the outside world, which offer a way to reduce internal unrest. For many of the authoritarian regimes of the world, the legitimacy of the state had been based on economic performance (that is "performance legitimacy"). In other words, many authoritarian regimes had purchased the loyalty of its citizenry via the material benefits derived from economic growth (such as jobs, access to education, social welfare benefits, etc.). However, the global economic downturn of the 1970s led to the increasing inability of these regimes to produce further economic growth, hence weakening their legitimacy in the eyes of their citizens, providing greater sources for mass grievances directed at these regimes.

Further the unprecedented economic growth of the 1960s also led to greater social mobilization and a greatly expanded middle class. The subsequent economic downturn in the 1970s affected this new middle class most directly, and it was this class that led the demands for greater openness and democracy in places like Spain and Portugal (Bermeo, 1987).

There were also external influences, beyond economic changes, that affected the emergence of the third wave. An important change was the shift in the activities of the Catholic Church and the reforms that were introduced under Pope Paul II from 1963–1965, collectively known as "Vatican II." This period saw the introduction of reforms (such as the nationalization of the Catholic liturgy so that it would be conducted in national languages rather than in Latin) but also signified a shift of the role of the national Catholic churches in politics. Indeed, the Vatican II reforms transformed the national Catholic churches from defenders of the status quo to opponents of authoritarianism.

In addition to the Vatican's reforms, other external actors moved away from unconditional support of authoritarian regimes. In particular, the European Community and the United States shifted in the 1970s (particularly in the wake of the Vietnam War and the emphasis of the Carter administration in the United States on the promotion of human rights) away from unconditional support of anti-communist authoritarian regimes. Although the confrontation between the West and the Soviet Union during the Cold War had made acceptable any regime that was anti-communist (including many brutal right-wing authoritarian regimes), this changed with the thaw in East–West relations brought about by the policies of détente and normalization of relations between the United States and its allies and the communist world. No longer did the West unconditionally support regimes whose human rights records were highly suspect in the name of anti-communism. This decline of Western (as well as Soviet) support of authoritarian regimes throughout the developing world accelerated after the collapse of the Soviet Union in 1991.

Certainly, an additional contributing factor to the spread of the third wave was something of a "demonstration" or "snowball" effect. As one country democratized this provided models for emulation elsewhere. Neighboring states are typically oriented to the same political-economic policies; in the language of spatial analysis, they share a regional positive diffusion effect or a regional learning curve (Shin, 1994, pp. 152–153). Starr (1991) as well as Modelski and Perry (1991), detected demonstration effects in analyses of regime changes towards democratization over time; however, neither study directly considered possible internal factors nor examined the regional heterogeneity of the world-system. Starr (1991) found some evidence of regional effects but concluded that "although we might posit emulation via awareness of events throughout the global system, those same diffusion effects were taking place at a regional level for *some* of the world system," but not all. This regional diffusion makes sense given the cultural and linguistic connections that regional neighbors share. However, these demonstration effects may also transcend regional boundaries, especially if countries share cultural or linguistic affinities. For instance, the fact that the early democratizers in Europe in the "third wave" were Portugal and Spain, and that both had such longstanding cultural and political ties with countries in Latin America, certainly contributed to the spread of democracy in South and Central America.

However, each "sub-wave" in the third wave was made up of countries with different sets of economic, cultural, and political characteristics (features that, as we saw in Chapter 2, impact greatly on the development of political democracy). The countries of the first "sub-wave," which included Greece, Portugal, and Spain, was economically developed, capitalist states with market economies (albeit with authoritarian regimes). All three had had previous historical experiences with democracy in the 1920s and 1930s, and all three were in geographical proximity to many democratic European states. Further, none (except for the possible exception of Spain) were divided by deep ethnic and linguistic cleavages. Thus, to some extent, these conditions made the transition to democracy relatively "easy" when compared to other states that were not so "endowed."

The second sub-wave in Latin American occurred in countries that were economically less developed than Portugal, Spain, and Greece, but were basically capitalist market economies (for the most part) and had had previous experiments with democracy. Nonetheless they were significantly more culturally diverse than the European states. The transitions to democracy in these countries were more drawn out and it took longer for these countries to consolidate democracy.

The third sub-wave included those countries of the former communist world. Although in relatively close proximity to democratic Europe, many of the countries of the former communist world were faced with the challenges of a "triple transition" – not only a transition from communist authoritarianism, but also a transition from central planned economies to market economies. Further for many of these countries, there was also the struggle to develop a new national identity, particularly important following the collapse of an ideology that had rejected the ideas of nations as capitalist phenomena. In addition, as the result of totalitarianism, there was little in the way of a developed civil society (see Chapter 5). Thus, the post-communist and particularly the post-Soviet states faced especially difficult challenges in building democracy as a result.

Finally, perhaps the greatest challenges face the countries of the "fourth" sub-wave in Africa and the Middle East. These countries not only lack many of the social, economic, and political "pre-conditions" for the development of democracy, but also are "cursed" with natural resources. For many scholars the existence of natural resources creates a "curse" for countries, preventing them from becoming political democracies. For instance, Hazem Beblawi (1987) argues that states rich in oil become rentier states, or states that generate revenues primarily by selling high value commodities like oil and natural gas (or diamonds) abroad rather than generating revenue via taxation. This prevents states from developing along democratic lines, because, in the absence of taxes, citizens have less incentive to place pressure on the government to become responsive to their needs. Further, the state has less incentive to be responsive to the demands of the population, because revenues are not derived from taxes but by generating external "rents" via the sale of resources. If the state is at all responsive, it is in the form of "bribes" where the citizenry buys off the population with extensive social welfare programs and the allocation of material resources, rather than broadening the scope of popular political participation (Feldman, 2003). Furthermore, Beblawi argues that this creates other impediments for the development of democracy in resource-rich states. In such countries, the bureaucracy becomes bloated and inefficient. Since access to resources is controlled by the state, this gives a strong incentive for corruption as access to political office provides for an opportunity to get rich (Quinn, 2002). Thus, not only do these countries in Africa and the Middle East lack the "pre-conditions" for the development of democracy, but even those "rich" with resources are further saddled with the curse of oil and gas and other valuable resources.

Processes of democratization

Although the third wave of democratization swept across the globe in the last part of the twentieth and early twenty-first centuries, the way in which democratic transitions took place varied across countries. Many theorists (for example, O'Donnell, Schmitter, and Whitehead, 1986; Przeworski, 1986, 1991; Huntington, 1993) have pointed to the independent effect of the democratic transition process on the future development of democracy. Although they argue that certainly contextual factors (economics, culture, social structure) correlate with the emergence of democracy, the democratization process itself impacts on whether or not a transition to democracy is "successful." These processes are affected by the relationship between whether there are hardliners or softliners in the previous authoritarian regime and moderates and radicals in the opposition. In the authoritarian regime, hardliners want to cling to power, whereas softliners are willing to negotiate with the opposition (particularly to preserve their authority in the face of change of circumstances brought about by external pressures). On the opposition side, there are the radicals who want the immediate replacement of the existing authoritarian regime, and the moderates, who are willing to negotiate to maintain a peaceful transition of power.

In particular, Huntington (1991) has identified three different types of transitions from authoritarian rule: *transformation, replacement,* and *transplacement.* Transformation is where "the elites in power [take] the lead in bringing about democracy" (Huntington, 1991, p. 153). In other words, the authoritarian regime itself (mostly reformers within the regime) plays a major role in making transition possible. Replacement occurs when "opposition [takes] the lead in bringing about democracy, and the authoritarian regime collapses or is overthrown" (ibid., p. 154). Finally, transplacement occurs when "democratization results largely from joint action by government and opposition group" (ibid., p. 156). Transplacement is where neither opposition nor the regime authorities are strong enough to dominate the process, and hence both sides adopt a strategy of negotiation. Successful transplacement requires that the reformers and the moderates control the hardliners in the authoritarian regime and the radicals in the opposition.

For Huntington, the preferable types of democratic transitions were either transformation or transplacement and NOT replacement. This is because replacements were often characterized by rapid turnover, leading to considerable political instability and the propensity of the new "democratic" regime to engage in the use of force to maintain its new authority. Indeed, even transformation was preferable to replacement in this regard because replacements often involve confrontation and violence. Indeed, "stable democracies and near-democracies are likely to result from rather slow evolutionary process than from revolutionary overthrow of existing hegemonies" (Huntington, 1984, p. 41).

What affects the types of transitions that occur? Although the type of transition that occurs is affected by social and economic factors (such as the wealth of a country and the level of development of a civil society), perhaps one of the more prevalent arguments in the literature on democratic transition is that the characteristics of the previous authoritarian regime are a crucial part in explaining what happens in post-authoritarian politics (Huntington, 1991; Bratton and Van de Walle, 1994). From this perspective, the nature of the previous regime affects the type of transition which occurs, which in turn structures the character of politics in the period following the transition (Huntington, 1991). Welsh (1994) finds such a connection in Eastern Europe, where regime type affected the extent to which bargaining and compromise took place during the transition period; countries which had an extended period of bargaining and compromise were more likely to produce a trained cadre of politicians within the contending political parties; politicians who had learned how to play according to the rules of democratic competition and electoral politics.

One of the more influential works on the effects of previous regime legacy on post-transition politics in Central and Eastern Europe after the collapse of communism is offered by Herbert Kitschelt (1994). Kitschelt argues that the extent to which personalist rule was in place (what he called patrimonial communism) had an important effect on the kinds of politics that followed the transition. Such systems relied heavily on hierarchical chains of personal dependence between leaders and followers, with low levels of inter-elite contestation, popular interest articulation and rational-bureaucratic professionalization. Such systems also tolerated little in the way of dissent in the leadership, and strongly emphasized the doctrine of democratic centralism. This stood in contrast to systems such as those in Hungary and Poland, or *national consensus communism*, where levels of contestation and interest articulation were permitted, and there was a degree of bureaucratic professionalization. In essence, the communist elites allowed for a measure of contestation and interest articulation in exchange for compliance with the basic features of the existing system. Such regimes also appealed to some degree of nationalism (in Poland and Hungary, for instance) and charted an economic course somewhat independent of the Soviet Union. This provided some legitimacy for these regimes, even though they had largely been imposed regimes by the Soviet Union after World War II. For Kitschelt, transitions from national consensus communist regimes are most likely to succeed, given that the regime allowed for enough internal competition (and to some extent the inclusion of an opposition) that made the relevant actors more willing to compromise and negotiate (that is transitions by transplacement) than in regimes that were patrimonial or bureaucratic authoritarian.

Another approach that focuses on the legacies of the previous regime is the work by Michael Bratton and Nicolas Van de Walle (1994, 1997) that examined different transitions from "neo-patrimonial" regimes in Africa. Generally a neo-patrimonial authoritarian regime is one in which authority is not derived from an ideology or a particular institution (such as the military), but from personal connections to the "big man." Thus, what characterizes a neo-patrimonial regime is the existence of networks of patron–client relations, at the pinnacle of which is the leader. In Africa, there were several types of authoritarian regimes, but the most prevalent were the *personalist dictatorship*, the *military oligarchy*, the *plebiscitary one-party system*, and the *competitive one-party system*.

Each of these were differentiated by the extent to which the regime allowed elite level competition (in other words, although there was a "big man," he was first among equals, as opposed to ruling alone) and the level in which mass participation in the regime was encouraged. Personalist dictatorships (which were exemplified by countries like Zaire under Mobutu Sese Seko) had low levels of elite completion and low levels of mass participation. The regime essentially revolved around one man, and through his manipulation of resources he was able to buy the temporary loyalty of key sections of the population. Military oligarchies, are characterized by some degree of competition among the elites (usually generals with a junta) but mass participation in political activities was discouraged. Nigeria, throughout most of its history since independence, exemplifies this type of neo-patrimonial authoritarian regime. Plebiscitary one-party systems are characterized by relatively low elite competition (there is generally clearly one "big man") but the regime encourages mass participation in politics (although this participation is officially mobilized and usually for purposes of demonstrating mass "shows of support" for the regime). An example of such a regime was Zambia under Kenneth Kaunda. Finally, there was the competitive one-party system (exemplified by Tanzania under Julius Nyerere). Such a system has relatively higher levels of inter-elite comple-tion, albeit within the confines of a single party, but also seeks to mobilize mass support for the regime. In addition to these four basic types, Bratton and van de Walle identify the *settler regimes* (such as South Africa and Rhodesia) which were in reality much more like European-dominated colonial regimes, which left a very different legacy than the other types of authoritarian regimes in Africa.

As with Kitschelt, Bratton and van de Walle point to the effects of dif-ferent previous regime types. The most likely to succeed are those regimes that most closely resembled the competitive one-party systems, for much the same reason that Kitschelt identified as advantaging the national con-sensus communist regimes in Eastern and Central Europe. On the other hand, the most difficult transitions would occur in countries where the previous regime was closer to the model of personalist dictatorship. This is because the personal survival of the dictator is inherently tied with the survival of the regime. Thus, any reform, any change, or any threat to the authority of the system is construed as a direct personal threat to the dicta-tor, which makes it much more unlikely that the big man in a such a per-sonalist regime would even countenance change, let alone step down voluntarily (unless of course, a deal was made to guarantee his personal safety). Transitions are much more difficult from personalist dictatorships than other types of authoritarian regimes.

The "clash of civilizations" and a reverse wave of democratization?

As Huntington noted, each previous wave of democracy was followed by a "reverse" wave. What is the likelihood, of another "reverse" wave and a democratic contraction in the twenty-first century? Huntington con-tends that this will not only be affected by the state of the world economy and continuing economic growth, but the "cultural" impediments will make a reversal more likely in certain geographic areas than others. Unlike our previous discussion of political culture in Chapter 4 which focused on attitudes vis-à-vis the political system (see Almond and Verba, 1963, for instance), Huntington thought of culture as something like civiliza-tional world views which were best indicated by the dominant religion in the various parts of the world. Further, he argued that some regional contexts are more amenable to political change than others. An identification of the factors by region thus helps understand why some contexts are mostly democratic (Europe) while other contexts are not (the Middle East).

For Huntington, these regions or zones can be divided into several large civilizations that have historically been in competition with one another. Some were more conducive to the development of democracy than others. These civilizational zones included the Western Christian zone that was defined by an emphasis on individual liberties, but also the important development of the notion of the separation of Church and State, and that the primary justification for the right to rule came from the consent of the governed (as opposed to the authority derived from God, or from the laws of history).

A second civilizational zone was in the Orthodox Christian world, particularly Eastern Europe and Russia. The religious tradition here, in part derived from the imperial tradition of the old Byzantine Empire, was the fusion of State and Church. Thus, for instance, in Russia there was a tradition to fuse the secular and religious authority into the hands of the Princes of Moscow (and later the Tsars). Moscow was called the "Third Rome" (with the idea that Christianity's home had moved from Rome, to Constantinople as the capital of the Byzantine Empire, and then ultimately to Moscow). Thus, the authority of the rulers of Russia (and elsewhere in the Orthodox Zone) was ultimately derived from the notion of "divine right" (or the idea that the right to rule came from God) as opposed to the consent of the governed. This tradition was in many ways continued by communist rule, that claimed that the party-state ruled in the name of the laws of history as opposed to the consent of the governed.

The third major civilizational zone is the "Confucian" one of East Asia. Unlike the other civilizational areas, Confucianism is less a religion and more a social ideology that promotes the hierarchical structuring of society (based on family-like hierarchies, at the pinnacle of which was the Emperor). In such a system, the emphasis is on hierarchy and collective interests rather than on individual rights in opposition to the state. Generally, these values are not conducive to democratic development, although there certainly have been cases of the emergence of democracy in several East Asian cases, recently. Two exceptional cases (Japan and the Philippines) may have been the product of both the lack of penetration of Confucianist ideology in both cases (almost not at all in the Philippines which for much of its modern history was under Portuguese, Spanish, and American control, and in Japan because Confucianism was introduced fairly late, and only affected the upper classes). However, the transition to democracy in Korea and Taiwan, demonstrates to some extent the Confucian impediment to democracy may not be as strong as Huntington originally thought.

Finally, there is the Islamic zone. For Huntington, there are characteristics of Islam that are supportive of democracy, particularly its emphasis on egalitarianism and popular participation in the political community. However, a major impediment to democracy that is part of Islam (according to Huntington) is the lack of separation between the secular state and religious authority. The emphasis on theocracy, or the fusion of religion and political authority, undermines the principle of popular sovereignty. Rulers can simply claim that they are executing the will of God, and that their authority derives from their connection to God (very much akin to divine right) which then undermines one of the central pillars of democratic thought. That authority is ultimately derived from the consent of the governed as opposed to the consent of the heavens. Thus Islamic doctrine contains elements that are both congenial and uncongenial to democracy.

There have, of course, been several criticisms of Huntington's "clash of civilizations" approach. Critics have argued that it is overly simplistic and does not take into account significant differences between countries within civilization areas. Further, others have pointed out that the taxonomy and classification system he used were rather arbitrary, particularly along the "borders" of the civilizations. Critics also argue that Huntington neglects factors such as ideological mobilization, and the unfulfilled socioeconomic needs of the population as the real causal factors driving conflict and the undermining of democracy, and that he essentially reduced the explanation of democracy and conflict to cultural determinism. Indeed, there is some danger of it becoming a self-fulfilling prophecy. The more that people think that politics and conflict are culturally determined, the more likely it will be so (see Rubinstein and Crocker, 1994, for a list of the major criticisms of the clash of civilizations thesis).

Some scholars have argued that the force of the third wave has essentially petered out, or have questioned the entire assumption of the "inevitability" of democratization. Indeed, as scholars like Thomas Carothers, Marina Ottaway, Steven Levitsky and Lucan Way have noted, the transitions of the 1990s have not really produced full-blown democracies, but rather something like *hybrid* systems, not fully democratic, but not fully authoritarian either (Carothers, 2002; Diamond, 2002; Levitsky and Way, 2002; Ottaway, 2003). In the third wave of democracy, a large number of regimes did not become liberal consolidated democracies. In many cases (most prominently in Africa and Latin America), human rights violations and military interference in politics were so widespread that many observers hesitated to label these regimes "democratic." After the break-up of the Soviet Union, the number of regimes that introduced free and fair elections but retained many authoritarian traits continued to grow (Levitsky and Way, 2002) At the time, the overwhelming number of democratization scholars held that these regimes were merely transitory and would soon become true democracies. This "transition paradigm" (Carothers, 2002) started to change around the middle of the 1990s and was seriously questioned by the beginning of the twenty-first century. A growing number of scholars suspected that these "hybrid" regimes were not transitional but displayed remarkable stability (Carothers, 2002; Ottaway, 2003).

Whatever the case, there is considerable evidence that something changed during the third wave, and that there is considerable consensus that this was brought about by changes in the international environment. Whether these waves actually produced consolidated democracies, or simply the proliferation of hybrid regimes, remains to be seen.

The Legacy of Colonialism

An oft-cited additional "international" factor affecting democratic development, particularly in the developing world, is the legacy of colonialism. On the one hand, there is the extremely Eurocentric view that the spread of democracy is the political outcome of the spread of European values and traditions via colonialism (for a discussion, see Huntington, 1984). This is because, theoretically, the colonial power may have transmitted some of its culture and language to the colony, which in turn may have led to the emergence of a "cooperative" political culture, or may have left institutions that were conducive to democracy in place when the colonizing powers exited (Weiner, 1989). However, some scholars (Barro, 1999; Quainoo, 2000) have found no relationship between colonial heritage and democracy, while others (Lipset *et al.*, 1993; Clague *et al.*, 2001) find that being a former British colony increases the probability that a country becomes democratic.

In particular, several scholars have argued that the type of colonizer was important in explaining whether a country was able to develop into a democracy after the end of colonial rule. Myron Weiner (1989), for instance, noted that by 1983 every country in the Third World that emerged from colonial rule since World War II with a population of at least one million (and almost all the smaller countries as well) with a continuous democratic experience was a former British colony. This would suggest that there was something about British colonial rule that made it different from the colonial administration of other European states, such as France and Belgium.

Khapoya (1998), for instance, distinguishes between two main types of colonial rule in Africa: indirect rule and direct rule. The British generally used a system of indirect rule, where the emphasis was not on the assimilation of Africans to become "black Britishers," but rather to share skills, values, and culture, to "empower" the Africans with the ability to run their own communities. Thus, instead of assimilating the Africans as British citizens, society was segregated between the natives and the whites living in the colony. The British also employed an indirect system of administrative rule. Generally this meant that the colonial authorities would co-opt the local power structure (the kings, chiefs, or headman) and via invitations, coercion, or bribery, incorporate them into the colonial administrative structure. In return, these local elites were expected to enforce laws, collect taxes, and serve as the "buffer" between the natives and colonial authorities.

A positive consequence of this system of indirect rule (a system used elsewhere in the British Empire, such as in India and Malaya) was that it provided native elites with important experiences in self-rule. Further, many British colonies adopted practices that mimicked British practices such as experience with electoral, legislative, and judicial institutions (Clague *et al.*, 2001). Given this level of preparedness, then following World War II, Britain was much more willing than other colonial powers to grant independence, which in turn made the newly independent states more willing to retain the institutions the British had put into place. Thus, from this perspective, Britain seems to have left its colonies in a better situation to develop democracy later than non-British colonies.

However, there was a negative side to this style of indirect rule – it tended to reinforce ethnic and tribal division. Generally, the British often arbitrarily empowered certain ethnic groups over others, extending privileges and authority to some at the expense of other groups. When they left, the legacy of these policies often led to the attempted creation of the hegemony of one privileged group over all others. Weiner and Huntington describe ethnic hegemonic states as countries in which "a single ethnic group has taken control over the state and used its powers to exercise control over others" (1987, p. 35). In turn, this created the increased tension and hostility between ethnic groups, leading to violence and decidedly less democracy.

Other colonial powers, however, exercised more direct forms of rule. For instance, French, Portuguese, and Belgian colonies essentially perceived their possessions as an extension of the "mother country" (Khapoya, 1998). This meant that European rule was essentially imposed on the Africans, and the African people were governed without any regard to the existing ethnic stratification. The French, for example, showed equal subjugation regardless of identity to the French state. All commands flowed from the mother country to the colonies and were enforced by regional governors. In the French case as well, there was a strong effort in some of their possessions (particularly in Algeria) to assimilate the subjugated populations to becoming French. Although the Belgian rule of Congo was somewhat different (given that early on it was considered a personal possession of the Belgian King as opposed to a Belgian colony), all power flowed from Brussels, and local elites were not empowered to rule. To be sure, under French, Belgian and Portuguese rule, there did develop a bureaucratic elite that served the colonial state, and many native peoples staffed the colonial state. However, these natives were trained to implement policy, not to make it.

Different political consequences resulted from this form of direct colonial rule. After World War II, unlike the British, the French resisted decolonization and attempted to maintain their assimilation policies throughout their empire (as did Belgium and Portugal). Further, given the equal treatment (and equal subjugation of all groups by the colonial authorities) and the unwillingness of the French, Belgian and Portuguese colonial authorities to cede power, this tended to polarize conflicts between the colonial powers and the indigenous peoples. This often led to an anti-colonial cooperative ethos developing among the inhabitants (regardless of ethnicity) directed against a common enemy, which have avoided the kinds of interethnic tensions that emerged in the wake of British rule. However, another consequence of direct rule colonies was that local elites really had no experience with self-government. Thus, in many cases, colonial elites in former French, Belgian and Portuguese colonies in Africa were poorly equipped for self-rule once independence came.

Globalization and Democracy

In recent years there has also been a great deal of attention paid to the phenomenon of globalization. For our purposes, *globalization* refers to the increasing interdependence of citizens and nations across the world. This interdependence is primarily economic, although it is facilitated by the multiplicity of linkages and interconnections between the states and societies which make up the modern world system (McGrew and Lewis, 1995, p. 23). Globalization, is a "process by which events, decisions, and activities in one part of the world can come to have significant consequences for individuals and communities in quite distant parts of the globe" (ibid., p. 23). According to Baker, Epstein, and Pollin (1998), globalization is globalized capitalism that has led to three things: (1) an increase in international economic interactions; (2) qualitative changes in the way nation-states operate within any country's economy; and (3) decrease in the power of nation-states and increase in the power of private business and market forces (ibid., p. 2). We can therefore define globalization as increasing economic interdependence among the countries of the world in which there is created a multiplicity of linkages, interconnections, and interdependence.

Does globalization help promote democracy? On the one hand, several scholars have pointed to the positive benefits of economic globalization in stimulating market growth and development (ibid.). Thus increasing economic development and the generation of wealth in the developing world should be positively related to the development of democracy. On the other hand, a longstanding argument made by several scholars has been that globalization and economic integration have activated latent cultural and ethnopolitical forces that have been unleashed on the world, or what Yahya Sadowski has labeled the "primodialist" or "chaos" perspective. From this point of view, increased conflicts result from a backlash against globalization's encroachments on identity. Thus, one would expect that in developing countries where rapid globalization has occurred, the probability of conflict is much higher than in countries that are less globalized.

A second perspective contends that although globalization has intensified conflict, conflicts have not resulted from the unleashing of "primordial forces." Rather, increased conflicts can only be understood as resulting from a backlash against globalization's encroachments on identity. The chaos theorists claim a direct connection between globalization and ethnic conflict. The general argument made by advocates of this approach is that globalization has intensified nationalistic and localist sentiments as a result of greater international economic integration. Inequities generated by globalization, or so the argument goes, generate parochial forms of resistance rooted in an imagined past that never was. The homogenization of culture brought about by globalization elicits reactions that exalt differences and local particularisms. Globalization forces a materialistic and superficially universalistic set of Western values on the rest of the world, and this elicits a violent reaction. The homogenizing influence of globalization creates strong opposition to wholesale adoption of the values and standards of the international community. Further, the growth of communication and electronic media (including television, but increasingly the internet) erodes traditional values and moral restraints, by introducing the "glitz of Hollywood." In addition, economic integration, perhaps the most seductive form of globalization, has tremendous social and political consequences, including potentially triggering ethnic and cultural conflict. The global spread of market capitalism, and its attendant shrinking transport costs and growing communications facilities means that both goods and people can more easily move from one country to another. The movement of peoples and goods leads to competition for jobs and other economic benefits, and an expanding set of material desires and aspirations, most of which are frustrated, creating greater resentments and the desire to single out scapegoats.

Many theorists thus suggest a direct connection between economic globalization and ethnic conflict. For instance, as Wright and Macmanus (1991) argued, although earlier there was considerable hope that economic interdependence would bring about "world harmony," in fact, the new intimacy brought about by increased trade and financial flows, and other forms of economic interdependence has provoked political and cultural backlashes that were the seeds of serious conflict. One of the reasons why conflict emerges as a consequence of globalization is because, as Joel Kotkin (1993) argues, economic globalization is breeding a new wave of ethnic awareness in reaction to the homogenizing influences of the global culture. This "great revival" of ethnic identity would promote prosperity for some groups, but for many others globalization would produce a "throwback to the basest kind of clannishness ... increased emphasis on religion and ethnic culture often suggest the prospect of a humanity breaking itself into narrow, exclusive and hostile groups." John Naisbitt (1994), like Kotkin, envisioned that globalization would lead to the growth of a new "tribalism" particularly a "belief" in the fidelity of one's own kind. For Naisbitt, just as economic globalization has led to the decentralization of large capital into smaller economic units, so would economic globalization lead to the break-up of states and the creation of a thousand new countries. The greater integration of economies has led to smaller productive units and the revolution in telecommunications has provided the means for ethnic groups to coordinate their actions and go it alone, so that there was emerging the shared sense that a particular group might do better economically if they were independent politically. This has provided a greater impetus for separatism, and from separatism emerges conflict.

Amy Chua (2002) also points to globalization as a trigger for conflict, but that conflict is particularly extreme because of the overlap between class and ethnic divisions. Chua's theory centers on the "market dominant minorities" who control a disproportionate amount of wealth in many countries where there is ethnic strife. She argues that globalization is a "catalyst" for ethnic strife in these countries because the minorities who control the economy become much wealthier, while the more impoverished majority gains very little. Thus globalization ignites ethnic conflict and ultimately undermines democracy, although the lines of conflict already existed.

Another body of literature has examined the effects of globalization on already democratic polities. From this perspective, globalization especially has undermined the political left in the countries of the developed world. This is because it undermines domestic actors because it leads to the opportunity for the owners of mobile capital to relocate abroad and increases competition for domestic producers in the face of competition from foreign producers. As Lowell Turner argues, the more dynamic, competitive, and interdependent global markets undermine older forms of production, particularly by promoting a movement towards smaller production units (Turner, 1991). As a result, the accompanying move to decentralized capital-intensive production has led to less labor solidarity and declining strength of organized labor, which in turn has weakened the parties of the Left.

These external pressures have caused the parties of the Left to forge new political identities for themselves (Kurtzer, 1993). The social democratic and socialist parties in the West have become increasingly conservative in economic issue areas such as the regulation of workplace practices, redistributive taxation, and expansion or maintenance of the welfare state (Piazza, 2001). Moreover, as Herbert Kitschelt contends, the changes that occurred in the 1970s and 1980s in the social, economic, and cultural structures of the advanced capitalist countries demanded that the social democratic parties alter their political appeals to attract new constituencies and remain electorally viable (Taylor, 1993; Kitschelt, 1994). However, different Left parties adapted differently, largely based on their internal organizational features. Parties that had relatively loose internal features (such as loosened ties with organized labor, less internal discipline, etc.) were better able to adapt to changed circumstances than were more "entrenched" parties, especially those with strong ties to the labor unions. These latter parties, because of internal constraints on their maneuverability, had relatively greater difficulty responding to change and lost ground in the elections.

Imposed Democracy

A more direct way in which the international environment impacts on the development of democracy is through *imposition* or where regimes are "democratic governments installed by a foreign power in which the foreign power plays an important role in the establishment, promotion, and maintenance of the institutions of government" (Enterline and Greig, 2008). Certainly this is not a new practice. A succession of leading countries (the Netherlands in the seventeenth century, the United Kingdom in the eighteenth and nineteenth centuries, and the United States in the twentieth century) have each promoted a respective global ideology and sought to reshape countries in their mold (Modelski and Perry, 1991; Taylor, 1996). The US has been especially forceful in the post-1945 period as the promoter of liberal democracy (Robinson, 1996).

Imposed democratic regimes can be installed following the defeat of a state in a war – two classic examples of imposed regimes are post-World War II West Germany and Japan. In these cases, the foreign power occupied the defeated state, removed the existing government, and established entirely new political institutions. More recent examples of such imposed democratic regimes are in Iraq and Afghanistan. As Enterline and Greig (2005, 2008) point out, there are other more incremental ways to impose a democratic polity, through the colonial process, for example, where the colonial power establishes the democratic regime to govern the colony after independence, or via covert activity, such as support of a *coup d'état*. Yet, what all these forms of imposition have in common is that *the means of governance are established through the actions and decisions of a foreign power.*

Generally, however, most scholars think of imposed democracy as democracy quickly forced upon a defeated state. Many scholars point out the inherent weakness of these imposed democratic systems. For instance, Gills *et al.* (1993) argue that at best, external intervention serves to promote only nominal, "low-intensity democracies" or relatively weak democratic (or semi-democratic) systems. Enterline and Greig (2008) argue that generally externally imposed democratic regimes can survive, depending upon certain conditions. They identify four key criteria that lead to the successful imposition of democracy: (1) the use of a large occupation force; (2) a clear message of sustained, long-term occupation to back the new state; (3) an ethnically homogenous society, and (4) democratic neighbors. However, these conditions do not exist in most countries of the "third wave" particularly in the third and fourth sub-waves (such as Iraq and Afghanistan), so the prospects for the success of imposed democracies are not particularly good, given these considerations.

Conclusion

In this chapter we focused on a variety of external factors that impact on the development of democracy, including waves of democratization, the legacies of colonialism, globalization, and democratic imposition. Although clearly these external forces do not determine whether or not democracy will emerge, the effects of democratic diffusion, globalization, and democratic imposition cannot be discounted. Taken together with the variety of environment factors (such as historical processes, culture, economics, and social structure), these external forces can powerfully shape political developments within a country. However, whether a country ultimately develops along democratic lines depends powerfully on the institutional choices that are made upon the inception of the democratic experiment. This is the topic for the next chapter.

References

Almond, Gabriel and Verba, Sidney (1963) *The Civic Culture*, Boston: Little Brown.
Baker, Dean, Epstein, Gerald, and Pollin, Robin (1998) *Globalization and Progressive Economic Policy*, New York: Cambridge University Press.

Barro, R.J. (1999) "Determinants of Democracy," *The Journal of Political Economy*, 107: S158–S183.

Beblawi, Hazem (1987) "The Rentier State in the Arab World," in Hazem Beblawi and Giacomo Luciani (eds.) *The Rentier State*, New York: Croom Helm.

Bergesen, Albert (1992) "Regime Change in the Semi-periphery: Democratization in Latin America and the Socialist Bloc," *Sociological Perspectives*, 35: 405–413.

Bermeo, Nancy (1987) "Redemocratization and Transition Elections: A Comparison of Spain and Portugal," *Comparative Politics*, 19: 213–231.

Bratton, Michael and van de Walle, Nicolas (1994) "Neopatrimonial Regimes and Political Transitions in Africa," *World Politics*, 46: 453–489.

Bratton, Michael and van de Walle, Nicolas (1997) *Democratic Experiments in Africa*, Cambridge: Cambridge University Press.

Carothers, Thomas (2002) "The End of the Transition Paradigm," *Journal of Democracy*, 13: 5–21.

Chua, Amy (2002). *World on Fire: How Exporting Free Market Democracy Breeds Ethnic Hatred and Global Instability*, New York: Doubleday.

Clague, C., Gleason, S. and Knack. S. (2001) "Determinants of Lasting Democracy in Poor Countries: Culture, Development, and Institutions," *The Annals of the American Academy of Political Science*, 573: 16–41.

Diamond, Larry Jay (2002) "Thinking about Hybrid Regimes," *Journal of Democracy*, 13(2): 21–35.

Enterline, Andrew J. and Greig, J. Michael (2005) "Beacons of Hope? The Impact of Imposed Democracy on Regional Peace, Democracy and Prosperity," *Journal of Politics*, 67: 1075–1098.

Enterline, Andrew J. and Greig, J. Michael (2008) "Against All Odds? The History of Imposed Democracy and the Future of Iraq and Afghanistan," *Foreign Policy Analysis*, 4: 321–347.

Feldman, Noah (2003) *After Jihad: America and the Struggle for Islamic Democracy*, New York: Farrar, Straus and Giroux.

Gills, B., Rocamora, J. and Wilson, R. (1993) *Low Intensity Democracy: Political Power in the New World Order*, London: Pluto Press.

Huntington, Samuel P. (1984) "Will More Countries Become Democratic?" *Political Science Quarterly*, 49: 193–218.

Huntington, Samuel (1991) *The Third Wave: Democratization in the Late Twentieth Century*, Norman, OK: University of Oklahoma Press.

Huntington, Samuel (1991–1992) "How Countries Democratize," *Political Science Quarterly*, 106: 579–616.

Huntington, Samuel (1996) *The Clash of Civilizations and the Remaking of World Order*, New York: Simon & Schuster.

Khapoya, V. (1998) *The African Experience: An Introduction*, Upper Saddle River, NJ: Prentice-Hall.

Kitschelt, Herbert (1994) *The Transformation of European Social Democracy*, New York: Cambridge University Press.

Kotkin, Joel (1993) *Tribes: How Race, Religion and Identity Determine Success in the New Global Economy*, New York: Random House.

Kurtzer, Paulette (1993) *Business and Banking: Political Change and Economic Integration in Western Europe*, Ithaca, NY: Cornell University Press.

Levitsky, Steve and Way, Lucan (2002) "The Rise of Competitive Authoritarianism," *Journal of Democracy*, 13: 51–65.

Lipset, S.M., Seong, K. and Torres, J.C. (1993) "A Comparative Analysis of the Social Requisites of Democracy," *International Social Science Journal*, 36: 155–175.

McGrew, Anthony G. and Lewis, Paul G. (eds.) (1995) *Global Politics*, Cambridge, MA: Blackwell.

Modelski, G. and Perry, G. III. (1991) "Democratization in Long Perspective," *Technological Forecasting and Social Change*, 39: 23–34.

Naisbitt, John (1994) *Global Paradox: The Bigger the World Economy, the More Powerful its Smallest Players*, New York: William Morrow & Co.

O'Donnell, Guillermo, Schmitter, Philippe, and Whitehead, Laurence (1986) *Transitions from Authoritarian Rule*, Baltimore, MD: Johns Hopkins University Press.

Ottaway, Marina (2003) *Democracy Challenged: The Rise of Semi-Authoritarianism*, Washington, DC: Carnegie Endowment for International Peace.

Piazza, James (2001) "De-Linking Labor: Labor Unions and Social Democratic Parties under Globalization," *Party Politics*, 7: 413–435.

Przeworski, Adam (1986) "Some Problems in the Study of the Transition to Democracy," in Guillenno O'Donnell, Philippe C. Schmitter, and Laurence Whitehead (eds.) *Transitions from Authoritarian Rule: Comparative Perspectives*, pp. 47–63, Baltimore, MD: Johns Hopkins University Press.

Przeworski, Adam (1991) *Democracy and the Market*, New York: Cambridge University Press.

Quainoo, S.E. (2000) *Transitions and Consolidation of Democracy in Africa*, Binghamton, NY: Global Publications, ICGS.

Quinn, John (2002) *The Road Oft Traveled: Development Policies and Majority State Ownership of Industry in Africa*, New York: Praeger.

Robinson, W.I. (1996) *Promoting Polyarchy: Globalization, US Intervention, and Hegemony*, Cambridge: Cambridge University Press.

Rubenstein, Richard and Crocker, Jarle (1994) "Challenging Huntington," *Foreign Policy*, 96: 113–128.

Sadowski, Yahya (1998) *The Myth of Global Chaos*, Washington, DC: Brookings Institution.

Shin, Doh Chull (1994) "On the Third Wave of Democratization: A Synthesis and Evaluation of Recent Theory and Research," *World Politics*, 47: 135–170.

Starr, Harvey (1991) "Democratic Dominoes: Diffusion Approaches to the Spread of Democracy in the International System," *Journal of Conflict Resolution*, 35: 356–381.

Taylor, A. (1993) "Trade Unions and the Politics of Social Democratic Renewal," in Richard Gillespie and William Paterson (eds.) *Rethinking Social Democracy in Western Europe*, London: Frank Cass.

Taylor, P.J. (1996) *The Way the Modern World Works: World Hegemony to World Impasse*, Chichester: John Wiley and Sons, Ltd.

Turner, Lowell (1991) *Democracy at Work: Changing World Markets and the Future of Labor Unions*, Ithaca, NY: Cornell University Press.

Weiner, Myron (1989) "Institution Building in India," in *The Indian Paradox: Essays in Indian Politics*, Newbury Park, CA: Sage Publications.

Weiner, Myron and Huntington, Samuel (eds.) (1987) *Understanding Political Development*, Boston, MA: Little, Brown and Company.

Wright, Robin and Macmanus, Doyle (1991) *Flashpoints: Promise and Peril in a New World*, New York: Alfred Knopf.

7

Electoral Systems

In previous chapters, we discussed the contextual factors that affect the development of political systems. However, the evolution of political systems is not merely a function of the economic, social, cultural, and international environments. Political democracy is also as much a product of human choices as it is a product of context, particularly the choice of institutions that help shape the behavior of political actors. As many scholars in political science have long argued, a crucial choice in building political democracy is the design of electoral systems. Indeed, given that elections are central to the functioning of democratic systems, scholars have sought to understand why different electoral systems are chosen and the impact those choices have on a range of political outcomes, both at the individual and the system level. These outcomes include the quality and breadth of representation, the fractionalization and polarization of political party systems, voter turnout and voting behavior, and the stability of government and the political system.

Much of the comparative work on electoral systems has focused largely on the experiences of countries in the West, particularly in Europe and the United States, although more recently there has been a considerable amount of attention paid to the role of electoral systems in new democracies (Ishiyama, 1997; Moser, 1999; Reynolds, 1999; Reilly, 2002; Benoit, 2007). Since electoral processes and outcomes exert such important effects on the real world of politics, understanding the impact of electoral systems helps connect theory and practice in political science.

Comparative Politics: Principles of Democracy and Democratization, First Edition.
John T. Ishiyama.
© 2012 John T. Ishiyama. Published 2012 by Blackwell Publishing Ltd.

What Is the Electoral System?

Generally, we can think of the electoral system as the method by which voters make a choice between different options. More specifically, we can think of the electoral system as being comprised of a set of crucial choices – in particular, who is to be elected, and how?

Elections are used to choose heads of state, heads of government, and members of the legislature, as well as a variety of other offices in political democracies. In the literature, however, the focus is largely on identifying different types of elections designed to determine national executive power and national legislative power. As far as Chief Executives are concerned, they can be elected via *direct* or *indirect* means. In a direct election, voters cast ballots directly for a set of eligible candidates. Political systems that use direct elections of the president include France, Russia, and Argentina. In an indirect election, a group of electors are selected who then elect the President. For instance, the United States employs an indirect method for electing the President, where voters (or state legislatures) select presidential electors, who then comprise an *Electoral College*. These electors then select the President. Although generally the electoral college reflects the popular vote, this has not always been the case in the history of the United States. The most recent example of this being the highly contested 2000 election where the Democratic candidate Al Gore had more popular votes than the Republican George W. Bush, but the latter had more electoral college votes – and was subsequently elected. In other countries, such as Germany and Italy, the President is elected by parliament. One of the advantages of the indirect election of the President is to help insulate the power of the executive from a populist demagogue. Certainly, this was the case with the US political system where the constitutional framers in 1787 were clearly suspicious of the general population's ability to choose wisely, and sought to establish an elite-level check on the political aspirations of the mass electorate.

There are also direct and indirect elections of legislators. For instance, for many years, prior to 1913, members of the upper house of the US Congress, the Senate, were elected by members of state legislatures. In France, Senators are also elected indirectly by approximately 150,000 local elected officials ("grands électeurs"), which includes regional council members, department councilors, mayors, city council members, and deputies of the National Assembly. This system tends to favor the more politically conservative rural areas of the country.

The second question relates to how candidates are to be elected. In general, we can think of electoral systems as being made up of a set of choices, which include: the *electoral formula, the district magnitude, ballot structure*, and *electoral thresholds* (Farrell, 1997, 2001).

In terms of electoral formula, there is a distinction between plurality, majority, and proportional representation formulae. Generally in Britain, and in many countries that were former British colonies (such as the United States, Canada, India, Kenya, and Nigeria), the most commonly used electoral formula is the plurality formula, sometimes called first past the post (FPTP) system. In such systems the candidate who receives the most votes (not necessarily the majority of the vote) wins the election. Indeed, under such conditions it is quite possible for a candidate to be elected with far less than a majority of the vote (depending on how many candidates run for office). Thus, in 1992, President Bill Clinton received only about 43 percent of the popular vote, but that was enough for his electoral victory, largely because a third party candidate Ross Perot, had also entered the competition. Similarly, in Russian State Duma elections, it was quite common for candidates to the single-member districts to be elected by a very small percentage of the vote (as low as 19 percent) because there were many candidates running for election (Moser, 1999).

Second, there is the majority formula, which is most often associated with "runoff" elections. In such an electoral contest, a candidate can win outright in a single round of voting by garnering an absolute majority of the ballots cast; however, when no one candidate captures 50 percent plus 1 of the eligible votes, a runoff round is held at a subsequent date, with the top two finishers from the first round squaring off. Several countries use this formula for the direct election of their chief executives (such as in France, Russia, Poland, and Argentina) as well as election to the legislature (as in the case of France). This method has the advantage of providing voters with a wide range of candidates from which to choose in the first round. If there is no majority winner in the first round, then this system provides for a second round, which yields a winner supported by a simple majority of those voting in the runoff.

Third, an alternative to single-member, winner-take-all systems of electing representative assemblies is one based on proportional representation (PR) in multimember districts. In PR systems, the goal is to have the proportion of a party's seats in the legislature reflect the strength of the party in the electorate. Thus, for example, a party securing 25 percent of the vote would be rewarded with 25 percent (either exactly or approximately) of the legislative seats. The party that won 10 percent of the popular vote would be entitled to 10 percent of the seats in the legislature (and so forth).

The second dimension of an electoral system is the *district magnitude*. District magnitude refers to the number of candidates who will be elected from any given constituency, with the basic distinction between systems that rely on single-member districts and those that employ multimember districts. In the single-member district system, a country is divided into electoral districts from which one individual will emerge as the elected representative. Often, particularly in countries that were once British colonies, single-member districts are set up in tandem with a plurality electoral formula. Generally this means that whichever candidate receives the most votes in a competitive election, wins. Thus such systems are often referred to as winner-take-all systems where there is no compensation for coming in second place. This system is used in the United States, Britain, Canada, Ghana, and India. Others, most notably France, employ a single-member district system with two rounds of voting. In such cases, individual candidates can win outright in the first round with an absolute majority of votes cast, or they can secure the most votes cast among eligible candidates in the second-round runoff.

Advocates of single-member district systems defend the system for generally two reasons. First, there is a clarity of responsibility and democratic accountability by giving citizens in each district the ability to hold their representative responsible. Further, such systems enhance constituency service, in as much as voters can call upon individual representatives to directly address their concerns. Second, and perhaps more importantly for new democracies, advocates of single-member district systems point to the "moderating" influence such systems have on political competition (Duverger, 1954). This is because since candidates have the incentive to win as many votes as possible (in order to win the election), there is a tendency to gravitate towards the ideological center of the political spectrum, or to regress to what Anthony Downs (1957) referred to as the "median voter." Thus single-member district systems are often lauded as way to hedge against extremism.

Detractors, however, find that aggregating district-level winner-take-all elections into a national whole can produce representational distortions in the national legislature. For example, a party that runs a consistent and respectable second place throughout the country but that fails to win any single district would be excluded from taking seats in the legislature. Such a system, then, has the potential to under-represent smaller parties in a democracy (Downs, 2010).

Although the most common combination is the use of a plurality formula with single-member districts, there are, however, multimember plurality systems as well, including the "block" voting system. This system uses multi-member districts in which electors have as many votes as there are candidates to be elected. Counting is identical to a first past the post/single-member district plurality system with the candidates with the highest vote totals winning the seats. Thus if there are three seats available in a district, and six candidates are running, then the top three finishers are awarded seats (for a description and application, see Ishiyama, 2009).

Proportional representation systems are characterized by the use of multimember districts, which often vary in size. Some countries, such as the Netherlands, use the entire country as a single "district" and seats are allocated based solely on the national constituency. On the other hand, in Belgium, there are eleven multimember electoral districts, which are apportioned seats proportionally according to population, and results are allocated based upon electoral performance of the parties in each district. Some multimember districts can be quite small as in the single transferable vote system, a form of PR, in Ireland, where district magnitudes range from 3–5 seats per district (Lijphart, 1994).

Further, for PR systems we can also distinguish between *closed party list systems*, and *open party list systems*. In a closed system, voters vote only for a party list (in a multimember constituency, often the whole country), whereas in an *open party list system*, voters can choose from a published list or select an individual candidate. In closed systems the party determines who is on the list and in what order they appear. The order on the list is important, in as much as if a party wins 5 percent of the vote, for example, then the top 5 percent on the list will be awarded seats. The closed party list mechanism clearly provides considerable power in the hands of the party leadership.

On the other hand, in an open list system, parties are generally allowed to place as many candidates on their lists as there are seats available. The formation of the list is an internal process that varies with each party. The place on the list is considered to play a role in the election of a candidate, by giving stronger visibility to those high on the list. Voters, however, in an open list have several options. For instance, in Belgium, they may: (1) vote for a list as a whole, thereby showing approval of the order established by the party; (2) vote for one or more individual candidates, regardless of his/ her ranking on the list (a "preference vote"); (3) vote for one or more of the "alternates" (substitutes); (4) vote for one or more candidates, and one or more alternates; or (5) leave the ballot blank so no one receives the vote. The open list system provides more opportunities for voter input and is touted as more democratic than its closed list counterpart (Downs, 2010).

Ballot structure refers to the way the ballot that appears before voters is organized. Generally, ballots can be organized along *categorical* or *ordinal* lines. A categorical ballot structure allows a single either/or choice of one candidate or one party. This is more commonly used in most electoral systems. The voter cannot divide their vote. On the other hand, an ordinal ballot structure allows the voters the opportunity to rank order their preferences or, in other words, the ability to divide their vote, to vote for more than one candidate. In some ordinal ballots, political parties devise rank ordered lists of candidates to determine which persons ultimately claim those seats. An example is "the single transferable vote" which is also called the "Hare-Clark system" in Australia. In the United States, electoral reform activists have taken to calling it "choice voting." Currently this system is used to elect parliaments in Ireland and Malta. In Australia, it is used to elect the federal Senate, as well as the legislatures in several states there. Instead of voting for one person, voters rank each candidate in their order of choice. By this method, voters rank candidates preferentially, and if a voter's first-choice candidate has already cleared a set threshold and does not need additional support to win, then that vote is transferred to a second choice. This process, exemplified most clearly by Ireland, is designed to avoid "wasting" votes, or where votes are cast that are not represented in some way (as is the case in many district-based plurality elections, where votes cast for losers are effectively "wasted") .

Finally, for proportional representation systems, there is the issue of thresholds. Generally, this involves setting some minimum threshold that would qualify parties to obtain representation in the legislature. A very common threshold is 5 percent (used in Germany and Belgium, for instance) but other thresholds, but lower and higher thresholds are also used. Israel has a very low threshold (at 2 percent) whereas Turkey's is quite high, with its 10 percent threshold for representation. These thresholds are an increasingly common way for PR systems to limit the entry of minor (and sometimes extremist) parties into legislatures.

In sum then, generally plurality systems involve a winner-take-all formula, small district magnitudes, and categorical ballot structures. On

the other hand, most proportional representation systems involve proportional formulae, large district magnitude, categorical ballot structures
– and on occasion ordinal ballots (as with the single transferable vote
system).

A variety of systems have sought to mix features of both district-based
plurality and PR systems into a hybrid type system. For instance, one type
of mixed system is the *additional member system* which is used for elections
to the lower house of the German Bundestag, the New Zealand House of
Representatives, and Scottish and Welsh Assemblies in the United Kingdom.
This system combines elements of the single-member district plurality
system with characteristics of party-list PR. In this mixed system voters get
two votes, and the ballot generally has two sides. In the first part the voters
vote for candidates and in the second party they vote for parties. The percentage of second or party-list votes won by a party determines the party's
overall number of representatives, and the number of seats won in single-
member districts is added to match that overall percentage received by the
party in the PR portion of the election. In the German case, there are two
sets of minimal thresholds. To qualify for additional seats, a party must win
at least three district seats or at least 5 percent of the PR list vote. In this
way the two parts of the ballot are linked (Lijphart, 1994). Another variation of the mixed system is the *parallel* system in which the two parts of
the ballot are unlinked. For instance, from 1993 to 2007, the Russian
Federation used such a system where seats elected via the districts were
separate from the list. In other words parties were not entitled to additional
seats based upon the percentage won on the list. One of the major pur-
ported advantages of the mixed systems is that it combines the accountability of the district-based system while at the same time assuring the
proportionality of representation. However, as some scholars have noted
(Ishiyama, 1997), this often creates different types of politicians that create
divisions within parties between those who were elected from the districts
and those who were elected from the PR list. This can create coordination
problems for parties during the legislative and policy-making process.

The Effects of Electoral Systems

What are the posited effects of electoral systems, and more specifically, how
do they impact the development of democracy? For many democratic
theorists, holding elections are the central component of the development

of democracy, and how they are conducted will vitally affect whether democracy evolves. For instance, Schumpeter (1942) argued that democracy is "that institutional arrangement for arriving at political decisions in which individuals acquire the power to decide by means of a competitive struggle for the people's vote" (p. 269). Przeworski, Alvarez, Cheibub, and Limongi (2000) also view contested elections as the primary litmus test for democracy. Whether sufficient or not, elections typically figure as necessary conditions for the existence of democracy (Downs 2010).

Generally, the scholarly work on the effects of electoral systems has focused on the longstanding debate between what is the "best" type of electoral system and (a) the relationship between electoral rules and the ideological polarization and size of political party systems; (b) the tendency of electoral systems to impact voter turnout and citizen participation; and (c) the potential for electoral systems to affect the course of democratic development.

Party systems effects

Much of the debate about the "best electoral system" revolves around the differences between single-member district FPTP systems versus List PR systems. On the one hand, advocates of the single-member district plurality electoral system point to a number of advantages of the system. First, such systems provide for incentives for political moderation in the party system and the political system generally. This is because of the incentive for candidates to maximize the number of votes received in an electoral competition, because only by winning the most votes will a candidate be elected to office. The best strategy to increase the number of votes is to appeal to the political center, as opposed to campaigning on the political fringes of the ideological spectrum. Thus candidates (and parties seeking to recruit candidates) have an incentive to present moderate political platforms (Powell, 2000).

On the other hand, critics of PR point out that no such incentive for moderation exists under the PR formula. Indeed, an extremist party could essentially win seats in the legislature, even if they were only able to attain a fairly small fraction of the vote (even with electoral thresholds). Thus there is no incentive to moderate a party's position on anything, especially if the party expects to win some representation. When combined with parliamentary government and coalitional politics, it is quite possible for even minor parties to gain access to executive power. Further, the openings created by PR can provide extremist, and even anti-democratic parties a "foothold" in government in which they can expand their recruitment efforts (by distributing patronage) and develop legitimacy to the extent that ultimately take power. This is what the detractors of list PR point out as the principal failing of the German Weimar Republic (1919–1933), in which the PR list system (with a very low threshold) "allowed" Adolph Hitler and the National Socialist Party to first gain a toehold in the German parliament in the 1928 election and from there spread their recruitment efforts and expand their activities (Duverger, 1954). Presumably, had the Weimar Republic had a district-based plurality system, this would not have happened.

A second posited effect of the single-member district plurality system is that it tends to reduce the number of parties and hence promotes governmental stability, particularly when governing coalitions are required (as is the case in many parliamentary systems) (Duverger, 1984). This is because there is a strong incentive for larger parties to form out of smaller ones. Consider this simple example. Suppose in a district competition, Party A's candidate receives 34 percent of the vote, Party B's candidate receives 33 percent of the vote, and Party C's candidate receives 33 percent of the vote. Under FPTP plurality rules, Party A would win the seat, although it won clearly far less than a majority of the popular vote. Further 66 percent of the vote is "wasted" or unrepresented in the final result. Suppose over time this distribution remained stable, with Party A winning again and again. This would provide an incentive for Party B and Party C to find some common ground to perhaps offer a single candidate, or perhaps merge as a single party, in order to defeat their common rival, Party A. Thus, over time, the number of parties should be reduced to nearly two parties in the system (a tendency which is known as "Duverger's Law" named after the scholar Maurice Duverger).

The notion that plurality elections using one-ballot single-member districts will create two-party systems whereas proportional representation rules with multimember districts will lead to multiparty systems has had considerable staying power. Duverger argued that electoral laws have both *mechanical effects* and *psychological effects*. The mechanical effects highlight the under-representation of third (and fourth, and fifth, etc.) parties, which is likely to occur over time in a single-seat legislative district that is used in an election. Given these mechanical impediments to minor party success, voters who generally support minor parties then have psychological incentives not to "waste" their votes and may often cast ballots against their preferred candidate in a strategic effort to exercise some influence over the most likely winner in the two-party competition. Sartori (1968) extended Duverger's assertion of a link between proportionality and party system size, arguing that district magnitude is the best predictor of the effective number of political parties in a district.

There has been ample empirical support for Duverger's claims that first-past-the-post, single-ballot elections produce two-party systems (Rae, 1967; Sartori, 1968; Riker, 1982; Taagepera and Shugart, 1989; Lijphart, 1994; Cox, 1997). Indeed, in elections for the UK House of Commons and the US Congress, the evidence seems to suggest a compelling link between electoral rules and strong, stable, two-party government. Electoral structures in the United States, for example, help explain the consistent failure of third parties to mount successful campaigns. Although smaller parties have been able to win parliamentary seats in the United Kingdom, their representation in the House of Commons does not match their overall support in the electorate, and they have had little chance at becoming the party of government or forcing a coalition. To illustrate, the perennial third-party Liberal Democrats won 22.1 percent of the vote in Britain's 2005 general election but secured only 9.6 percent of the 646 seats in the House of Commons. Tony Blair's Labour Party, having won only 35.3 percent of the votes nationwide, nevertheless captured 55.2 percent of the seats in Parliament and 100 percent of the Cabinet positions in government.

On the other hand, PR systems do not have this reductive effect on the number of political parties. This is because there is far less incentive for parties to coalesce, if they gain representation with a small percentage of the vote. Take, for instance, our example above, with Parties A, B, C. If we had the same vote distribution for the parties under PR, then Party A would be entitled to 34 percent of the seats in parliament, Party B, 33 percent and Party C, 33 percent. Thus, no votes are "wasted" and each party gains representation, providing less incentive to merge as parties. Thus PR, according to Duverger's law, would tend to promote a multiparty as opposed to a two-party system.

However, PR systems also present a problem when forming stable governing coalitions. When no single political party secures a legislative majority, which is generally the case when elections are governed by PR election rules, the post-election period is usually marked by formal negotiations and backroom deals between parties in the process of forming a governing coalition. For instance, in Belgium, which uses a PR List system with a 5 percent threshold for representation in the federal Chamber of

Representatives, the general election of 2007 resulted in 11 parties gaining parliamentary seats. The largest party was the Flemish-speaking Christian Democratic Party, which won only 18 percent of the 150 seats in parliament. Protracted negations continued for 196 days after the election, and even then only an interim caretaker government was formed. Seventy-nine more days passed until a full government was agreed upon. The government failed to survive the year and the coalition collapsed.

The impact on voter choice, turnout and citizen participation

Beyond party systems effects, many scholars have argued that electoral systems also impact voter behavior, both choices and turnout (see Downs 2010). For instance, as mentioned above, single-member plurality systems tend to encourage *strategic voting*, or where voters will opt to vote for their second, or third choices, in order to prevent their least preferred choice from getting elected. This means that many voters under such conditions vote against their least preferred candidates, as opposed to voting for their most preferred. This "voting against" behavior makes voters susceptible to negative campaigning, or where electoral campaigns are often conducted to "villainize" opposing candidates to make them the least preferred candidates for voters. Further, according to Arend Lijphart (1994, 1999), majoritarian and plurality electoral systems dilute citizen enthusiasm and voter turnout because so many supporters of minor parties conclude that casting their ballots will have little to no impact on electoral outcomes, government formation, or policy choices. Thus, they simply stop voting.

On the other hand, PR systems, especially those with low electoral thresholds and large district magnitude tend to allow voters to express their preferred choices, and minimizes the practice of strategic voting (Katz, 1980). This is because larger district magnitudes and lower electoral thresholds should increase the likelihood that smaller parties are able to secure seats and obtain a voice in the legislature (and potentially a role in a coalition government). With the greater likelihood of electoral success for minor (and even extreme parties), voter efficacy (the sense that one's vote counts) and hence the incentives to cast ballots should increase. Thus, voter turnout is generally much higher in countries that use PR systems when compared to countries that use FPTP electoral rules (Lijphart, 1999, p. 284). According to Norris, "Institutional rules do indeed matter: voting participation is maximized in elections using PR, with small electoral districts, regular but relatively infrequent national contests, and competitive party systems, and in presidential contests" (2004, pp. 257–258).

Electoral systems and democratic transition

Recently, several scholars have examined how electoral laws impact the processes of democratic transition and consolidation. Indeed, there has been much recent attention in the political science literature given to the potential for the successful *electoral engineering* of political democracy. There has been certainly no shortage of potential cases to test these theories, ranging from the post-communist states, and post-authoritarian countries throughout Africa, Latin America, and Asia. Further, hotspots such as Iraq and Afghanistan present possibilities to further test our theoretical assertions.

However, as Pippa Norris (2004) notes, the impact of electoral systems on democratic transition and consolidation may be tempered by other cultural factors. Indeed, she identifies two theoretical traditions in the literature on democratization – *rational choice institutionalism* and *cultural modernization*. The rational choice approach emphasizes that political actors adopt different strategies based on the incentives generated by district magnitudes, electoral thresholds and ballot structures. Further, citizens adapt their voting behavior in response to the incentives generated by different electoral rules. Thus, from this perspective, changing the structure of incentives through electoral engineering "should have the capacity to generate important consequences for political representation and for voting behavior" (Norris, 2004, p. 15). On the other hand, the cultural modernization approach argues that cultural habits arising from processes of social modernization place constrain how rules can alter behavior. This culturalist argument is often employed to explain why the wholesale introduction of electoral rules into culturally divided countries frequently fails to produce transformations of individual behavior.

Whatever the case, there certainly are efforts currently to build democracy where it had not existed before, and the cross-national lessons from other countries have informed the design of electoral systems in such world hot spots as Iraq and Afghanistan. When parliamentary elections were held in December 2005 to constitute a post-Saddam Council of Representatives in Iraq, a PR-list system governed 230 of the total 275 seats in 18 multi-member districts (*governorates*). An additional 45 seats were then allocated to political entities that did not win any seats outright in the governorates but that did clear a minimum national threshold of 5 percent. Also Iraq's electoral law requires that at least 25 percent of the members of those elected be women. In Afghanistan, post-Taliban elections have struggled to secure domestic and international legitimacy. The 2005 elections for Afghanistan's lower house of parliament employed the single non-transferable vote (SNTV) method in 34 multimember constituencies (a system similar to the Block Vote) and specifically designed to address the ethnic divisions within the country. Candidates, however, ran independently because parties and lists were not recognized by the governing law.

Other effects of electoral systems

Beyond party systems effects and effects on voter behavior, there is also evidence that the type of electoral system can impact the political opportunities for women and minorities (Rule and Zimmerman, 1994). For instance, the countries that consistently sit atop comparative rankings of the proportion of women winning seats in national parliaments, that is Sweden, Iceland, Finland, and the Netherlands, all use PR electoral systems with relatively low thresholds. Further, advocates of PR systems point to the inclusive nature of the system, and contend that inclusion of even extreme parties and their voters will have a moderating effect on politics, in as much as inclusion provides these parties and voters with a "stake" in maintaining the political system (Liphart and Grofman, 1984; Grofman and Lijphart, 1986).

Perhaps one of the most interesting arguments in favor of the use of proportional representation is made by advocates of the *consociational* school, who have long argued that by promoting the emergence of ethnic politics and then representing groups broadly, this will facilitate the integration of as many subcultures as possible into the political game, thus creating the conditions for inter-ethnic cooperation (Lorwin, 1971; Nordlinger, 1972; Daalder, 1974; Lijphart, 1974; McRae, 1974). Indeed, by securing representation for minority groups, rules such as PR serves to facilitate the integration of groups into the political system, which ultimately leads them to moderate their demands. Frank Cohen (1997, p. 613) states, "By making institutions more accessible and making ethnic cleavages more explicit, ethnic groups will engage in more frequent but less intense conflict. They will use moderate means of resistance to effect change in the status quo."

However, there has been considerable debate as to whether PR list systems in fact "freeze" ethnic cleavages and promote the development of ethnic parties, which Donald Horowitz (1985) views as fundamentally inimical to the development of democracy. Indeed, the ethnification of politics, which inevitably results from the appearance of ethnic parties, is something to be avoided in countries in transition. Whereas Lijphart advocates power sharing and list PR (for example, Lijphart, 1974), Horowitz (1985) advocates a variation of a single-member district system with an ordinal ballot structure known as the alternative vote (AV).

The *alternative vote*, although not widely used (it has been employed in Australian Senate elections, as well as in local elections in Canada and elsewhere) has been touted as an institutional remedy for politics in ethnically divided societies. The alternative vote system allows voters to express their preferences for candidates in a single-member district (much like the single transferable vote, but for single-member districts). If there is not a single candidate who wins a majority (50 percent) of the first preferences votes, then the lowest polling candidate is eliminated and that candidate's second preferences are redistributed to candidates remaining in the race, until a single candidate surmounts the 50 percent threshold.

Horowitz views the alternative vote, despite its similarity to other district-based systems, as less divisive for ethnically divided societies than FPTP voting. Horowitz views AV as a means to foster interethnic accommodation and moderation through as the result of two effects. First, since voters are asked to express their preferences, even supporters from one ethnic group may choose to express support for interethnic accord by ranking moderate parties associated with the other ethnic group ahead of radical parties associated with their own ethnic group. Although Horowitz acknowledges that in many ethnically divided society, "voters will generally not cross ethnic lines" (1991, p. 179), he also argues that with a preferential ballot, voters might be willing to give support to moderate parties from another ethnic group. As he explains, "The purpose of incentives is to create floating voters at some level of preference" (ibid., p. 179). Thus, it could be the case that a radical party of a given ethnic group might be a plurality winner but still lose out to a moderate party of either its own or the other ethnic group as a result of eventual lower order ballot transfers.

Second, in Horowitz's view, under AV, political parties seek as many second or lower preferences votes outside their own ethnic group. Thus they have an incentive to appear acceptable as a second choice, and hence may adopt more conciliatory or moderate stances on ethnically divisive issues.

> Electorally, the way to induce politicians to be moderate is to structure voting
> arrangements so politicians must rely, in part, on votes delivered by members

of a group other than their own. Such incentives are effective because those votes will not be forthcoming unless the candidates receiving them can be portrayed as being moderate on inter-ethnic issues. (1993, p. 24)

Since the moderate parties are more likely to be able to obtain such cross-ethnic support than extremist parties, in Horowitz's view, AV will "make moderation rewarding and penalize extremism" (Horowitz, 1991, p. 452).

A third effect is that AV is likely to provide an incentive for parties to make post-election deals to for policy adjustments on divisive issues, and ultimately to create an incentive for cross-ethnic electoral alliances. "The exchange of second or third preferences, based on reciprocal concessions on ethnic issues, is likely to lead to an accommodative interethnic coalition if no party can form a government alone" (see ibid., p. 189). These coalitions are likely to be more robust "coalitions of commitment" than the "coalitions for convenience" which are often established by parties after an election under PR systems) (see Horowitz, 1985: 365–388; 1991).

Thus, in these ways, Horowitz believes that the alternative vote is a workable solution for promoting interethnic accommodation in divided societies. This argument, however, has come under some criticism particularly by those who have studied the AV in operation (in Fiji, which is ethnically divided between indigenous Fijian and Indian populations). Fraenkel and Grofman (2004, 2006) question the merits of AV, and have argued that list PR would have been more effective in promoting accommodation between the two groups. Nonetheless, there remains considerable debate over which electoral system would best promote interethnic accommodation in ethnically divided societies.

Another posited effect of electoral systems is that proportional electoral systems should also generally improve overall citizen satisfaction with the political system (Anderson and Guillory, 1997). Thus, in is study of democratic performance in 36 countries from 1945 to 1996, Lijphart (1999) establishes empirically that electoral systems favoring consensus-oriented governance yield gains in citizen satisfaction. Because of multipartism and coalition government, this provides a greater chance that the interests of more people will at least be partially represented. This is not true for FPTP system where the losers' interests are not represented at all. Lijphart's empirical results indeed demonstrate this, where the greatest dissatisfaction occurs in countries that use FPTP systems (like the United States and the United Kingdom) and the most satisfaction in more proportional systems (with Ireland and its single transferable vote system producing the greatest level of satisfaction). Lijphart's study supports the work of Klingemann (1999), who found that Danes and Norwegians – each with highly proportional systems – scored the highest levels of democratic satisfaction among Western democracies.

Electoral System Change

Given the great attention that political science scholarship has paid to the consequences of electoral systems, it is not surprising that electoral systems have been manipulated to elicit certain political outcomes. For instance, the framers of the 1958 Fifth Republic sought to use electoral rules to avoid the problems that had plagued the French Fourth Republic (from 1946–1958) in particular, the series of weak and frequently collapsing multiparty coalition governments, which were incapable of dealing with the numerous post-war crises that faced France (such as decolonization, the Indo-Chinese War and the Algerian Civil War, etc.). The framers of the French Fifth Republic sought to replace the list PR system used by the previous Fourth Republic with a single-member district, two rounds, majority formula system. In the first round, seats were awarded to candidates who won an outright majority of the votes. If no candidate received a majority, then all candidates that received at least 12.5 percent of the votes in the first round were eligible to contest the second round runoff election, where, whoever won the most votes won the election (in other words the second round was a simple plurality contest). The system was designed to encourage multipartyism (especially with the low threshold to get into the second round) but to provide incentives for parties to gravitate towards the center of the ideological spectrum. In particular, extreme parties are left out of the system, such as the case with the far-right-wing National Front. However, in 1986, the Socialist government of President François Mitterrand altered the system to PR list system, in hopes of fragmenting the right-wing opposition. However, much to the consternation of the Socialists, the National Front won 9.6 percent of the vote and captured 35 of the 577 national legislative seats. In the next parliamentary election, the government altered the electoral system back to the single-member district two-round system. Although the National Front did slightly better (winning 9.7 percent of the vote), they won only one seat in the legislature.

In Japan, there was also a major electoral reform in 1994, when the old system of multimember plurality elections, the single non-transferable votes (block vote system) was scrapped and replaced by a mixed-member system. In part, this was due to the victory of the left opposition (who held power for a brief time in 1994) who sought to "craft a competitive two-party, issue-oriented politics and a cleaner, more efficient government" (Norris, 1994, p. 5). The new system for the lower house of the parliament, the House of Representatives, adopted a mixed parallel system (as opposed to the mixed additional member system in Germany) with 300 single-member district plurality seats, along with 200 PR lists seats. Prior to the reform, Japanese politics was dominated by the conservative Liberal Democrats, and a fragmented opposition. With the new system, there was a coalescing of the opposition into a new Japanese Democratic Party, who won the 2007 legislative elections and took power from the LDP.

In New Zealand, there were also reforms undertaken to replace the single-member district plurality system with a mixed system. Currently the system resembles Germany's – 70 of the 120 national parliamentary seats continue to be elected via single-member districts via plurality rules. The remaining 50 seats are apportioned so that party seats will reflect the proportion of the vote parties win nationally. The change in electoral system had been endorsed via a referendum in 1993 and has had a notable impact on the party system of New Zealand. Prior to the reform, there were only two large parties that dominated politics. However, after 1993, seven parties have consistently gained representation in the New Zealand parliament.

Conclusion

A powerful tool for constitutional engineers is the design of electoral systems. As discussed above, the rules governing and guiding voting are a crucial part of building democracy. The very rich literature on electoral systems over the past several decades not only provides important insights for countries in transition, but has implications for how to address issues that threaten the health of democracy in the developed world (such as the United States). Issues such as declining voter efficacy, declining voter turnout rates, negative campaigning, the lack of third party alternatives, etc., are in many ways the product of problems with existing electoral systems. Changing electoral rules can alter citizen participation and satisfaction, can enhance or diminish the congruence between voter preferences and public policy outputs, and can have profound consequences for system stability. Electoral system design is one of the clearest areas where political science scholarship can have practical effects – particularly in new democracies Taking lessons from the Western experience (such as from the United States, Western Europe, and other cases of consolidated democracy) can inform policies and enhance the role of political scientists in that policy process; however, these experiences cannot be casually transported across the globe to new democracies or systems in transition without considering the constraints defined by a country's social, economic, cultural, and political contexts. Nonetheless the insights they provide, with adaptation, can be invaluable in addressing some of the most vexing problems in building democracy.

References

Anderson, C. and Guillory, C. (1997) "Political Institutions and Satisfaction with Democracy," *American Political Science Review*, 91 (1): 66–81.

Benoit, Kenneth (2007) "Electoral Laws as Political Consequences: Explaining the Origins and Change of Electoral Institutions," *Annual Review of Political Science*, 10: 363–390.

Cohen, Frank S. (1997) "Proportional versus Majoritarian Ethnic Conflict Management in Democracies," *Comparative Political Studies*, 30: 607–630.

Cox, Gary (1997) *Making Votes Count: Strategic Coordination in the World's Electoral Systems*, Cambridge: Cambridge University Press.

Daalder, Hans (1974) "The Consociational Democracy Theme," *World Politics*, 26: 604–621.

Downs, Anthony (1957) *An Economic Theory of Democracy*, New York: Harper & Row.

Downs, William (2010) "Comparative Electoral Systems" in John Ishiyama and Marijke Breuning (eds.) *21st Century Political Science*, Thousand Oaks, CA: Sage.

Duverger, Maurice (1954) *Political Parties: Their Organization and Activity in the Modern State*, London: Methuen.

Duverger, Maurice (1984) "What is the Best Electoral System?" in Arend Lijphart and Bernard Grofman (eds.) *Choosing an Electoral System: Issues and Alternatives*, New York: Praeger.

Farrell, David (1997) *Comparing Electoral Systems*, London: Prentice Hall.

Farrell, David (2001) *Electoral Systems: A Comparative Introduction*, New York: Palgrave.

Fraenkel, Jon and Grofman, Bernard (2004) "A Neo-Downsian Model of the Alternative Vote as a Mechanism for Mitigating Ethnic Conflict in Plural Societies," *Public Choice*, 121: 487–506.

Fraenkel, Jon and Grofman, Bernard (2006) "Does the Alternative Vote Foster Moderation in Ethnically Divided Societies?: The Case of Fiji," *Comparative Political Studies*, 39 (5): 623–651.

Grofman, Bernard and Lijphart, Arend (eds.) (1986) *Electoral Laws and Their Political Consequences*, New York: Agathon Press.

Horowitz, Donald (1985) *Ethnic Groups in Conflict*, Berkeley, CA: University of California Press.

Horowitz, Donald (1991) *A Democratic South Africa? Constitutional Engineering in a Divided Society*, Berkeley, CA: University of California Press.

Ishiyama, John (1997) "Transitional Electoral Systems in Post-Communist Eastern Europe," *Political Science Quarterly*, 112 (1): 95–115.

Ishiyama, John (2009) "Alternative Electoral Systems and the 2005 Ethiopian Parliamentary Election," *African Studies Quarterly*, 10 (4): 37–56.

Katz, Richard (1980) *A Theory of Parties and Electoral Systems*, Baltimore, MD: Johns Hopkins University Press.

Klingemann, Hans-Dieter (1999) "Mapping Political Support in the 1990s: A Global Analysis," in P. Norris (ed.), *Critical Citizens: Global Support for Democratic Government*, Oxford: Oxford University Press, pp. 31–56.

Lijphart, Arend (1974) *The Politics of Accommodation: Pluralism and Democracy in the Netherlands*, 2nd edn., Berkeley, CA: University of California Press.

Lijphart, Arend (1994) *Electoral Systems and Party Systems: A Study of Twenty-seven Democracies, 1945–1990*, New York: Oxford University Press.

Lijphart, Arend (1999) *Patterns of Democracy: Government Forms and Performance in Thirty-six Countries*, New Haven, CT: Yale University Press.

Lijphart, Arend and Grofman, Bernard (eds.) (1984) *Choosing an Electoral System: Issues and Alternatives*, New York: Praeger.

Lorwin, Val R.(1971) "Segmented Pluralism," *Comparative Politics*, 3: 141–175.

McCrae, Kenneth D. (1974) *Consociational Democracy: Political Accommodation in Segmented Societies*. Toronto: McClelland and Stewart.

Moser, Robert G. (1999) "Electoral Systems and the Number of Parties in Postcommunist States," *World Politics*, 51 (3): 359–384.

Nordlinger, Eric A. (1972) *Conflict Regulation in Divided Societies*. Cambridge, MA: Center for International Affairs, Harvard University.

Norris, Pippa (1994) "Labour Party Factionalism and Extremism," in Anthony Heath, Roger Jewell and John Curtice (eds.) *Labour's Last Chance?* Aldershot: Dartmouth.

Norris, Pippa (2004) *Electoral Engineering: Voting Rules and Political Behavior*, Cambridge: Cambridge University Press.

Powell, G. Bingham (2000) *Elections as Instruments of Democracy: Majoritarian and Proportional Visions*, New Haven, CT: Yale University Press.

Przeworski, A., Alvarez, M., Cheibub, J., and Limongi, F. (2000) *Democracy and Development*, Cambridge: Cambridge University Press.

Rae, Douglas (1967) *The Political Consequences of Electoral Laws*, New Haven, CT: Yale University Press.

Reilly, Ben (2002) "Electoral Systems for Divided Societies," *Journal of Democracy*, 13 (2): 156–170.

Reynolds, Andrew (1999) *Electoral Systems and Democratization in Southern Africa*, Oxford: Oxford University Press

Riker, William (1982) "The Two-Party System and Duverger's Law: An Essay on the History of Political Science," *American Political Science Review*, 76 (4), 753–766.

Rule, W. and Zimmerman, J. (1994) *Electoral Systems in Comparative Perspective: Their Impact on Women and Minorities*, Westport, CT: Greenwood Press.

Sartori, Giovanni (1968) "Political Development and Political Engineering," in J. Montgomery and A. Hirschman (eds.) *Public Policy*, Cambridge, MA: Harvard University Press.

Schumpeter, Joseph (1942) *Capitalism, Socialism, and Democracy*, New York: Harper & Row.

Taagepera, Rein and Shugart, Matthew (1989) *Seats and Votes: The Effects and Determinants of Electoral Systems*, New Haven, CT: Yale University Press.

8

Legislatures and Executives

An extremely important set of institutional decisions facing constitutional designers relates to the relationship between the executive and legislative branches of government (the judicial branch is also important, but we will deal with this topic in Chapter 9). This, fundamentally, involves the choice between *presidential* versus *parliamentary* systems. Indeed, there is considerable empirical evidence that presidential and parliamentary systems have very different effects on a whole range of political issues, ranging from public spending, trade policy to political stability (Linz, 1990; Shugart and Carey, 1992; Keech and Pak, 1995; Evans, 2004; Cheibub, 2006; Tavits, 2009). Thus, some consideration of the features of presidential versus parliamentary system is crucial to an understanding of how institutional choices affect the development of democracy.

What are the key differences when comparing between presidential and parliamentary systems? Further, what are the characteristics of the internal structuring of executive offices and legislatures, and how do these affect the development of political democracy? These topics are the focus of this chapter.

Presidentialism

What are the primary features of presidential systems? Essentially, presidential systems are those in which there is a directly elected executive who represents an entire country and whose tenure in office is not dependent

Comparative Politics: Principles of Democracy and Democratization, First Edition.
John T. Ishiyama.
© 2012 John T. Ishiyama. Published 2012 by Blackwell Publishing Ltd.

upon legislative support. There are of course many countries that also have Presidents, such as Germany, Hungary, and India, but these are largely ceremonial heads of state, in many ways serving the same role as the monarch in constitutional monarchies such as the United Kingdom, the Netherlands, and Japan. Thus merely having a president does not make for a presidential system.

In general, there are four key characteristics of presidential systems. First, there is the *separation of powers* between the various branches of government (Shugart and Carey, 1992). This refers to a division of responsibility between the executive, legislative, and judicial branches, where the executive branch administers the law, the legislature writes the laws, and the judiciary interprets or reviews the constitutionality of the laws. In parliamentary governments, this separation is lacking inasmuch as the executive and legislative branches are fused together (Robbins, 2010).

Second, Shugart and Carey (1992) note that presidents are *directly elected* through some type of nationwide vote. Thus, ascendance to office is not dependent on sufficient legislative support as in parliamentary systems, but rather upon support of the entire country as a constituency. Various countries use different electoral rules to govern such elections. Some countries use a simple-majority (or plurality) electoral system, in which the winner is the candidate who secures the most votes. The plurality method is used in the presidential elections in Bosnia and Herzegovina, Cameroon, the Comoros Islands, Equatorial Guinea, Guyana, Honduras, Iceland, Kiribati, South Korea, Malawi, Mexico, Palestine, Panama, Paraguay, the Philippines, Rwanda, Singapore, Taiwan, Tunisia, Venezuela, and Zambia. On the other hand, other countries, such as France and Poland, employ a majority system with two rounds, where the winner must possess more than 50 percent of the nationwide vote to be elected in the first round, or a plurality of the vote in the second round. Another approach uses an indirect method, which is best illustrated by some type of *electoral college*, used to elect the president. Although it is not the only country to use this system, the United States is perhaps the best-known country to employ it. In the case of the United States, both the Republican and the Democratic Parties select a slate of electors for each state equal to the number of House of Representative members and Senators from that state. The presidential candidate who wins a plurality of a state's popular vote receives the Electoral College votes of that state. Each candidate's electoral votes are then summed, and the candidate with a majority of the Electoral College votes (that is, 270) is declared the winner of the election (Robbins, 2010).

A third feature of presidential systems is that presidents serve *fixed terms*, and these terms are not dependent on the continued confidence (or support) of the legislature. In most cases these terms last from four to five years (although the term of the French President is seven years). Although presidents' terms in office are not dependent on support in the legislature, most systems have some provisions for the removal of a president from office for some major offenses, via a process called *impeachment*. For example, during the 1990s, after the Monica Lewinsky scandal, the US Congress impeached President Bill Clinton, although there were not enough votes in the Senate to remove him from office. In the early 1990s, the Russian legislature similarly sought to impeach Boris Yeltsin (who also survived). Thus, in contrast to a parliamentary system where the Prime Minister and the Cabinet need to maintain the support of parliament, a president can be eternally at odds with legislators and not jeopardize his or her own political survival.

A fourth characteristic of presidential systems is that presidents, as chief executives, *form their own cabinets*. Indeed, this appointed cabinet (which in some systems like the United States requires the confirmation of the upper house of the legislature, the Senate) acts largely as a set of advisors to the President, and serve at his/her behest. This authority is significantly different under parliamentary regimes, in which cabinet appointments are typically more of a cooperative endeavor.

The final primary attribute of a presidential system relates to the chief executive's law-making authority. In some countries, presidents have virtually independent law-making authority. The President of the United States, for example, can issue executive orders and executive treaties that can, but do not always, carry the same weight as congressional legislation. In other countries, such as in Russia and the Ukraine, the president has powers that rival that of the legislature (Ishiyama and Kennedy, 2001; Protsyk, 2004). For instance, Steven Fish (2000, pp. 22–23) refers to the Russian and Ukrainian presidencies as *superpresidencies*, which are characterized by

> an apparatus of executive power that dwarfs all other agencies in terms of size and the resources it consumes; a president who enjoys decree powers; a president who *de jure* or *de facto* controls most of the powers of the purse; a relatively toothless legislature that cannot repeal presidential decrees and that enjoys scant authority and/or resources to monitor the chief executive; provisions that render impeachment of the president virtually impossible; and a court system that is controlled wholly or mainly by the chief executive and that cannot in practice check presidential prerogatives or even abuse of power.

Superpresidentialism is a regime. It many be contrasted with autocracy, insofar as the chief executive does not enjoy total power and is subject to bona fide, periodic challenge in national elections.

Parliamentarism

The other major type of democratic system is parliamentarism. Parliamentary systems actually outnumber presidential states in the world. The classic parliamentary system is often referred to as the *Westminster model*, named after the United Kingdom's government. The first key defining characteristic of this model is that, unlike in presidential systems, where the heads of state and government are often embodied in the same person, parliamentary systems separate the two roles, with the head of state in a largely ceremonial role (as is the case of the role of the Crown in the United Kingdom) and the prime minister as head of government.

Second, unlike in presidential systems where the head of government (the president) is powerful and has a separate electoral constituency, in a parliamentary system the head of government's authority is dependent on maintaining support in the legislature. Indeed, the prime minister and the cabinet are generally selected by the parliament to govern. Thus there is the *fusion* of the executive and legislative branches. Although presidential systems generally have a separation of powers among the various branches of government, such separation is not found in most parliamentary regimes. Instead, parliamentary governments often combine the responsibilities of both the legislative and the executive branches.

Generally, the process of government (or cabinet) formation in a parliamentary system involves the following steps (Laver and Shepsle, 1996). After the general election, in which voters decide how many seats are allocated to the various political parties, the elected representatives in a parliament are then given the task of establishing or forming the government. The majority party (the party that has the majority of seats in parliament) or a coalition of parties that can demonstrate they control enough seats to ensure passage of legislation then puts forward a government (a prime minister or premier and cabinet). If one party wins a clear majority of the seats in the parliament, then government formation is fairly straightforward—the majority party selects the prime minister/premier and the cabinet, as well as the leadership of the legislature (such as Speaker of the House, committee chairs and other legislative officers). At other times, when there is no majority party, the party with the most seats (often referred to as the *formateur* party) is responsible for constructing the governing coalition. This party will seek a coalition partner – or sometimes multiple partners – and, after negotiations, attempt to cobble together enough support to provide the coalition with a majority of parliamentary seats, and then jointly decide the composition of the government (generally dividing ministerial offices, or portfolios among themselves). When no clear majority winner emerges, occasionally, there is the formation of a *minority* government. For instance, the Canadian government for the past few years has had a minority government led by the Conservative Party. In the Canadian case, no majority party was elected and subsequent attempts to form a coalition failed. However, the Conservative Party was able to gain the acquiescence of the Bloc Québécois and other smaller parties to provisionally go along with the legislation introduced by the government, but the latter would not join the government (hence they would not be held accountable for government failures). Remarkably the Conservative government has survived, although its minority status clearly constrains what it can do, policy-wise (Robbins, 2010).

After forming the ruling coalition, those in power make a number of key appointments, particularly the prime minister. The prime minister serves until he or she loses the support of the legislature, either because of the results of election or because the legislature for one reason or another no longer supports the government. When the prime minister loses support of the legislature, as evidenced through a loss in *vote of confidence* which is an act initiated by the government or a *vote of no confidence* (called for by the opposition), then the government must step down, and either a new coalition is cobbled together, or a new election is held (Clark et al., 2009). Some states use a slightly different version of the confidence vote, referred to as a *constructive vote of confidence*. In Germany and Hungary, two countries where such a tool is in use, the legislature must agree on a replacement government prior to dissolving the current government. This is designed to promote a stable transition to power, as opposed to continual instability resulting from repeated votes of no confidence (Robbins, 2010).

Indeed, a distinguishing feature of parliamentary governments, as indicated in the discussion above, is the absence of fixed terms. The confidence votes used to sustain a coalition government suggest that a government can fail at any time. Although most parliamentary states have provisions that require elections to be held every four or five years, very often parliamentary terms are cut short. At times, the government itself cuts short a term, even without a vote of confidence. Indeed, when a government is viewed in a positive manner, the government may ask for new elections to be held earlier (usually requesting this of the head of state, who is formally charged with the power to grant new elections, and almost invariably does so) to capitalize on high levels of public approval. However, when public approval ratings are low or decreasing, then the governing coalition will often postpone elections. Some scholars have found that since political leaders possess more accurate information than voters, early elections will be held if elected officials anticipate political strife or economic turmoil which will allow the government to survive longer (Smith, 2003). As a corollary, other works have found that voters are cognizant of this practice and, in some cases, may punish coalition members for holding elections too early (Robbins, 2010).

In a parliamentary system, party discipline is crucial. If parties cannot ensure that their representatives will vote as a bloc (and hold to the coalition agreement), then they will not appear to be attractive coalition partners. Thus, political parties have, under the conditions of parliamentary democracy, developed many mechanisms to ensure that individual representatives "toe the party line." These include controlling campaign finances, control of nomination processes (such as to a district or placement on a party list in the case of proportional representation system) and other incentives.

In addition, there are a few other features of parliamentary systems. Behaviorally, because their own political survival depends on cooperating with the executive, members of the legislature are more willing to work with the executive branch than are legislatures in presidential regimes (who often find their agendas and interest to be at odds with the sitting president's). Further, generally, most parliamentary systems are also characterized by the use of a *proportional representation* (PR) electoral system to translate votes into seats. There are some exceptions to this. Great Britain and India each employ a *single-member district* (SMD) plurality electoral system to fill legislative seats. The use of the SMD electoral system in Great Britain has largely favored the two major parties – the Conservatives and the Labour Party – at the expense of the Liberal Democrats. Generally, this has not led to coalition governments, but in places like India and Canada, where there are significant ethnic and regional differences, coalition governments have been the norm in recent years. However, the elections in 2010 in the UK created a coalition government of the Conservatives and the Liberal Democrats.

Nonetheless, in most parliamentary systems, multiparty systems are the norm. To some extent, parliamentary structures can be attractive alternatives for societies that might be deeply divided along ethnic or religious lines. Thus, given the deep sectarian divides in Iraq, it should not be surprising that the architects of the constitution there opted for a parliamentary system (along with a PR electoral system). These structures allow for multiple interests to be represented in the center of power, including religious and ethnic interests.

Hybrid Systems

Beyond the archetypes of presidential and parliamentary systems, there are also *hybrid regimes* (sometimes called *semi-presidential systems*), which combine elements of both. Generally these systems have developed in reaction to some particular crisis (as in the French case) or as a legacy of some authoritarian past, which had a tradition of a strong, independent executive (such as in Russia). For instance, the French system is a mixed system, with the features of both a presidential system and a parliamentary system. Resulting from the constitutional changes introduced in 1959 with the foundation of the Fifth Republic, the system was a reaction to the previous weaknesses of the Fourth Republic (1953–1959). The Fourth Republic had been a parliamentary system with a proportional representation electoral system, and produced as series of weak coalition governments, which were unable to deal with the series of crises, both domestic and international that culminated in an attempted coup by elements of the French Foreign Legion. To address these problems, the designers of the French Fifth Republic changed the electoral system (as discussed in Chapter 7) and appended a far strengthened Presidency to the parliamentary system. The president was charged with significant executive powers and a lengthened presidential term of seven years.

These powers include:

1 The president is Head of State.
2 The president has the ability to make laws via decrees and may refer these laws for review to the Constitutional Council prior to promulgation.
3 The president may dissolve the National Legislature and call for new elections.

4　The president may refer treaties or certain types of laws to a popular referendum, but needs the agreement of the prime minister or the parliament.
5　The president is the Commander-in-Chief of the military.
6　The president names the prime minister, who is confirmed by the legislature. However, the prime minister cannot be dismissed by the president. The president can name and dismiss ministers in the cabinet, but only with the consent of the prime minister.
7　The president names certain members of the Constitutional Council, the primary court dealing with constitutional judicial issues.
8　All decisions of the president must be countersigned by the prime minister.

However, despite these enumerated powers, the division of labor between the strengthened presidency and the prime minister is not always clearly delineated. To some extent the prime minister is responsible to the president (inasmuch as the president nominated the candidate for the prime minister, subject to approval from the parliament). On the other hand, the prime minister is also subject to votes of confidence in the parliament, and hence, must muster parliamentary support for the government. When the president and the majority in parliament are from the same party or party coalition, the prime minister acts as "second" to the president, and the latter has significant influence of domestic policy. However, when the president and prime minister are from different parties, then there is the practice of *cohabitation*. During cohabitation, in which the legislature and executive are controlled by different political parties, there is a division of labor, or sorts. Under such conditions, the prime minister leads the government and handles domestic policies, but the president handles foreign affairs. However, the French President, as can the US President, can exercise *veto power*, whereby the executive can prevent a bill from becoming a law, even during periods of cohabitation.

On paper, the Russian system also resembles the French system. The Russian President is also elected directly, as is the case of the French presidency, and there is a parliamentary system, with a prime minister and cabinet, simultaneously responsible to the president and parliament. In reality, however, the prime minister is primarily responsible to the president, and acts as the president's head of government, at least on paper. When Boris Yeltsin and Vladimir Putin were president, this was clearly the case, with the prime minister playing a subordinate role to the president. However, with the election of Dmitri Medvedev in 2007 (Putin's hand-picked successor) and the selection of Putin as prime minister, the roles reversed, with Putin as the dominant personality in the executive partnership.

Further, the Russian presidency is far more powerful than most presidents elsewhere, with significant executive, legislative, and even judicial powers (Fish, 2000). Not only does the Russian President have significant appointment and decree powers (which have the force of law and are not subject to overturn by the legislature) but the president also has important judicial powers. For instance, in the case of disputes between various regions in the Russian Federation, the president, not the courts, has first jurisdiction. Further regarding issues of constitutionality and judicial review, again the Russian President, and not the courts, makes first determination if a regional law circumvents the constitution, and he then refers it to the Russian Federation Constitutional Court. Thus, although in form, the Russian system appears to be a hybrid system, it is in reality a "super-presidential" system.

The Effects of Presidentialism and Parliamentarism

When considering whether to choose a presidential or parliamentary model, it is necessary to consider the attributes of each system and their posited effects on democracy. What are the posited benefits of presidentialism and parliamentarism?

As far as presidentialism is concerned, the literature emphasizes three key benefits of presidential systems: (1) government efficiency; (2) the representativeness of the entire populace; and (3) the checks and balances (Robbins, 2010). First, an attractive aspect of most presidential systems is that they promote *efficiency*. In this sense, efficiency means that voters know, prior to casting a ballot, what the new government will look like. That is not to say that the outcomes are preordained but rather that the most likely scenarios are widely known. This efficiency provides voters with a wealth of information as they decide which candidate to support. Being able to view the candidates who will govern when elected (as opposed to the wheeling and dealing after an election which is characteristic of most parliamentary systems), allows voters to have an idea of what they are voting for. They also know that, if elected, their candidate should pursue the policies supported by his or her electorate. In parliamentary systems, on the other hand, it is quite possible that a voter who votes for a certain party may not see their preferred policies enacted because of the need for compromise among the participants in a coalition government.

A second attractive attribute of presidential systems is that the president represents a national constituency, as opposed to a particular constituency or particular political party. By definition, this also means that for presidential candidates to win, they cannot appeal to narrow partisan or constituent interests, and must expand their appeal enough to be appealing to a large number of different points of view. This provides some incentive for political moderation on the part of the presidential candidates (Horowitz, 1990).

A third appealing attribute of presidential systems is the separation of powers that characterize these systems. This provides multiple points for citizens to influence the policy process. Further, it provides for representation of different interests in the center of power. For instance, one party might control the presidency and the opposition the legislature (or the existence of *divided government*). Thus, people from different ideological backgrounds should have some say in policy-making as long as there are multiple political actors or institutions with some semblance of power. Finally, separation of powers prevents one branch from becoming too powerful relative to others, thus acting as a "hedge" against potential dictatorship. This certainly was one of the justifications for the institution of separation of powers in the United States, as the framers of the US Constitution saw this as way to prevent the emergence of "tyranny."

On the other hand, advocates of parliamentary systems point to several features of parliamentarism that make it superior to presidentialism. For instance, it is argued that parliamentarism and not presidentialism is better at promoting the accountability of the political leadership. First, unlike presidential systems where an ineffective president can scapegoat the legislature for policy failures, the unified legislature executive relationship prevents this from happening in a parliamentary system. Second, parliamentary systems allow for the removal of a prime minister and cabinet at any time, via votes of no confidence. Barring any significant scandal or an attempted *coup d'état*, most presidents cannot be removed from office until the expiration of their term. Consequently, a nefarious or incompetent president cannot be removed prematurely (unless impeachment proceedings are initiated), thus enabling the president to wreak further havoc. Third, unlike presidential systems where the president rarely appears before the legislature to address questions of policy (unless there are very special circumstances, or because there is an occasional ceremonial requirement, as exists in the United States with the Presidential State of the Union address), in parliamentary systems, prime minister and cabinet are often required to appear before the legislature and address questions posed by the parliamentary membership, a process known as *interpellation*. This allows the legislature's continuous monitoring of the activities of the executive. Thus, advocates of the parliamentary model would suggest that this style of governance is better able to reward or punish the politicians at the head of the government.

Finally, parliamentary systems are thought to be more conducive to the formation of organizationally strong and disciplined political parties. This is because in parliamentary systems, parties have a strong incentive to promote organizational coherence because of the need to maintain party coherence to participate in coalition governments (Steffani, 1995). Parties that are unable to ensure the discipline of their party's representatives are unlikely to be attractive coalition partners. Creating and maintaining disciplined parties, moreover, can help legislators overcome collective action problems through organizing members, delivering necessary information, and rewarding loyal rank-and-file members (Aldrich, 1995).

On the other hand, presidential systems tend to constrain party-building efforts. Hale (2007), Fish (2000) and Mainwaring (1993) have argued that strong presidencies tend to be inimical to the development of political parties. There are several reasons cited as to why presidentialism militates against the development of political parties. First, by concentrating authority in the hands of a single individual, the politics of personality prevails, making it more difficult for parties to develop coherent programs and identities. Thus, presidentialism affects party building because it encourages greater personalism in politics than a parliamentary system (Mainwaring, 1993). Fish (2000) contends that this effect is exhibited throughout the states of the former Soviet Union where presidentialism "chills party development in part by holding down incentives for important political and economic actors to invest in politics." Most importantly, candidates have relatively little incentive to associate with political parties, when the legislature (the principal arena for party politics) has such little say in policy. Rather, individuals tend to focus on forming personal attachments with presidential hopefuls, bypassing association with political parties.

Thus, there are both positive and negative attributes of presidentialism and parliamentarism. In part, this explains why hybrid systems are also attractive options for constitutional engineers (as in France and in Russia) where the system allows for the combination of the best of both presidentialism and parliamentarism. But what are the effects and consequences on the development of democracy of choosing such systems?

The Perils of Presidentialism: Do Presidential Systems Produce Democratic Instability?

The decision as to whether to implement a parliamentary or a presidential system has been one of the more contentious debates among scholars in comparative politics. In particular, some scholars, largely based upon observations from the Latin American experience, have argued that presidential systems are not particularly conducive to the development of democracy. The reasons for this skepticism rest on four primary criticisms, all of which were first put forward by Juan Linz, when he pointed to what he called the "perils of presidentialism."

Linz begins by noting that the fact that only a few stable democracies are characterized by presidential systems – indeed, the "the superior historical performance of parliamentary democracies is no accident" (Linz, 1990, p. 52). Essentially Linz argues that the choice of presidentialism is a bad one for many new democracies.

First, in presidential systems, the separation of powers, although held out as a check against tyranny by its proponents, actually leads to the president and assembly having competing claims to legitimacy. Both are popularly elected and hence have separate claims to legitimacy (Shugart and Carey, 1992, especially Chapter 2). These competing legitimacies can lead to deadlock and policy paralysis if the leadership of the legislature and the president have fundamental disagreements, largely because "no democratic principle exists to resolve disputes between the executive and the legislature about which of the two actually represents the will of the people" (Linz, 1990, p. 63). Although in consolidated democracies, such as the United States, this problem can be resolved via peaceful means, such is not often the case in new democracies, or countries in transition, where such policy conflicts can lead to broader, and sometimes, more violent confrontations. On the other hand, in parliamentarism, the fusion of the executive and the legislature, prevents such problems from emerging.

Second, the fixed nature of the presidential term in office presents problems as well. Since a president cannot easily be removed from office once elected, this makes it difficult to remove someone who has engaged in particularly egregious behavior. Further, just as presidentialism makes it difficult to remove a democratically elected head of government who no longer has support, it usually is quite difficult, if not impossible, to extend the term of popular presidents beyond constitutionally set limits. Presidents thus are tempted to accomplish as much as possible in a very short period of time and this "exaggerated sense of urgency on the part of the president may lead to ill-conceived policy initiatives, overly hasty stabs at implementation, unwarranted anger at the lawful opposition, and a host of other evils" (ibid., p. 66).

Third, the winner-take-all nature of electoral competition also contributes to conceiving of politics as a "zero sum" game, where there can only be one winner and all others are losers. Thus,

> the danger that zero-sum presidential elections pose is compounded by the rigidity of the president's fixed term in office. Winners and losers are sharply defined for the entire period of the presidential mandate ... The losers must wait at least four or five years without any access to executive power and patronage.
>
> (ibid., p. 56)

Normally this is not a problem in consolidated democracies, where the opposition has the opportunity to return to power, and there is a general acceptance of defeat. However, for many countries in transition, where there is no certainty that future elections will take place, and that the opposition may not have another chance for power, the acceptance of defeat becomes more problematic. Such was the case after the highly contested 1994 election in Angola, which was supposed to end the civil war between the governing Marxist MPLA and the opposition UNITA party led by the charismatic Jonas Savimbi. After losing the presidential elections, Savimbi declared the elections fraudulent and simply returned to the bush to relaunch the civil war.

On the other hand, in parliamentary systems, since "power-sharing and coalition-forming are fairly common, and incumbents are accordingly attentive to the demands and interests of even the smaller parties" (ibid., p. 56) politics are not zero sum. Rather it is likely that cooperation between warring parties and the empowerment of the opposition will forestall the recurrence of what happened in Angola after 1994.

Fourth, Linz argues that the "style of presidential politics", with its focus on personal power, is also less supportive of political democracy than parliamentary systems. Since the president is both head of state and head of government, and also generally charged with substantial executive powers, there is considerable incentive to personalize politics, to equate the survival of the state with the personality of the President. In other words, to paraphrase Lord Acton, a nineteenth-century British historian: "Power tends to corrupt, and absolute power corrupts absolutely." The pressure towards dictatorship is stronger in a presidential system than in parliamentary systems, where there are substantial checks on the ability of the executive to act unilaterally.

Although much has been written about the perils of presidentialism, other scholars have questioned the connection between presidentialism and political instability. For example, Donald Horowitz (1990) argues that there are several things wrong with Linz's argument. First, he contends that the thesis was accepted without much in the way of evidence. He points out that Linz's evidence is predominantly based on the Latin American experience and that Linz neglects stable presidencies found in other regions, as well as unstable parliamentary systems in Asia, such as Thailand and Malaysia or in Africa, such as Nigeria in the 1960s. Second, he argues that the problems that have been associated with presidentialism (such as zero sum politics) are really the result of the use of first past the post (FPTP) electoral rules. Further, the FPTP winner-take-all system used to elect many presidents often results in disproportional outcomes and the lack of representation of significant minorities or regional groups. This exclusion can potentially exacerbate significant tensions and instability, particularly in ethnically or religiously divided societies. Finally, those who point to the perils of presidentialism also overlook the potential beneficial aspects of presidential systems, such as the incentive for moderation of politics that was discussed above.

Further, the empirical evidence is rather mixed regarding the "perils of presidentialism" thesis. Alfred Stepan and Cindy Skach (1993) provided some empirical support for the idea that presidentialism was correlated with weaker democracies, and parliamentarism with more stable democracies. However, in their data, most of the parliamentary states they included were European states (which have a long history of political stability) and most all of the presidential states were Latin American countries. These "sampling bias" problems (or that the countries considered do not represent the entire population of countries) may color the results. The real issue is whether such systems affect developing democracies, NOT already consolidated ones. Timothy Power and Mark Gasiorowski (1997) criticize the sampling problems associated with the Stepan and Skach study and find in their more representative sample of 50 developing countries that there was no real relationship between presidentialism and democracy or stability. Ishiyama and Velten (1998) found evidence to support Horowitz's contention that it was the electoral system and not presidentialism that explained the development of democracy in their study of 27 post-communist states in East-Central Europe and the Former Soviet Union. Jose Antonio Cheibub (2007) found evidence to support Power and Gasiorowski's conclusions, and argues that that it is not presidential systems that are dangerous; rather, he demonstrates that it is the underlying social conditions or background characteristics that jeopardize democratic stability. Specifically, he suggests that whether or not a military regime had previously existed is far more important than whether a presidential system is in place, a finding that provides a different explanation for why presidentialism appears to be associated with instability in Latin America, which also has had a long history of military intervention in politics.

Thus, despite the popularity of the "perils of presidentialism" thesis, and the suggestion that it is somehow related to political instability and democratic failure, there remains considerable debate. It remains to be seen whether such choices, such as parliamentarism in Iraq or presidentialism in Afghanistan, will ultimately affect the development of democracy in places where the social, economic, and cultural conditions are not particularly conducive for democracy.

Organizing Executives and Legislatures

Beyond issues related to the general structural relationship between the executive and legislative branches (either in the form of presidentialism or parliamentarism), there are also questions related to how these branches are internally structured – what, for instance, is the relationship between the members of cabinet and the chief executive, and how are decisions generally made? How are legislatures internally organized, and what characterizes the policy process?

The role of cabinets in parliamentary, presidential, and hybrid systems

In parliamentary systems, prime ministers are elected by their governing coalition but not all prime ministers are equally powerful. Unlike in presidential systems, prime ministers must persuade other cabinet ministers go along with policy decisions, since especially in coalition governments members of cabinet are often not from the same political party as the prime minister, and decisions made by the cabinet are made collectively, via some kind of vote of the ministers. However, this does not mean that prime ministers are of equal status when compared to other ministers. Indeed, Giovanni Sartori (1994) explains that there are at least three scenarios common to most parliamentary governments: A prime minister may be *first above unequals, first among unequals,* or *first among equals.* The power of the prime minister is most powerful in the first case (that is, first above unequals) and can be found in places such as Germany, Greece, and the United Kingdom (Lijphart, 1999). In contrast, among the weakest prime ministers (that is, first among equals) are the heads of government in Italy, the Netherlands, and Norway (ibid.). How does one discern between powerful and weak prime ministers? Typically, researchers have relied on the prime minister's authority vis-à-vis fellow members of the executive branch (for example, the Exchequer – or finance minister – in the United Kingdom compared with the prime minister), the prime minister's ability to navigate through the policy-making process, and his or her ability to remove and appoint members of the executive branch (see King, 1994; Lijphart, 1999).

In parliamentary systems, particularly those that use some variant of the Westminster system, the cabinet collectively decides the government's policy direction, especially legislation that is to be introduced by the cabinet for passage by the legislature. This generally is done by an internal debate in the cabinet, followed by a collective, secret vote, where a simple majority prevails (although this sometimes depends on the issue debated). However, once the decision is made, the cabinet is expected to put up a unified front when presenting legislation to the legislature.

In most parliamentary systems, the cabinet is made up of about 10–20 ministers, although in some cases, such as in Kenya, cabinets can be quite large (in Kenya the number of ministers exceeds 50). Cabinet ministers are selected from among sitting members of the parliament, and remain members of the legislature while simultaneously serving as cabinet ministers. In coalition governments, cabinet ministers are often members of very different parties, and in the coalition agreement the parties jostle and negotiate for the ministerial position they most value. There are of course exceptions. Occasionally ministers may be selected who are not legislators (such as in governments of specialists in times of emergency, which has not been uncommon in countries such as Slovakia and Latvia during times of political deadlock) but this has been generally rare in consolidated democracies. In most governments, members of the cabinet hold the title of minister and each is charged with a different portfolio of duties that are associated with the ministerial rank (such as for Minister of Defense, or Minister of Interior, or Minister of Foreign Affairs, etc). Occasionally ministerial offices are called something different such as "Home Secretary" or "Chancellor of the Exchequer" or Attorney General. The day-to-day role of most cabinet members is to serve as the head of one of the ministries that comprise the national bureaucracy.

In a parliamentary system, generally the opposition also forms a "shadow cabinet" which is designed to be a government-in-waiting of sort. These opposition party members are charged with shadowing sitting cabinet members and keeping informed about decisions made and to propose policy alternatives. Shadow cabinets are particularly important in countries that require "constructive" votes of no confidence (as in Germany and Italy) where the opposition must demonstrate that they have a ready-made government to replace the current sitting government in case the no confidence vote succeeds (Robbins, 2010).

In presidential systems, on the other hand, cabinet members (in the United States and the Philippines called "Secretaries") do not have status independent of the president. In presidential systems of government, the cabinet is part of the executive branch. Theoretically, the cabinet is meant to execute or carry out policy as opposed to making policy, but generally cabinet members have a great deal of influence in policy-making as well. In addition to heading up the departments they administer, cabinet members are generally seen as advisors to the president and primarily responsible to the president and not the legislature. Thus unlike in parliamentary systems, cabinet members serve at the pleasure of the president and are strongly subordinate to the head of government. The president has wide latitude in selecting cabinet members, and often cabinet members are selected outside of the president's party (particularly if the president wishes to demonstrate the non-partisan or multipartisan nature of his or her administration). In addition to cabinet, Presidents also have other advisors who are directly attached to the presidential office, usually including policy areas such national security, the economy, or other areas of importance to the chief executive.

In hybrid, or semi-presidential systems, such as those that exist in France and Russia, the relationship between the president, prime minister, and cabinet is more complex. Generally as in presidential systems, the president appoints the members of the cabinet (including the prime minister) subject to confirmation by the legislature. Further, as in presidential systems, the president is free to choose whomever he or she sees fit to be a minister, even including members of parties other than the president's own party, and ministers do not have to be sitting members of parliament (as is the case in most parliamentary systems). However, as with parliamentary systems, the cabinet is responsible to parliament and subject to interpellation and votes of confidence. Further the cabinet is not merely a set of advisors to the president, but formulates policy much along the same lines as in parliamentary systems.

The structuring of the legislative process

Besides the internal structuring of the executive, there is also the design of the legislative process. Although there are a variety of different ways to structure the legislative process, two examples are illustrative of the different ways in which this process can be structured – the internal workings of the US Congress and the UK Parliament.

In both cases, legislative officers are selected by the majority party to lead the legislative proceedings. In both the lower house of the US Congress (the House of Representatives) and the lower house of the British Parliament (the House of Commons), the principal presiding officer is the Speaker of the House. However, in the US House, the Speaker is much more powerful, doling out powerful committee assignments, and guiding the course of debate over legislation on the house floor, for example. On the other hand, the Speaker of the House of Commons is largely a ceremonial position, who purpose is to act as a neutral arbiter of the proceedings on the house floor. The Speaker presides over the House's debates, determining which members may speak, and is responsible for maintaining order during debate. The Speaker, although a Member of Parliament, must renounce all affiliation with his or her political party when becoming Speaker.

Further, in both cases, a committee system exists which is part of the legislative process. In the US Congress, there is a complex system of legislative committees that handles the 6000–8000 bills that are introduced in a two-year session of the House of Representatives, Generally, the committees do much of the legislative work on a bill even before it makes it to the floor of the House of Representatives for a vote. In the US House of Representatives, there are different types of committees: (1) the standing committees, which have a fixed membership and jurisdiction, and are permanent fixtures of the committee system in both the House and the upper chamber, the US Senate. These standing committees are generally set up to deal with legislation in important policy areas, such as Finance, Agriculture, Foreign Affairs, Defense, etc.; and (2) the "select committees" which are temporary committees appointed to deal with a specific issue or problem – such as organized crime, or issues of corruption. Committees in turn are subdivided into subcommittees that allow for more specialized consideration of legislation.

In the British House of Commons, there is also a dense network of committees, made up mostly of what are referred to as "select committees." Select Committees in the Commons are designed to oversee the work of departments and agencies, examine issues affecting the country or individual regions, and review and advise on the procedures and rules of the House of Commons. These select committees, as permanent structures, are a fairly recent addition to the legislative process, having only been adopted in 1979–1980. There is also a set of committees that are part of the upper House of Lords as well.

The key difference between the US Congress and the British Parliament is the role these committees play in the legislative process, or the process by which laws are made. In the US system, committees and subcommittees are extremely powerful, and can effectively alter and block legislation, even before it reaches the floor of Congress for a vote. On the other hand, the committees in the British House of Commons do not have such power to block legislation.

Thus, in the US House of Representatives, for instance, a bill or resolution is introduced by a Member of Congress, or *congressional sponsor*. Once introduced, the House Speaker or the Senate presiding officer (if the bill is introduced in the Senate) refers the proposal to the appropriate committee (or committees if the presiding officer deems that the issue transcends committee jurisdictions). The Chair of the committee, which is generally a member of the majority party in the House of Senate, passes the proposed legislation on to the appropriate subcommittee, and this is where the real work begins on the proposed bill. If the subcommittee takes bill seriously, it will schedule hearings and then after the hearings on the bill are completed, the "mark-up" period begins, where the bill is revised, and sections are added or deleted, in preparation for presentation to the full committee. The subcommittee can choose to ignore the bill and not act, thus killing it. The full committee may repeat the process, or it may largely accept the work of the subcommittee and pass it on for report to the full House or Senate or the full committee can also kill the legislation.

If the bill is passed onto the House or Senate, and is passed on the floor, then the bill is passed onto the other chamber, where the process begins again. To be sent on to the President of signature, the bill must be passed in identical form by both chambers. If one version is passed by the House and another version is passed by the Senate, then a special conference committee made up of members of the House and Senate works to create a compromise version, which then goes back to each chamber for a vote. If this version is passed, then it is sent through an appropriations process (if the bill requires expenditures of funds) and then the appropriations are brought up for a vote. Once this is completed, the bill is passed on to the President for signature.

In the British Parliament, the process is very different. First, most legislation is not introduced by individual members of the parliament but by the government. Individual members' bills may be introduced, called "private member's bills" that deal with general issues, and "private bills", which are limited in scope and usually apply only to particular regions of the country. Once the government introduces legislation, the bill is set for first reading on the House of Commons floor, where the bill is presented and ordered to be printed. In the case of private bills, there is usually a second reading that is scheduled, and a vote is held to see if it will be passed on to the committees (most private member's bills are stopped at this point, particularly those introduced by the opposition).

The next stage is the committee stage, where proposed legislation is passed onto the appropriate committee. The committee considers each clause of the bill, and may make amendments to it. However, unlike the United States, the committee cannot kill the legislation by refusing to act on the legislation. After the committee considers the bill, it is sent as a report to the floor of the House, where there is a further opportunity to amend the bill. Unlike committee stage, the House need not consider every clause of the bill, only those to which amendments have been tabled. Finally, a third reading is scheduled on the final text of the bill as it is amended, and then put to a vote. If the bill passes, it is then sent to the other House (to the Lords, if it originated in the Commons; to the Commons, if it is a Lords bill), which may amend it. Following this, there is consideration of Lords/Commons amendments: The House in which the bill originated considers the amendments made in the other House (the House of Commons is NOT required to accept amendments from House of Lords – but the House of Lords IS required to accept amendments from the House of Commons). Once this process is completed, it is passed onto the Queen for royal assent, and the Queen is required to sign the bill by law.

Generally, most parliamentary systems have legislative processes similar to Britain's. However, in many systems, the upper house is not powerless, but the lower house can override the upper house and veto legislation (as in France, Germany, Japan, Russia, the Netherlands, etc.).

Conclusion

There are several different ways to design the relationship between the executive and legislative branches of government as well as the internal structure of the executive and the legislature. These choices include presidential, parliamentary, or hybrid (or semi-presidential) systems. Although each choice has its advantages and disadvantages, many newer democracies have opted for some version of the hybrid system that seeks to combine the best of both presidentialism and parliamentarism (as in Russia and in Afghanistan). Although it is unclear as to the exact effects the choice of regime type has on the development of democracy, there is considerable evidence that such designs have at least indirect effects (such as via the development of political parties, or the structure of political competition). Further, it is certainly the case that constitutional designers believe that they do have effects. Thus the selection of regime type remains one of the most debated, and perhaps least understood, principles of comparative politics.

References

Aldrich, John (1995) *Why Parties? The Origin and Transformation of Party Politics in America*, Chicago, IL: University of Chicago Press.

Cheibub, J.A. (2006) "Presidentialism, Electoral Identifiability, and Budget Balances in Democratic Systems," *American Political Science Review*, 100, 353–368.

Cheibub, J.A. (2007) *Presidentialism, Parliamentarism, and Democracy*, New York: Cambridge University Press.

Clark, W.R.M. Golder and Golder, S.N. (2009) *Principles of Comparative Politics*, Washington, DC: CQ Press.

Evans, D. (2004) *Greasing the Wheels: Using Pork Barrel Projects to Build Majority Coalitions in Congress*, New York: Cambridge University Press.

Fish, M. Steven (2000) "The Executive Deception: Superpresidentialism and the Degradation of Russian Politics," in Valerie Sperling (ed.) *Building the Russian State: Institutional Crisis and the Quest for Democratic Governance*, Boulder, CO: Westview Press, pp. 177–192.

Hale, Henry (2006) *Why Not Parties in Russia*, New York: Cambridge University Press.

Horowitz, Donald. (1990) "Comparing Democratic Systems," *Journal of Democracy*, 1: 783–794.

Ishiyama, John T. and Kennedy, Ryan (2001) "Superpresidentialism and Political Party Development in Russia, Ukraine, Armenia and Kyrgyzstan," *Europe-Asia Studies*, 53, 1177–1191.

Ishiyama, John and Velten, Matthew (1998) "Presidential Power and Democratic Development in Post-Communist Politics," *Communist and Post-Communist Studies*, 31: 217–233.

Keech, W.R. and Pak, K. (1995) "Partisanship, Institutions and Change in American Trade Politics," *Journal of Politics*, 57, 1130–1142.

King, A. (1994) "Chief Executives in Western Europe," in I. Budge and D. McKay (eds.) *Developing Democracy: Comparative Research in Honor of J. F. P. Blondel*, London: Sage, pp. 150–163.

Laver, Michael and Shepsle, Kenneth A. (1996) *Making and Breaking Governments: Government Formation in Parliamentary Democracies*, New York: Cambridge University Press.

Lijphart, Arend (1999) *Patterns of Democracy: Government Forms and Performance in Thirty-Six Countries*, New Haven, CT: Yale University Press.

Linz, Juan (1990) "The Perils of Presidentialism," *Journal of Democracy*, 1: 51–69.

Mainwaring, Scot (1993) "Presidentialism, Multipartism, and Democracy: The Difficult Combination," *Comparative Political Studies*, 26: 198–228.

Power, Timothy. J. and Gasiorowski, Mark J. (1997) "Institutional Design and Democratic Consolidation in the Third World," *Comparative Political Studies*, 30: 123–155.

Protsyk, Oleg (2004) "Ruling with Decrees: Presidential Decree Making in Russia and Ukraine," *Europe-Asia Studies*, 56: 637–660.

Robbins, Joseph (2010) "Presidentialism versus Parliamentarism" in John Ishiyama and Marijke Breuning (eds.) *21st Century Political Science*, Thousand Oaks, CA: Sage.

Sartori, Giovanni (1994) "Neither Presidentialism Nor Parliamentarism," in J.J. Linz and A. Valenzuela (eds.) *The Failure of Presidential Democracy*, Baltimore, MD: Johns Hopkins University Press, pp. 106–118.

Shugart, Matthew. S. and Carey, John M. (1992) *Presidents and Assemblies: Constitutional Design and Electoral Dynamics*, Cambridge: Cambridge University Press.

Smith, A. (2003) "Election Timing in Majoritarian Parliaments," *British Journal of Political Science*, 33: 397–418.

Steffani, Winfried (1995) "Semi-Präsidentialismus: ein eigenständiger Systemtyp? Zur Unterscheidung von Legislative und Parlament," *Zeitschrift für Parlamentsfragen*, 26 (4): 621–41.

Stepan, Alfred and Skach, Cynthia (1993) "Constitutional Frameworks and Democratic Consolidation," *World Politics*, 46: 1–22.

Tavits, Margit (2009) *Presidents with Prime Ministers: Do Direct Elections Matter?* Oxford: Oxford University Press.

9

Comparative Judicial Politics and the Territorial Arrangement of the Political System

Another key set of institutional choices when fashioning together a political systems is: (1) the structure and the role of the judicial system and courts; and (2) the relationship between the central government and local governments. In this chapter we will explore how different judicial systems are structured, the role played by judicial independence and judicial activism, and the effects of courts on the development of democracy. The chapter then will turn to a discussion of the various ways in which the relations between the central government and the local governments can be structured, particularly via unitary systems, federalism, and confederal arrangements.

Judicial Systems

As C. Neal Tate (1992) has noted, the comparative study of courts by scholars has had a long tradition in political science. Although the role of courts in democracies was a favorite topic of the discipline in the earlier part of the twentieth century, the coming of the behavioral revolution pushed the study of courts to the sidelines. However, by the late 1960s, the behavioral study of the courts began again, and since then there has been a considerable amount of new work on the role of courts in democratization and democratic consolidation.

To understand the role courts play in the democratic process, it is first necessary to have some idea of what one means by a "court." Becker (1970, p. 13) defined a court as

Comparative Politics: Principles of Democracy and Democratization, First Edition.
John T. Ishiyama.
© 2012 John T. Ishiyama. Published 2012 by Blackwell Publishing Ltd.

a man or body of men [*sic*] …with power to decide a dispute, before whom the parties or advocates or their surrogates present the facts of a dispute and cite existent, expressed, primary normative principles (in statutes, constitutions, rules, previous cases) … and that they may so decide, and as an independent body.

Shapiro (1981) contended that courts serve three primary functions in democracies – the resolution of conflict, social control, and the making of laws. By *law-making*, Shapiro meant that courts not only shape policy by filling in the gaps in existing statutory law (via judicial interpretation of the law) but also can create law and policy via court rulings on issues such as constitutionality of existing laws, or judicial review.

Although all courts may have similar functions, there is wide variation in terms of legal traditions and judicial structures (Weiden, 2010). In general there are three types of legal traditions that can be found in the world – common law, civil law, and religious law. *Common law* legal systems are found primarily in Anglo-American nations, and is generally based on the idea of precedent, that is legal rulings should be based upon the principles established by previous court cases. Judges have considerable flexibilty in interpreting precedent, and hence considerable autonomy in making rulings. On the other hand, *civil law* systems, which are found in much of the rest of the world (particularly in continental Europe and Latin America) rely more on the use of specifically codified laws and written rules that guide judges in their rulings. This provides relatively little latitude for judges in interpreting law. *Religious law* systems (such as Sharia law, found in some Muslim states) rely extensively on sacred texts to direct judges in their legal decisions (Merryman, 1985).

Courts and judicial review

Beyond different legal traditions, there are also very different ways to organize court systems, largely based on the principle of judicial review. For instance, there is a distinction between "European" and "American" models in terms of how courts are structured and how they deal with the principle of *judicial review*, or the ability of a court to overturn a piece of legislation, an act of the executive, or a lower court decision. Most countries have some form of judicial review, but two notable exceptions are Great Britain and the Netherlands, where the courts are not charged with the power to review the constitutionality of statutes.

The tradition of judicial review has long historical roots. Early forms of constitutional review existed in France by the middle of the thirteenth century. Similar codes regarding judicial review were introduced in Portugal in the seventeenth century and later in the constitutions of Norway, Denmark and Greece in the nineteenth century. In 1867, the Austrian State Court acquired the power to make decisions on constitutional complaints. While the current British system does not have constitutional review, there certainly are precedents for the idea for judicial review, that is, the principle of the supremacy of the law over the acts of the Crown. However, the major defining moment for the development of constitutional review was exerted by the famous *Marbury v. Madison Case* (1803), in which the Supreme Court asserted the power of judicial review. This set the precedent for the US Supreme Court to carry out the judicial review of statutes (Capeletti, 1994).

Generally judicial review can take a number of different forms, but the two primary dimensions to distinguish different forms of review are:

1   *A posteriori* (or *concrete*) *review* versus *a priori* (or *abstract*) *review*. This principle is used in the United States, but also is enshrined in the Japanese Constitution, and in Denmark, Estonia, and several countries in Africa. In *a posteriori* review, judicial review occurs only after law has taken effect and there has been a concrete case brought before the court to review. On the other hand, in *a priori* (or *abstract*) *review*, the judicial review may take place before a law takes effect and thus without an actual case or controversy brought before the court (Stone, 1992). However, generally in such systems, courts also rule *a posteriori* as well as *a priori*. Such systems exist in Austria, Portugal, Spain, Germany, and in France, as well as in most of newly democratizing states of Central and Eastern Europe.

2   The *all courts model of judicial review* (used in the United States) versus *concentrated* or *constitutional courts model of judicial review*. In the former (as in the United States), both higher and lower courts can declare a statute unconstitutional, whereas in the latter, a special court is charged with rendering decisions on the constitutionality of laws and statutes (Tate, 1992).

Judicial review, or a court's power to invalidate a legislative or executive act on grounds of its unconstitutionality, is structured very differently in Europe than in the United States. First, in European systems, the form of constitutional review takes the form of an *abstract review*. When constitutional courts practice abstract review, they need not examine the specific circumstances of a particular case. In other words, the court can rule on issues of principle that are not being raised in the case. In the United States, however, review can only be in concrete form, or only in the context of a particular case brought before the courts.

The second difference is that the European model features a concentrated, or centralized, system of review. Under a system of concentrated judicial review, only specialized courts that have been specifically created to decide constitutional issues can exercise constitutional review. Thus, while the US system of diffuse judicial review authorizes all courts to consider the constitutionality of legislation, the European model concentrates the power of judicial review in one court. Although, ordinary European courts generally are not permitted to exercise judicial review of constitutional questions, these courts may be allowed to refer such issues to constitutional courts for decision.

Courts and independence

In addition to issues of judicial review (and the structures performing the function of judicial review), there is also the issue of *judicial independence*, or the extent to which the judicial authorities are shielded and independent from other political actors. In other words, can judges make decisions without being influenced by policy-makers and elected officials? Generally, one would want judicial independence to act as the neutral arbitration and conflict resolution function that was identified by Shapiro (1981).

A number of institutional characteristics can increase the level of independence of the courts. First, there is life tenure or very long terms for judges (rather than fixed shorter terms), which is designed to ensure that they are insulated from potential retaliation from other political actors. To a large extent, the longer the term of the judges, the more likely they will be to possess some degree of independence from other actors. However, to some extent this depends on how long the term is relative to the terms of other actors. For instance, if the term of judges is *less* than a single parliamentary term, then parliament has a theoretical opportunity within a single session to punish a judge via removal or non-renewal (Smithey and Ishiyama, 2000).

A second institutional characteristic relates to the number of political actors involved in the nomination and confirmation processes when judges are selected for office. It is likely that judges who are selected as the result of a process which involves several political actors possess far more potential independence than judges who are all selected by the same actor.

There is also the question of who controls judicial procedure, that is, who sets the rules for the proceedings of court cases? A constitutional court that determines its own procedures is likely to possess considerably more potential independence than one that has all of its procedures determined by another political actor.

Finally, there is the degree of difficulty in removing judges from office. The easier the constitution makes it to remove a judge, the less independent the judges will be. With regard to removal, we consider constitutional vagueness to be to the advantage of judicial independence, since such vagueness allows judges to interpret vague constitutional provisions to their benefit (Smithey and Ishiyama, 2000).

Although judicial independence may be related to judicial activism, independent courts are not necessarily active in their exercise of judicial review. For instance, Ginsburg (2003; see also Epstein *et al.*, 2001) found that in the early years of a court's existence, judges in these developing nations are less likely to make rulings that challenge other political actors. Similarly Smithey and Ishiyama (2000) found that in post-communist Central and Eastern European countries, the extent to which courts in these countries were judicially independent did not really explain whether they exercised judicial review.

The judicialization of politics

Recent comparative works have suggested that there has been an increase throughout the world of what some have referred to as the "judicialization" of politics (Stone, 1992; Tate and Vallinder, 1995). That is, courts have increased their influence over the policy process and politics generally. For instance, Tate and Vallinder (1995) argue that politicians adjust their policy positions in advance of adoption of legislation in order to avoid nullification by the courts (see also Shapiro and Stone, 1994). Martin Shapiro and Alec Stone note that judges in some European constitutional courts "actually provide the draft statutory language that the judges say they would find constitutional" (1994, p. 404) to legislators, thus having a direct effect on the legislative process.

Further, Stone (1990) argues that judicial power has also expanded most significantly in Europe with the cooperation of other policy-makers, through the use of the reference procedure. As he notes,

> Referrals to courts act as a kind of jurisprudential transmission belt: the more petitions the court receives, the more opportunity they have to elaborate jurisprudential techniques of control; this elaboration, in turn, provides oppositions with a steady supply of issues, expanding the grounds of judicial debate in parliament and in future petitions. (Stone, 1990, p. 90)

The process of judicialization has also led to greater attention being paid to the "constitutionalization of politics" or the focus on the "politics of rights." For instance, Shapiro and Stone (1994, p. 417) describe this process when they note that constitutionalization of politics

> comes to infect the entire political system because opposition political parties, lawyers, citizen groups, and others can see that rights claims are an effective avenue of social change. These actors have become, in essence, the political constituencies of the judges and of constitutional review.

In part, this explosion in rights-based claims is due to what Epp (1998) calls the increase in the "support structure" for legal mobilization. By "support structure," Epp refers to the financial resources and legal expertise that allow litigants to pursue claims that they almost certainly could not finance on their own.

Finally, the judicialization of politics has been spread internationally by the influence of the developing system of supranational judicial structures. These include the European Union tribunals such as the European Court of Justice, the European Court of Human Rights, and the International Court of Justice, whose rulings are now used as precedent in cases before European constitutional courts (Weiden, 2010). Additionally, the European Conference of Constitutional Tribunals, which is composed of all the presidents of the highest courts in Europe, meets regularly at conferences in which their rulings are discussed among each other. Thus, the constitutionalization of the political process is being encouraged at the supranational level as well.

Trial courts and juries in comparative perspective

In the literature on comparative judicial politics, most of the focus has been on high courts, or the general features of the judicial system. However, there has been relatively little work on comparative trial courts. As Weiden (2010) notes, this is somewhat surprising given that there are rather substantial differences between how trials are conducted in Anglo-American countries and those procedures used in the rest of the world. For instance, the trial system employed in Anglo-American countries such as Canada and the United States is known as the *adversarial model* and is based on the premise that truth in a court case will emerge as the result of direct competition between the litigants, and the arguments are then evaluated by a jury.

In most of the rest of the world, the trial procedure is referred to as the *inquisitorial model*. This system is based less on confrontation and is more akin to an investigation where the judges control the proceedings, call, and question the witnesses, and make the ultimate determination in the case. These fundamentally different approaches towards trial procedures have prompted some interesting research into the differential effects of adversarial and inquisitorial systems. For instance, Bruno Deffains and Dominique Demougin (2008) and Block and Parker (2004) conducted research analyzing whether the adversarial or inquisitorial trial system tended to be more equitable; they found that the adversarial trial system could lead to inequality in treatment of litigants, particularly in criminal cases, whereas inquisitorial systems tended to be more equitable in treatment of litigants.

Courts and democracy

Although there has been a growing literature on how the actions of other institutional actors have affected the process of democratic consolidation (such as presidentialism, multipartyism, and the drafting of electoral laws), there has been remarkably little work done that investigates the impact of judicial action.

Understanding the effects of judicial intervention is important to understand the process of democratic consolidation. Given that democratization is a delicate process during which democratic procedures of government are established and maintained, the promotion of the rule of law is an essential task facing these transitional regimes. This is because the submission of the state to law helps the newly democratizing states achieve two crucial goals: (1) a clear break with the authoritarian past; and (2) the development of a culture which teaches state actors that the legal bounds of the system cannot be ignored for the partisan political gains. The significance of the establishment of the rule of law in newly democratizing countries creates a crucial point for the courts in transitional countries, inasmuch that the judicial branch is the institution charged with the enforcement of the constitution, rights, and other democratic procedures (Larkins, 1996).

The possibility of judicial activism in democratizing countries raises important questions about the legitimacy of judges as policy-makers. Many scholars cautioned against creating too much judicial power in new democracies, agreeing with Landfried that judicialization is "dangerous for democracy" (Landfried, 1985, p. 522). Two main reasons were offered as to why strong judiciaries would be inimical to the development of democracy. The first was that the new constitutions entrenched the power of judicial review (allowing judges to act in a counter-majoritarian fashion) while insulating judges from political pressure – a combination that contradicts the modern push for democratic accountability. The second complaint was that increased judicial power reflected a failure of more accountable political institutions. Some scholars see increased judicial power as symptomatic of democratic breakdown, since transferring disputes to the courts allows elected decision-makers to dodge controversial policy questions (Linz, 1978; Valenzuala, 1978). Others argue that transferring decision-making authority from the legislatures to the courts decreases a society's ability to achieve political conciliation. Judicial decisions, emphasizing rights and zero-sum solutions at the expense of compromise, can harden conflict and escalate partisan-ideological disagreement – a particularly dangerous situation in new democracies. From this perspective, increased power for courts signifies an increasing crisis of democracy.

The foregoing criticisms are based on a procedural critique "that having important policy matters decided by non-majoritarian institutions like courts is inherently undemocratic and damaging to the legitimacy and effectiveness of majoritarian institutions like legislatures and elected executives" (Tate, 1997, p. 280). This approach ignores the democracy-enhancing role that courts can play. Other scholars argue that judicial power can be good for democracy, at least if exercised in particular ways. Judges may help keep the democratic process open and fair, by protecting minority rights and making sure that no one is excluded from participation (Ely, 1980; Melone and Mace, 1988). The presence of judicial review may also encourage faith in democracy since it suggests respect for limited government and the rule of law (Shapiro, 1999). From this perspective, a healthy democracy actually requires an active and independent judiciary (Tate, 1995).

The Territorial Arrangement of the Political System

One of the basic challenges in organizing a political system is how power should be territorially or spatially divided. Indeed, the vertical division of power (that is, between central, regional, and local authorities) is as important a consideration for constitutional engineers as is the horizontal division of power between the various branches of government. With rise of the political relevance of ethnicity and nationalism in the late twentieth and early twenty-first centuries, the issues of decentralization and deconcentration of power has become even more important, from the rich developed countries of the West (such as the United Kingdom, and the European Union itself) to poorer developing countries like Ethiopia.

In the comparative politics literature on the spatial dispersion of power, there have generally been three ways to classify different kinds of states. These are *unitary, federal,* and *confederal systems.* There are of course variations within each type, but each type represents distinctly unique ways to structure relations between the central government and regional and local political authorities.

Unitary systems

Unitary systems are characterized by the concentration of powers in the hands of the central government. Important powers such as law making, revenue raising, and defense powers are the purview of the central authorities. Although there may be regional subnational units in the country, the powers that these regional or local governments possess are delegated to them by the central government. Most of the states in the world are unitary systems in one way or another, and include countries such as France, Japan, and the People's Republic of China. The United Kingdom has also historically been a unitary state, but has experienced significant devolution of power (since 1997) to regional governments in Scotland, Wales, and Northern Ireland, including the power to tax in the case of Scotland. Significant devolutions of authority from national to subnational levels have occurred in Africa (for example, Côte d'Ivoire, Ghana), Asia (for example, Bangladesh, India), Europe (for example, Belgium, Britain, France, Italy, and Spain), and Latin America (for example, Argentina, Colombia, and Mexico) (Elazar, 1996).

There are a number of cited advantages to a unitary state (see Hague *et al.,* 1998). These include clarity in the lines of political accountability, greater coordination of policy and ability to ensure equality in treatment of all parts of the country via the uniform application of laws and policies, and the promotion of political unity in the face of regional or ethnic differences. However, there are many cited disadvantages as well. Among the most important are the difficulty in accommodating local differences (or the sense that local interest are trampled under the weight of national interests) and the excessive concentration of power and the emergence of a bloated central bureaucracy.

Federal systems

Federal systems involve shared rule between the central government and regional and local governments. For Riker (1964, p. 11), a system is federal if:

> 1) two levels of government rule the same land and people, 2) each level has at least one area of action in which it is autonomous, and 3) there is some guarantee (even though merely a statement in the constitution) of the autonomy of each government in its own sphere.

Thus, power is shared across different levels of government, and this distribution of powers is defined constitutionally as opposed to being due to the discretion of the central government (Downs, 2010).

Federalism takes a wide variety of forms, although there are some central features that generally characterize this type of system. First, most all federal systems have a bicameral legislature, largely so that the upper house can represent state, regional, or provincial interests (Downs, 2010). This is the case in countries like the United States, Germany, Russia, and Mexico. Second, generally the courts in federal systems have the important role of adjudicating and mediating disputes between regions (although sometimes this power is shared with other branches, such as in the Russian Federation where the president has the power to adjudicate regional disputes).

Generally federalism tends to exist in countries that are quite large and populous (such as the United States, Germany, Brazil, and Mexico) and/or countries that also have significant ethnic, linguistic or regional differences (Russia, India, Canada, Belgium, and Ethiopia). Federalism has been praised as promoting consensus in culturally divided societies (Lijphart, 1999) and facilitating local responsiveness. However, federalism has also been criticized for being overly redundant in terms of multiple bureaucracies (national, state, and local), overlapping and unclear jurisdictions, and being excessively slow to act, due to multiple decision-makers (or "veto players"). Further, federalism has been thought of as promoting regional or ethnic separatism, because it creates institutional and regional bases as "jumping off" points for secessionist movements. Indeed, regional and provincial identities persist as challenges to national unity under federal systems.

There are also different types of federal systems. One of the classic ways to categorize different forms of federalism refers to the relationship between the central government and regional and local governments, or the extent to which power is shared. For instance, *dual federalism* is a theory about the proper relationship between government and the states, portraying the states as powerful components of the federal government – nearly equal to the national government. Dual federalism (Schütze, 2009) is composed of four essential parts:

1 The national government rules by enumerated powers that are only specifically listed in a constitution.
2 The national government has a limited set of constitutional purposes.
3 Each government unit – national, regional, local – is sovereign within its sphere.
4 The relationship between national and regional governments is one of managed tension rather than cooperation.

Dual federalism tends to emphasize the importance of regional authorities and emphasizes state rights relative to the central government. Centrally important is the idea that regions or states reserve powers to them that are not specifically granted to the central government by a constitution. Under the conditions of dual federalism, a rigid wall separates the central government from the regional and local governments.

Cooperative federalism (Schutze, 2009) refers to the cooperative relationship between the regional and central governments, or powers that are shared between the two levels. This system is defined by three core elements:

1 National and regional agencies typically undertake government functions jointly rather than exclusively (such as education, or health).
2 The central and the regional governments routinely share power.
3 Power is dispersed in such a way as to provide citizens with access to many venues of influence.

Generally, the distinction between dual and cooperative federalism is associated with studies of US politics, and generally refers to only the dispersion of power from the center to the regions. On the other hand, Arend Lijphart

(1999) has offered a very different way of differentiating between types of federalism, noting the difference between *congruent* and *incongruent* federalism. Essentially, this distinction refers to whether there is more or less regional distinctiveness relative to the features of the central government. Congruent federalism is the situation where each of the regional sub-units is essentially a smaller replica of the whole. Thus, for example, the classic case of a congruent form of federalism is the United States, where the individual states are replicas of the nation as a whole. Each state is culturally heterogeneous (as is the nation as a whole) and the state governments tend to be mirror images of the central government (complete with bicameral legislatures, mini-presidential systems – led by governors). On the other hand incongruent federalism is where each of the sub-units represents a distinct subsection of the whole. Countries that exemplify cultural homogenous regions that together make a broader heterogeneous whole include Canada (with the combination of French-speaking Quebec with the rest of English-speaking Canada) India, and Belgium (with the combination of the Dutch-speaking Flemish and the French-speaking Walloons). Lijphart saw some advantages for the use of incongruent federalism, particularly in ethnically or culturally divided societies. Indeed, this system ensures political representation and control for sub-groups in society, and thus can serve to create stability in an otherwise volatile society if there are longstanding tensions or conflicts between groups.

Some argue that ethnically based federalism (a form of incongruent federalism) is a way to prevent ethnic conflict and promote the unity of a multi-ethnic state. Ethnic- or identity-based federalism is appealing to many developing countries, particularly in the post-colonial context. A state adopting an ethnic-based federal system gives the "nations" within its borders some degree of self-governance as regions or states in a federal system (Smith, 1995; Tully, 1995).

Examples of emerging ethnofederal systems are Belgium, Bosnia-Herzegovina, and Ethiopia (and potentially Iraq). Perhaps the most extreme form of ethnofederalism has occurred in Ethiopia. In 1991, following the collapse of communist rule, Ethiopia established a federal system creating largely ethnic-based territorial units. The development of ethnic-based federalism was consistent with traditional program of the Tigrayan People's Liberation Front (TPLF) (which had favored the self-determination of ethnic groups during the war against the Derg) and its framers claimed that only through ethnic and regional autonomy would it be possible to maintain the Ethiopian state as a unified political unit. The initial process of federalization lasted four years, and was formalized in a new constitution in 1995 (Mengisteab, 1997, 2001; Habtu, 2005; Kellor and Smith, 2005). The traditional Ethiopian provinces were recombined into nine ethnic-based regional states and two federally administered city-states. The regional states that formed the federation in 1991 were: 1. Tigray; 2. Afar; 3. Amhara; 4. Oromiya; 5. Somali; 6. Benishangul-Gumuz; 7. Southern Nations, Nationalities, and Peoples Region (a merger of five regions); 8. Gambella; and 9. Harari. Addis Ababa and Dire Dawa were made federal cities with a special status. The result has been the development of an asymmetric federation that combines populous regions like Oromiya and Amhara in the central highlands with sparsely populated and underdeveloped ones like Gambella and Somali. Although the constitution vests all powers not attributed to the federal government in them, the regional states are in fact quite weak and subject to political manipulation by the central state (Chanie, 2007, 2009). However, each region has the ability to institute its own official language, and one of the largest, Oromiya, has not only adopted its own language as the language of the state, but also has abandoned the traditional Ethiopian (Amharic) script for a written language based on the Latin alphabet.

Iraq is another example of a potentially ethnofederal state. In Iraq, the principle of federalism was proposed and adopted in 2005 as a way to solve the inherent crisis in modern Iraq and potentially to address the significant regional and sectarian divisions between Kurds and Arabs, and Shiia and Sunni Muslims. Although Kurdistan's autonomy in the federation was acknowledged, the federative form of the rest of the country remains largely undetermined. Currently, the constitution allows for the formation of autonomous regions from the one or more existing governates (provinces) or two or more existing regions. There is no limit to the number of governorates that can form a region. Once formed, each new autonomous region can elect its own president and its own legislature. Although such regions have not yet formed, the current proposed ones include the creation of homogenous Shiia regions in the South. This has sparked considerable debate as to whether federalism in Iraq will be based largely on ethno-sectarian lines.

Lijphart also notes that there are some additional characteristics (or "secondary characteristics") of federalism. These institutional features generally ensure that the federal system will persist (that is, that the national majority will not be able to move power away from the federal units and back to the central government):

- bicameralism with a strong federal (territorial) chamber;
- a written, rigid constitution;
- a judicial review to ensure constitutionality of legislation.

Another distinction in the political science literature on federalism deals with the status of different regions, or the difference between *symmetric* versus *asymmetric* federalism (Elazar, 1991; Stepan, 1999). Symmetric federalism is where all regions or states have the same status and no distinction is made between the constituent states. A classic example of the symmetric federalism is the United States (although certainly there are units that comprise the country, such as the District of Columbia and Puerto Rico, that have a different status when compared to the states). Asymmetric federalism is where different constituent regions possess different powers: one or more of the regions, states, or provinces has considerably more autonomy than the other sub-states, although they have the same constitutional status. Thus, in contrast to a symmetric federation, where no distinction is made between constituent states, in asymmetric federals there is such a distinction.

Two examples of asymmetric federalism include India and the Russian Federation. In India, the federal union is made up of 28 states and 7 union territories (that generally are smaller and less populous, but includes the national capital territory of Delhi). States are generally self- governing with executives and legislatures elected locally, whereas Union Territories are administered directly by the national government (although the Union Territories of Puducherry and Delhi now have the right to elect their own legislatures). Further there are differences among the states as well, with special provisions that provide degrees of autonomy over cultural and educational affairs for Andrhra Pradesh, Arunchal Pradesh, Assam, Goa, Mizoram, Manipur, Nagaland, and Sikkim. Further Jammu and Kashmir are subject to special provisions under Article 370 which specifies that except for Defense, Foreign Affairs, Finance and Communications, the Indian government needs the State Government's concurrence to apply all other laws. Thus, residents of Jammu and Kashmir live under a separate set of laws (for example, citizenship, ownership of property) than other citizens of India (Johnson, 1996).

The Russian federal system, like that of India, is far more complex than that of the United States. The Russian Federation is currently divided into 83 "subjects" of the federation (reduced from 89 up until 2004). Of these, 46 carry the official name *oblast* (in English also translated as "region"); 21

are republics (*respublika*) which are technically tied to the Russian Federation via a series of bilateral treaties concluded in the 1990s; 4 are autonomous districts (*avtonomny okrug*); nine are territories (*krai*); two – Moscow and St. Petersburg – are federal cities; one is an autonomous region (Jewish Autonomous Oblast/Birobidzhan). Generally there is little distinction between *oblasts* and *krai* in terms of governing structure. Both have their own governors (which up until 2003 were directly elected) and their own legislatures. Autonomous districts are generally sparsely populated, and reserved for tribal peoples of the North (in many ways somewhat similar to the status of native peoples in North America, but with much less political autonomy).

The very different feature of the Russian Federation (and perhaps most asymmetric feature of Russian federalism) is the existence of the 21 republics. The republics are organized along non-Russian nationalities, and include Adygea, Altai, Bashkortostan, Buryatia, Republic of Dagestan, Ingushetia, Kabardino-Balkaria, Kalmykia, Karachay-Cherkessia, Karelia, Komi, Mari El, Mordovia, Sahkha Yakutia, North Ossetia-Alania, Tatarstan, Tuva, Udmurtia, Khakassia, Chechnya, and Chuvashia. Each is headed by an elected President, and is bound with the Russian Federation as equal partners with the Russian State, in a voluntary treaty arrangement. Republics differ from other federal subjects in that they have the right to establish their own official language and have their own constitution. Other federal subjects do not have this right. The level of actual autonomy granted to such political units varies but is generally quite extensive. The parliamentary assemblies of such republics have often enacted laws which are at odds with the federal constitution. In the 1990s there were also fairly strong secessionist movements in Chechnya, Bashkortostan, Tatarstan, and Sakha, but only in Chechnya did this turn violent.

Confederal systems

Finally, there are *confederal systems* which are far less common than either unitary or federal systems (Forsyth, 1981). Examples are mainly historical and are most frequently associated with the United States under the Articles of Confederation (1781–1789), the Confederate States of America (1861–1865), Switzerland (1291–1847), the Commonwealth of Independent States (the former USSR), and the emerging European Union (EU).

In confederal systems, a central government coexists alongside subnational units, but in this model, the provincial, regional, or state governments are much stronger than the national authority. The central government relies heavily on the resources and authority of the subnational units and is otherwise powerless to act without the consent of the states, regions, or cantons. Generally in a confederation, the participation in national politics is voluntary on the part of the subnational units, and they are generally free to leave the arrangement at will (although in practice there were some restrictions on leaving a confederacy). Typically, national level decisions require the unanimous agreement of the subnational unit, which makes individual states important veto players in country-wide decisions. In short, a confederal arrangement is really an alliance of independent political entities, and emphasizes local autonomy, although the central government is afforded some limited powers (such as national defense and the conduct of foreign policy).

One of the great weaknesses of confederal systems is that they struggle mightily when weak central governmental authorities are unable to enforce national laws, generate resources or to adjudicate disputes between regions, states, or provinces. Further, they struggle mightily even when attempting to perform basic functions assigned to it (such as national defense and foreign policy). Indeed, these problems explain why, in the modern era, confederations exist in only a few isolated places in the world.

Evolution of unitary and federal states

In recent years many changes have occurred in existing unitary and federal systems. In particular, many unitary systems have transformed into less centralized forms. Much of this was a product of the adaption to the economic contractions beginning the 1970s designed to pass on programmatic and bureaucratic burdens to regional and provincial governments. A second factor was that opposition groups pushed to dismantle unitary states as a campaign promise to mobilize votes (as with the Labour Party in the United Kingdom, relative to Scottish and Welsh autonomy) and once in power sometimes delivered on their promises (Ishiyama and Breuning, 1998). For other cases, decentralization has been driven by the desire to pacify persistent regional nationalisms (as in Italy). These persistent regionalisms have been assisted by the opportunities afforded by new forms of supranational governance (such as the European Union) to embolden subnational movements to seek greater local autonomy (Kincaid and Tarr, 2005).

Thus, many unitary states have experienced a "devolution revolution" of sorts (Hueglin and Fenna, 2006). For instance, in the United Kingdom, the Labour Party, which had lost four consecutive general elections in the 1980s and 1990s, seized on the issue of decentralization as a popular campaign pledge in 1997, and then adopted this as policy once in power. This was particularly popular in Scotland where the discovery of North Sea oil in the 1970s – with its potential for revenues – had fueled a resurgent Scottish nationalism (Ishiyama and Breuning 1998). Cultural autonomy was popular in Wales. With devolution as a centerpiece of Prime Minister Tony Blair's new government, Northern Ireland's elected Assembly convened in 1998 (only to be suspended by London on many occasions from 2002 to 2007) and new Scottish and Welsh parliaments were elected in 1999. However, devolution has not moved in the direction of federation as the local assemblies remain subordinate to the national government.

In France, devolution occurred largely as the result of the Socialist Party's belief that democratization could be furthered through decentralization of the French unitary state. French Socialists, led by President François Mitterrand, after 1981, created 26 directly elected regional councils (each with an indirectly elected president) (Tiersky, 2002; Hueglin and Fenna, 2006). In Italy, social pressures from below were certainly present in the 1970 reforms that created and devolved powers to new administrative regions although decentralization has had greater success in the north, and less in the south of the country (Putnam, 1994).

At times, the development of decentralization and federalism is a natural consequence of development or, as Ivo Duchacek (1970) points out, there may simply be no practical alternative to the adoption of federalism. Belgium is a case in point. Since its foundation in 1830, Belgium was a classical unitary state sitting atop a combination of very different linguistic communities – French-speaking Wallonia and a Dutch-speaking Flanders. Although traditionally politically dominant, over time the Wallonia region fell behind Flanders in the twentieth century, as Flanders became more economically vibrant. This new economic reality led to greater demands by the Flemish population, which resulted in constitutional reforms in 1970 and in 1980, which in turn led to the fundamental transformation of Belgium into a federal country in 1993 (Ishiyama and Breuning, 1998). For Kris Deschouwer (2005, p. 51), Belgium's metamorphosis from a unitary state to a federal state was not the result

> of a deliberate choice but of incremental conflict management … Federalism
> just happens to be the system of government that emerged, to some extent

as the unwanted consequence of the search for a way to keep two increasingly divergent parts of the country together.

Conclusion

The choice of judicial and territorial institutions is a crucial decision for any developing political system. How executive and legislative power is checked is an important consideration in constitutional design. Judiciaries are held out as the best check against the political excesses of other branches of government, but there remains considerable debate over how independent and/or how active an unelected (and for some critics, an unaccountable) branch of government should be in shaping policies and laws. Others, as we have seen, have argued that only through an empowered judiciary can democracy be promoted and consolidated.

The territorial dispersion of power has also been held out as a way to protect regional and local interests, and provide representation to those whose interests might be trampled by a political majority, or politically dominant group. But how far should decentralization go? How should subnational units be organized? Should they be organized along ethnolinguistic lines or other identity markers (as in Ethiopia, and potentially Iraq)? Or should more congruent forms of federalism be adopted, especially to deal with the political problems associated with cultural pluralism? These are questions that every constitutional designer must face, in addition to the choice of electoral system and the structure of legislative-executive relations.

References

Becker, T.L. (1970) *Comparative Judicial Politics: The Political Functionings of Courts*, Chicago: Rand McNally.

Block, M.K and Parker, J.S. (2004) "Decision Making in the Absence of Successful Fact Finding: Theory and Experimental Evidence on Adversarial Versus Inquisitorial Systems of Adjudication," *International Review of Law and Economics*, 24, 89–105.

Capeletti, Mario (1994) "The Judicial Process in Perspective", in D. Beatty (ed.) *Comparative Constitutional Law*, Toronto: Faculty of Law, University of Toronto, pp. I-7/I-8.

Chanie, Paulos (2007) "Clientelism and Ethiopia's Post-1991 Decentralisation," *Journal of Modern African Studies*, 45 (3): 355–384.

Chanie, Paulos (2009) "Disconnect Between Public Sector Management System and Decentralization Reforms: An Empirical Analysis of the Ethiopian Situation," *Eastern Africa Social Science Research Review*, 25 (1): 59–91.

Deffains, B. and Demougin, D. (2008) "The Inquisitorial and the Adversarial Procedure in a Criminal Court Setting," *Journal of Institutional and Theoretical Economics*, 164, 31–43.

Deschouwer, Kris (2005) "Kingdom of Belgium," in J. Kincaid and G. Tarr (eds.) *A Global Dialogue on Federalism*, Montreal: McGill-Queens University Press.

Downs, William (2010) "Comparative Federalism, Confederalism, Unitary Systems" in John Ishiyama and Marijke Breuning (eds.) *21st Century Political Science*, Thousand Oaks, CA: Sage.

Duchacek, Ivo D. (1970) *Comparative Federalism: The Territorial Dimension of Politics*, New York: Holt, Rinehart & Winston.

Elazar, Daniel (1987) *Exploring Federalism*, Tuscaloosa, AL: University of Alabama Press.

Elazar, Daniel (1991) *Federal Systems of the World: A Handbook of Federal, Confederal and Autonomy Arrangements*, London: Longman.

Ely, John Hart (1980) *Democracy and Distrust*, Cambridge, MA: Harvard University Press.

Epp, C.R. (1998) *The Rights Revolution: Lawyers, Activists and Supreme Courts in Comparative Perspective*, Chicago, IL: University of Chicago Press.

Epstein, Lee, Knight, J. and Shvetsova, Olga (2001) "The Role of Constitutional Courts in the Establishment and Maintenance of Democratic Systems of Government," *Law & Society Review*, 35: 117–164.

Forsyth, M. (1981) *Unions of States: The Theory and Practice of Confederation*, Leicester: Leicester University Press.

Ginsburg, T. (2003) *Judicial Review in New Democracies: Constitutional Courts in Asian Case*, New York: Cambridge University Press.

Habtu, Alem (2005) "Multiethnic Federalism in Ethiopia: A Study of the Secession Clause in the Constitution," *Publius: The Journal of Federalism*, 35 (2): 313–335.

Hague, Rod, Harrop, Martin, and Breslin, Shaun (1998) *Comparative Government and Politics: An Introduction*, London: Macmillan Press.

Hueglin, T. (2003) "Federalism at the Crossroads: Old Meanings, New Significance," *Canadian Journal of Political Science*, 36 (2): 275–294.

Hueglin, T.O. and Fenna, A. (2006) *Comparative Federalism: A Systematic Inquiry*, Toronto: University of Toronto Press.

Ishiyama, John and Breuning, Marijke (1998) *Ethnopolitics in the New Europe*, Boulder, CO: Lynne Rienner.

Johnson, Gordon (1996) *Cultural Atlas of India*, New York: Facts on File.

Keller, Edmond and Smith, Lahra (2005) "Obstacles to Implementing Territorial Decentralization: The First Decade of Ethiopian Federalism," in Phillip Roeder and Donald Rothchild (eds.) *Sustainable Peace: Power and Democracy after Civil Wars*, Ithaca, NY: Cornell University Press.

Kincaid, J. and Tarr, G.A. (eds.) (2005) *Constitutional Origins, Structure, and Change in Federal Countries*, Montreal: McGill-Queen's University Press.

Landfried, C. (1985) "The Impact of the German Constitutional Court on Politics and Policy Outputs," *Government and Opposition*, 20 (4): 520–535.

Larkins, Christopher M. (1996) "Judicial Independence and Democratization: A Theoretical and Conceptual Analysis," *The American Journal of Comparative Law*, 44 (4): 605–626.

Lijphart, Arend (1999) *Patterns of Democracy: Government Forms and Performance in Thirty-Six Countries*, New Haven, CT: Yale University Press.

Linz, Juan (1978) "Crisis, Breakdown and Reequilibration," in Juan Linz and Alfred Stepan (eds.) *The Breakdown of Democratic Regimes*, Baltimore, MD: Johns Hopkins University Press.

Melone, Alberte and Mace, George (1988) "Judicial Review: The Usurpation Question," *Judicature*, 71 (2): 202–210.

Mengisteab, Kidane (1997) "New Approaches to State Building in Africa: The Case of Ethiopia's Ethnic-Based Federalism," *African Studies Review*, 40 (3): 111–132.

Mengisteab, Kidane (2001) "Ethiopia's Ethnic-Based Federalism: 10 Years After," *African Issues*, 29 (1): 20–25.

Merryman, J.H. (1985) *The Civil Law Tradition: An Introduction to the Legal Systems of Western Europe and Latin America*, 2nd edn., Stanford, CA: Stanford University Press.

Putnam, Robert (1994) *Making Democracy Work: Civic Traditions in Modern Italy*, Princeton, NJ: Princeton University Press.

Riker, William H. (1964) *Federalism: Origin, Operation, Significance*, Boston: Little, Brown.

Schütze, Robert (2009) *From Dual To Cooperative Federalism: The Changing Structure Of European Law*, Oxford: Oxford University Press.

Shapiro, Martin (1981) *Courts: A Comparative and Political Analysis*, Chicago, IL: University of Chicago Press.

Shapiro, Martin (1999) "The Success of Judicial Review," in Sally Kenney, William Reisinger and Joseph Reitz (eds.) *Constitutional Dialogues in Comparative Perspective*, New York: Macmillan, pp. 193–219.

Shapiro, Martin and Stone, Alec (eds.) (1994) "The New Constitutional Politics of Europe" Special issue, *Comparative Political Studies*, 26 (1): 397–561.

Smith, B.C. (1985) *Decentralization: The Territorial Dimension of the State*, London: Unwin Hyman.

Smith, Graham (1995) "Mapping the Federal Condition: Ideology, Political Practice and Social Justice," in Graham Smith (ed.) *Federalism: The Multi-Ethnic Challenge*, New York: Prentice Hall.

Smithey, Shannon and Ishiyama, John (2000) "Judicious Choices: Designing Courts in Post-Communist Politics," *Communist and Post Communist Studies*, 33: 163–182.

Stepan, Alfred (1999) "Federalism and Democracy: Beyond the U.S. Model," *Journal of Democracy*, 10 (4): 19–34.

Stone Alec (1990) "The Birth and Development of Abstract Review: Constitutional Courts and Policy-Making in Western Europe," *Policy Studies Journal*, 19 (2): 81–95.

Stone, Alec (1992) *The Birth of Judicial Politics in France: The Constitutional Council in Comparative Perspective*, New York: Oxford University Press.

Tarr, G., Williams, R., and Marko, J. (eds.) (2004) *Federalism, Subnational Constitutions, and Minority Rights*, Westport, CT: Praeger.

Tate, C. Neal (1992) "Comparative Judicial Review and Public Policy: Concepts and Overview," in D.W. Jackson and C.N. Tate (eds.) *Comparative Judicial Review and Public Policy*, New York: Greenwood Press, pp. 3–14.

Tate, C. Neal (1995) "Why the Expansion of Judicial Power?" in C. Neal Tate and Torbjorn Vallinder (eds.) *The Global Expansion of Judicial Power*, New York: New York University Press, pp. 27–38.

Tate, C. Neal (1997) "Courts and the Breakdown and Re-creation of Philippine Democracy: Evidence from the Supreme Court's Agenda," *International Social Science Journal*, 49 (3): 278–298.

Tate, C. Neal and Vallinder, T. (eds.) (1995) *The Global Expansion of Judicial Power*, New York: New York University Press.

Tiersky, R. (2002) *François Mitterrand: A Very French President*, New York: Rowman and Littlefield.

Tully, James (1995) *Strange Multiplicity: Constitutionalism in an Age of Diversity*, Cambridge: Cambridge University Press.

Valenzuala, Arturo (1978) "Chile," in Juan Linz and Alfred Stepan (eds.) *The Breakdown of Democratic Regimes*, Baltimore, MD: Johns Hopkins University Press.

Weiden, David. L. (2010) "Judicial Politicization, Ideology and Activism at the High Courts of the United States, Canada and Australia," *Political Research Quarterly*, 63 (3): 1–13.

10

Conclusion
Principles in Application

As stated in the opening chapter of this book, the primary goal of this text was to identify the fundamental principles of comparative politics that political science students should know. Thus, the previous chapters have outlined how one might address the problems (at least in terms of a problem-based learning perspective) associated with democracy and democratization. More specifically, how does one promote the development of political democracy? What are the factors that help explain the emergence of political democracy? This is not because the book sought to argue that democracy should exist everywhere – in fact, it may not be possible for this to happen. However, *knowing* the factors that affect the development of democracy can help students understand why "building" democracy is so difficult (or perhaps impossible) in places such as Iraq or in Afghanistan. Thus the question is not prescriptive – rather, it presumes that students need to ask this question first to realize that democracy may *not* be the best institutional arrangement, given a set of historical, economic, social, cultural, and international circumstances.

In many ways, the focus on addressing the problem of democracy and democratization (as opposed to a broader survey of the comparative literature) sacrifices breadth for depth. Thus there are some areas that were not explicitly addressed in this text (such as political violence, or political organizations). However, by touching upon the historical, social, economic, cultural, and international factors that impact democracy, the framework that was presented can also be used to explain political violence and the development and evolution of political organizations.

Comparative Politics: Principles of Democracy and Democratization, First Edition.
John T. Ishiyama.
© 2012 John T. Ishiyama. Published 2012 by Blackwell Publishing Ltd.

With this in mind, what have we identified as those factors that help shape the context in which institutional choices are made? Certainly, as Chapter 2 demonstrates, history matters, and matters a great deal. What preceded the attempted transition to democracy (if there was one) has important "legacy" effects on the development of democracy. Although much of the "historical" approach focused on the Western experience and especially the timing of economic modernization, social mobilization, political institutionalization, and democracy (and may be of questionable applicability to countries outside of the West), the notion that the past provides legacies for future developments *is relevant everywhere*. Thus, for instance, several scholars have pointed to the legacies of the authoritarian past to explain why some countries seem to make a transition to democracy more easily than others. These historical legacies not only include the type of regime that existed before the emergence of political democracy (as mentioned in Chapter 2), but also the influence of the democratization process itself (as mentioned in Chapter 6). Generally, in countries where feudalism or quasi-feudal relations do not persist, and where the transition process (when it did occur) was one in which negotiated settlements (as opposed to sudden replacements) occurred, conditions emerged that were, *ceteris paribus*, more conducive to the development of democracy than otherwise.

Second, as was discussed in Chapter 3, the level of economic development and wealth impacts the development of democracy. Although it is not entirely clear whether that relationship is causal or merely correlational, there is little doubt that some kind of relationship exists. In other words, countries that are wealthier generally have an easier time transitioning to democracy than countries that are poorer and less developed (but of course economic factors are not the only explanation for the emergence of democracy).

An additional contextual factor that was covered in Chapter 4 was political culture and ethnicity. Generally, as was discussed in Chapter 4, there has been a great deal of debate in the scholarly literature over whether culture has a truly independent effect on the development of democracy, and whether ethnic diversity leads to conflict and the demise of incipient democratic experiments. However, whatever the case, we do know that, as with economics, culture and ethnic politics have some kind of effect on the development of democracy. Indeed, there is little question in the scholarly literature that countries that have political cultures that value tolerance, moderation, compromise, and civility, have an easier time developing democracy, than those countries that are not characterized by these features. Further, countries that are not faced with deeply divided societies along cultural, religious, racial, or ethnic lines have an easier time developing democracy than those that are deeply divided. Although cultural and ethnic politics may not determine whether democracy succeeds, they certainly are important variables to consider when designing political institutions. For instance, consideration of culture and ethnicity has certainly informed the debate over whether consociational institutional arrangements are better than other forms of institutional structuring.

Chapter 5 identified features of the social structure, and cited the important role played by civil society in the development of political democracy. Further, this chapter examined the historical effects of feudalism, the existence of socioeconomic inequality and the impact of civil society. Generally, it was argued that societies that do not have stark differences between very rich and very poor, and those that have some development of civil society, or social networks that link people together, are better at promoting democracy than societies that are characterized by large gaps between rich and poor and that do not have many features of civil society. Indeed, there has been considerable consensus in the literature that democracy is easier to develop than in countries that do not have such features.

Chapter 6 identified both the impact of the international environment (particularly democratization via diffusion) and the legacies of colonialism. Based upon the literature covered in Chapter 6, being geographically proximate with other democratic countries raises the probability that a country will itself become democratic. Further, the legacies of colonialism also impact the likelihood of democracy, with British colonies posited to be more likely to evolve into democracies than countries that have emerged from other colonial systems.

However, as was discussed in Chapter 6, globalization may or may not promote democracy. On the one hand, globalization, from the liberal economic perspective, may promote economic growth and development, which promotes democracy. However, on the other hand, globalization has also been posited as a catalyst for ethnic conflict, which can serve to undermine the development of democracy, particularly in ethnically divided countries.

Finally, a recently expanding area of empirical research is the impact of "imposed" democracy, and whether such efforts and creating democracy from the outside will lead to democratic outcomes or not. Although much of the theoretical work (see Huntington, 1984, 1991) and the empirical work (Enterline and Greig, 2005, 2008) has suggested that imposed democracy is unlikely to survive, the story has not ended regarding places like Iraq and Afghanistan.

Thus, in sum, a number of different factors serve to shape the context in which democratic experiments take place. Table 10.1 illustrates these factors and list the ways in which they shape the social, economic, and political context. This is not an "exhaustive" list of factors but it will prompt the reader to think in terms of factors that shape the context in which institutional choices are made.

These factors shape the social, economic, and international contexts in which political development occurs, and set the stage for institutional choices for constitutional designers. The first of these choices, or electoral systems was discussed in Chapter 7. The choice of electoral system has important ramifications for the development of political parties and party systems, voter turnout and participation, representation of women and minorities, and democratic development generally. For brevity, Table 10.2 summarizes the general effects of the two modal types of electoral systems: list proportional representation and single-member district plurality systems.

As was noted in Chapter 7, because each single member district plurality electoral systems and list PR have numerous advantages and disadvantages, many countries have sought to mix the elements of electoral systems, such as the additional member system in Germany (and a variant of this in Hungary) and parallel mixed systems (as in the Russian Federation). Other variations include the block vote and the single non-transferable vote (plurality systems with multimember districts, used in Afghanistan, for instance, and historically in Spain and Japan), as well PR systems with small district magnitudes (such as the single transferable vote – used in Ireland – and the much touted alternative vote system, used in ethnically divided countries, such as Fiji). Indeed, most new democracies and countries in transition have employed electoral systems that have sought to combine the positive elements of both plurality and PR systems.

Chapter 8 focused on the effects of presidentialism and parliamentarism on democratic development. As with electoral systems choices, there is a variety of ways to design the relationship between the executive and legislative branches of government as well as the internal structure of the executive and legislature. In terms of the overall constitutional relationship between executive and legislature, the basic choices include presidential, parliamentary, or hybrid (or semi-presidential) systems. As Chapter 8

Table 10.1 Summary of contextual factors impacting on democracy and democratization.

Factor	Positive effect on development of democracy	Negative effect on development of democracy	Relevant chapter
Historical legacy	Feudalism disappears, development of bourgeoisie; early development of national identity	Feudalism does not disappear, bourgeoisie does not develop, or only develops as comprador bourgeoisie; late development, or incomplete development, of national identity	Chapter 2
	Transition process = transplacement	Transition process = replacement, transformation (that does not evolve into transplacement)	Chapter 6
Economic development	Economic development and wealth	Poverty and lack of development	Chapter 3
Political culture	Participant political culture dominant	Subject and parochial political culture	Chapter 4
Ethnic, cultural, politics	Relative ethnic homogeneity or at least no deep, politicized, ethnic or cultural cleavages	Deep-seated and politicized ethnic or cultural cleavages	Chapter 4
Social structure	Society not structured hierarchically; Not large gaps between rich and poor	Large gaps between rich and poor	Chapter 5
Civil society	Existence of dense networks of interest groups; promotion of cross-cutting cleavages	No, or poorly developed, civil society	Chapter 5
External factors	Country is geographically proximate with other democracies	Country is geographically isolated from other democracies	Chapter 6
	Globalization is high (debate in literature)	Globalization is high (debate in literature)	Chapter 6
	British colonial legacy	Non-British colonial legacy	Chapter 6

Table 10.2 Advantages and disadvantages of electoral systems.

Electoral system	Advantages	Disadvantages
Single-member district plurality (the United States, the United Kingdom, Canada, India, Nigeria, Ethiopia)	Provides incentives for political moderation, and disincentives for political extremism Reduces the number of parties and hence promotes governmental stability Promotes constituency service by legislative representatives	Leads to large number of wasted votes, and excludes from representation large portions of the population Reduces competition to conflict between personalities as opposed to competition over programs (weakens political parties) Lowers sense of voter efficacy and reduces voter turnout
List proportional representation (The Netherlands, Belgium, Israel, South Africa, Iraq, Poland, Czech Republic, Slovakia)	Provides for broad representation and cooptation of political interests (thus promoting long-term political stability, particularly in ethnically/ culturally divided societies Provides for competition based on party programs as opposed to competition over personalities Higher sense of voter efficacy and higher voter turnout	Leads to fractionalization of the party system. Often produces weak coalition governments May provide openings for extremists to enter politics and gain a foothold in government Eliminates direct connection between voter and representative. Reduces level of constituency service

pointed out, there are a number of advantages and disadvantages when comparing presidential and parliamentary systems, as well as considerable debate over "the perils of presidentialism." Although each choice has its advantages and disadvantages, many newer democracies have opted for some version of hybrid system that seeks to combine the best of both presidentialism and parliamentarism (as in Russia and in Afghanistan). Chapter 8 also examined the different ways in which the legislative process can be structured, particularly contrasting the existence of a powerful committee system as illustrated by the United States, and a weaker, largely consultative committee system in the United Kingdom.

Finally, Chapter 9 reviewed the literature on the choices and effects of judicial systems, particularly the distinction between the American model and the European model of judicial review. In particular, we noted the contrast between the two systems, particularly the ability of the courts to intervene in the political process, and the impact of judicial independence and activism on the development of political democracy. As was noted in Chapter 9, there remains considerable debate over just how independent the courts should be relative to elected authorities, and whether an active court is a good thing for democratic development.

The second major issue covered in Chapter 9 was the territorial dimension in the design of political systems. Critics of unitary system have argued that the territorial dispersion of power is the best way to protect regional and local interests, and provide representation to those whose interests might be trampled by a political majority, or politically dominant group. How should these subnational units be organized? Should they be organized along ethnolinguistic lines or other identity markers? Or should more congruent forms of federalism be adopted, especially to deal with the political problems associated with cultural pluralism?

Table 10.3 illustrates the variety of combinations that have been employed in various political systems throughout the world. As Table 10.3 indicates, there is a variety of different combinations that can be employed when designing different political systems.

In sum, this book has been about how one defines the contours of the problem, that is, what the social, economic, political, and international conditions are that frame context in which action takes place, AND the range of institutional choices that are available to address this context in the effort to build democracy. To illustrate the application of these principles of democracy and how the design of political institutions has been applied, the next section briefly discusses the case of Afghanistan.

The Case of Afghanistan

Historical background

Afghanistan's history and its internal political development have been vitally shaped by its location at the crossroads of Central, West, and South Asia. The country has long been inundated with waves of migration, which made the country quite diverse in terms of ethnicity, religion, and languages. Afghanistan has also been the center of confrontations between the "Great Powers" over time with the armies of great empires, including Alexander the Great, the Persian Empire, and the Mongols, passing through

Table 10.3 Examples of combinations of different institutional designs.

Country	Electoral system	Presidential/parliamentary	Unitary/federal	American/European model of judicial system
The United States	Single-member district plurality (SMDP)	Presidential	Federal	American
The United Kingdom	SMDP	Parliamentary	Unitary (with devolution)	No judicial review
Germany	Mixed additional member system	Parliamentary	Federal	European
The Netherlands	List PR	Parliamentary	Unitary	No judicial review
France	SMDP	Semi-presidential	Unitary	European
Russian Federation	List PR (since 2007)	Semi-presidential	Federal	European
	Mixed parallel (1993–2007)			
Japan	Mixed (since 1995)	Parliamentary	Unitary	American
	Single non- transferable vote (1948–1995)			
Hungary	Mixed additional member system	Parliamentary	Unitary	European
Poland	List PR	Parliamentary	Unitary	European
Argentina	List PR	Presidential	Federal	American
Brazil	List PR	Presidential	Federal	American
South Africa	List PR	Presidential (but president is responsible to parliament similar to prime minister)	Federal	European
Ethiopia	SMDP	Parliamentary	Federal	American
Iraq	List PR	Parliamentary	Federal	American
Afghanistan	SNTV	Presidential	Unitary	American

the region and establishing at least temporary control over the area (Vogelsong, 2002; Sabahuddin, 2008).

For centuries, Afghanistan was a zone of conflict among strong neighboring powers, and was not really an integrated unified political entity until the reign of Ahmad Shah Durrani, who founded a monarchy in 1747. His successors (the so-called Durrani dynasty) ruled the country (at least in name) until the coup in 1973. However, the history of Afghanistan has been marked by almost continuous infighting among the various clans in the country, who ruled their own areas autonomously from the central state.

In the nineteenth century, Afghanistan became the site for the collision between the expanding British and Russian Empires in what was called "The Great Game." The British, ensconced in India, sought to expand northward to secure its prized possession (India) and the Russian Empire was expanding in the nineteenth century into Central Asia. The Russians and British vied for influence in Afghanistan, which represented a border region separating the two empires. After several wars between the Afghans and the British (who had sought to officially occupy Afghanistan), a peace was brokered in which the boundaries of Afghanistan were set by the British and Russians. Afghanistan became nominally self-governing, but a British protectorate, with the British retaining effective control over the country's foreign affairs (Dupree, 1973).

In 1919, King Habibullah was assassinated by anti-British family members and his brother Amanullah became king and regained control of Afghanistan's foreign policy after the Third Anglo-Afghan War. The war-weary British, having just emerged from World War I, relinquished their control over Afghan foreign affairs on August 19, 1919 (which remains the independence day of Afghanistan).

In the twentieth century, Afghanistan remained the center of great power intrigues. Mohammed Zahir Shah, who ruled from 1933 to 1973, promulgated a new constitution that allowed elections. Although Zahir Shah's "experiment in democracy" produced few lasting reforms, it allowed the growth of unofficial extremist parties on both the left and the right, including the communist People's Democratic Party of Afghanistan (PDPA), which had ties to the Soviet Union. In 1967, the PDPA split into two major rival factions: the Khalq (Masses) headed by Nur Muhammad Taraki and Hafizullah Amin, supported by elements within the military, and the Parcham (Banner) led by the intellectual Babrak Karmal (Ishiyama, 2005).

The July 1973 *coup d'état* ended 226 years of royal rule controlled by the Durrani tribal confederacy. In turn, in 1978, the communists seized power in Kabul (known as the Saur Revolution) in 1978. Once in power, the PDPA implemented a Marxist-Leninist social and economic agenda. It moved to replace religious and traditional laws with secular and Marxist-Leninist ones. Men were obliged to cut their beards and mosques were placed off limits. The PDPA promoted women's rights and banned forced marriages. The regime was overtly pro-Soviet, more so the Parcham faction than the Khalqists. However, due to internal infighting, and general incompetence in implementing reforms, as well as a growing Islamic insurgency, the Khalqist regime began to unravel, and reached a crisis with the death (likely murdered at the orders of Amin) of Taraki. The Soviets intervened militarily in December 1979, overthrowing Hafizullah Amin, and installed the Parchami leader, Babrak Karmal as the new president. For the next nine years the Soviet Union militarily propped up the PDPA regime, and fought a military campaign against the Mujahideen (the Islamic insurgents). Taking the opportunity to bog down the Soviet Union, the Afghan rebels received billions in US military aid (Ishiyama, 2005).

In 1988, the Soviet Union withdrew, and the Parchami-led PDPA regime hung onto power for another four years (now led by the former head of the Afghan Secret Police, Mohammed Najibullah, who had replaced Karmal in 1986). This regime was overthrown in 1992 by the Mujahideen and former PDPA militia that defected to the sides of the insurgents (such as the Uzbek PDPA militia general Abdul Rashid Dostum). From 1992 to 1996 the country was in a state of perpetual civil war, with a variety of warlords vying for control of the capital, Kabul. In 1997, a Muslim fundamentalist movement, the Taliban (or "students") reputedly supported by Pakistani intelligence services, began to gather support, and ultimately were able to drive out the warlords and institute a brutal form of *Sharia* law across most of the country. From 1996 to 2002, a civil war continued between the Taliban, and loose assortment of deposed warlords, grouped together in the Northern Alliance. Generally, the Taliban was strong among the Pashtun-speaking parts of the population, with the Northern Alliance supported by Persian-speaking Tajiks and other ethnic groups in the north of the country.

In 2002, after the US invasion of Afghanistan and the overthrow of the Taliban regime, Afghan factions met in Germany and chose a 30-member interim authority led by Hamid Karzai, a Pashtun from Kandahar. After governing for six months, former King Zahir Shah convened a Loya Jirga (Council of Elders) which elected Karzai as president and gave him interim authority for two years. On October 9, 2004, Karzai was elected as president of Afghanistan in the country's first ever presidential election. Karzai ran for re-election in 2009 and won a hotly contested election. In 2006 a new Taliban insurgency began, and the civil war continued. The resurgent Taliban retook parts of Afghanistan and are at war with the newly created Afghan state and international coalition forces.

Economic factors

Afghanistan is one of the world's poorest countries, with an estimated $366 GDP per capita in 2009 (World Bank, 2010). Only about 28 percent of the adult population is considered literate. Afghanistan's economy has historically been based on subsistence agriculture, and the Afghan economy continues to be overwhelmingly agricultural, despite the fact that only 12 percent of its total land area is arable and less than 6 percent currently is cultivated. Agricultural production is almost entirely based on runoff from winter snow, and to this day agriculture is largely done without machinery. Other than illicit poppies (Afghanistan has the dubious distinction of being the largest producer of poppies in the world), agricultural exports include pistachios and fruits.

Industry is limited. Afghanistan embarked on a modest economic development program in the 1930s, with the government introducing banks, paper money, and other infrastructural construction. In the 1950s, the government launched a series of development plans, but most of these produced only modest economic gains. By the late 1970s, these had achieved only mixed results (Edwards, 2002).

More recently the Afghan economy has grown considerably over the past five years at an average rate of about 11.23 percent per year between 2004 and 2009 (*CIA World Factbook*, 2004–2009). Much of this growth was due to the provision of international aid. By 2009, GDP growth had been reduced to a mere 3.4 percent, signaling a potential slowdown in further growth in the Afghan economy.

Ethnicity, religion, and civil society

In addition to the fact that of incomplete statehood in part because of the influence of foreign powers throughout its history, Afghanistan is also a deeply divided society on both ethnolinguistic and religious lines. Approximately 42 percent of the population is Pashtun, who are largely Sunni and speak a language related to the languages spoken in Pakistan.

The Pashtun are divided into numerous tribes, of which the Durrani have been historically dominant, but other important tribal clans include the Ghilzai and the Kasi. The Pashtun tend to be rural dwellers and concentrated in the southern and eastern parts of the country. On the other hand, about 27 percent of the population is ethnic Tajik, concentrated in Kabul and the north of the country. The Tajiks historically comprised the urban elite in the country and were also the backbone of the Northern Alliance in opposition to the Taliban. Further, about 9 percent of the population are Hazara, a group descended in part from the Mongol population that had migrated southward during the Mongol conquest of the region in the Middle Ages. The Hazaras, unlike most of the rest of the population, are Shiite Muslim, as opposed to Sunni Muslim, and have long experienced significant discrimination at the hands of other populations. They inhabit the central areas of the country. Uzbeks, who comprise about 9 percent of the population, inhabit the northern parts of the country adjacent to Uzbekistan, and had been aligned with the Parchami regime prior to 1992. They largely supported the Northern Alliance in the war with the Taliban. Religious divisions also exist, although about 80 percent of the population is Sunni Muslim and about 19% are Shia Muslim, including most of the Hazara (*Afghanistan, A Country Study*). Religion has always played an important political role in Afghanistan, and religious leaders have historically been political leaders as well.

Although ethnicity plays some role in Afghan society, the real organizing unit is the *qaum* (or community) which really refers to a complexity of affiliations, a network, of families or occupations. These communities are not always defined by ethnicity. Every individual belongs to a *qaum* which provides protection from outside encroachments, cooperation, support, security, and assistance, either social, political or economic. Frequently a village corresponds to a *qaum*, but it does not necessarily exist in a precise geographic setting. In many areas *qaum* refers to a common genealogy from extended family, or clan.

Clan politics is important in Afghanistan, and clan politics represent a kind of civil society that exists apart and autonomous from the state (Collins, 2002). However, as Collins notes, the clans are more interested in promoting their own economic and political interests rather than promoting democracy. The clans in Afghanistan, are headed by strongmen, or warlords, such as Abdul Rashid Dostum (former communist militia general and PDPA supporter) an Uzbek leader, and Mohammed Farim, a Tajik warlord who is currently Minister of Defense in the Karzai government.

However, the "pacts" that were made in Afghanistan (and throughout Central Asia for that matter) did not lead to democracy (as they have elsewhere in the world) because, unlike elsewhere where these were negotiated settlements between the government and the opposition, the pacts that have occurred in Central Asia (including Afghanistan) have been between the clans who have divided up the state among themselves, and then sought an authoritarian solution to protect this division of spoils. Hence, it is unlikely that clan-based civil society will be very conducive to the development of democracy in Afghanistan.

Summary of contextual factors in Afghanistan

In general, the social and economic contexts that frame institutional choices in Afghanistan are not particularly conducive to democratic development. Afghanistan has not had a long history of statehood, and for much of its history was internally divided along clan and ethnic lines, divisions that were actively promoted by external powers. This has not been particularly supportive of a united Afghan national identity, although Islam (and particularly Sunni Islam) is a shared identity for most of the population. However, the country remains deeply divided, particularly between southern Pashtuns and northern Tajiks.

Economically, Afghanistan remains poor, and dependent on foreign aid, with little in the way of export crops (except opium poppies) and industry. Although society is not structured along deeply hierarchical lines, and clan/tribal groups constitute something like a "civil society", as noted above, clan politics are not generally supportive of the development of democracy in Central Asia. Further, Afghanistan itself is not surrounded by geographically proximate democracies with Iran to the West, the authoritarian regimes of Uzbekistan and Tajikistan to the North, and Pakistan to the East. Finally, the "imposed" nature of the Karzai regime and the sudden transition to "democracy" has created difficulties in promoting the legitimacy of the current regime. Thus, overall, the contextual factors in Afghanistan do not appear to be particularly conducive to the development of democracy in the country.

Institutional choices

Given the above context, what have been the institutional choices made in Afghanistan? The current Constitution of Afghanistan was adopted by the

Loya Jirga on January 4, 2004. The Constitution provides for a presidential system with a bicameral legislature (see Afghan Constitution of 2004). The president is both head of state and head of government, and can name his two vice-presidents (a first and a second vice-president). The powers and duties of the President include:

- the power to introduce laws and policies in the National Assembly;
- being the Command-in-Chief of the armed forces of Afghanistan;
- the right to declare war (subject to approval of the National Assembly);
- declaring states of emergency, appointing of Ministers, the Attorney General, the Director of the Central Bank, Head of the National Security Directorate and the President of the Afghan Red Crescent Society with the approval of the lower House of Representatives;
- appointing the head and members of the Supreme Court with the approval of the House of Representatives.

Although the creation of a strong presidency and a relatively weak national parliament was the subject of some controversy in the debates over the Constitution, it was seen by the interim administration and its Western backers as being essential to securing the stability of Afghanistan.

The bicameral legislature (National Assembly) is made up of an upper house, a Council of Elders (*Meshrano Jirga*) with 102 members, and a House of Representatives (*Wolesi Jirga*) with 249 members. One-third of the members of the Council of Elders are elected by provincial council members (four-year term of office), one-third by district council members (three-year term of office); one-third are appointed by the President (five-year term of office). The House of Representatives is elected via a single non-transferable vote system, a plurality system with multimember districts. However, the district magnitudes are quite large, with 36 seats representing Kabul. This means that the top 36 vote winners gain seats in Kabul, and that candidates can win seats with relatively few votes. Indeed, in Kabul, in the 2005 election, most candidates elected received well under 1 percent while over 30 percent of the votes cast went to three candidates, with the leading candidate receiving over 25 times the vote of the candidate elected with the lowest vote share.

Further, political parties are very weak in Afghanistan and have been systematically marginalized during the post-2001 political process. The political parties law came too late for the 2005 parliamentary election.

During that election, parties were not even allowed to register their candidates' party affiliation on the ballot papers. For the 2010 election, this has changed, but Afghanistan's electoral law still only allows parties to field individual candidates, not party lists.

The House of Representatives has the right to interpellate ministers (if one-tenth of its members request it) and can institute votes of no confidence directed at individual ministers, but not the government as a whole.

In addition to the legislature, there is also an additional institution that was borrowed from past tradition and incorporated into the 2005 Constitution, the *Loya Jirga* (or Grand Council). The Loya Jirga had been traditionally assembled to make major decisions and appointments (such as selection of the King). According to Article 110 of the Constitution, the Loya Jirga is "the highest manifestation of the people of Afghanistan" and is made up of members of the National Assembly, and chairpersons of provincial and district councils. The Loya Jirga is convened to do the following: (1) to take decisions on the issues related to independence, national sovereignty, territorial integrity, other "supreme interests of the country"; (2) to amend the provisions of this Constitution; and (3) to prosecute the President in accordance with the provisions of Articles of impeachment.

The Supreme Court is composed of nine justices who have terms of ten years (not life) and cannot serve a second term. The justices are nominated by the President subject to approval by the House of Representatives. Although basically modeled after the American system, the Supreme Court is empowered with some measure of *a priori* judicial review, where it can review the constitutionality of laws, legislative decrees, and international treaties without a particular case brought before it, at the request of the government or lower courts (Article 121).

In terms of territorial administration (covered in Chapter 8 of the Constitution), Afghanistan is a unitary state, where local administrative government is subject to the principle of "centralism" (Article 138). There are local and district elected councils, but their powers are delegated to them by the central government. Thus, Afghanistan, despite its ethnic and regional diversity, has been designed as unitary state.

Although the effects of these institutional choices included in the 2005 Constitution may not be seen for several years (or perhaps decades), it is clear that the emphasis of the designers of the constitution intended to centralize authority via a strong presidential system and the creation of a unitary state. Further, the effect of the SNTV system has been to create a highly fragmented parliament, which has also enhanced the political authority of President Karzai relative to the National Assembly.

Despite the formal constitutional features of the system, the realities on the ground, at least in the short run, will have far more impact on the political development of Afghanistan. For instance, despite the constitutional centralization of power, Karzai has had to rely heavily on making deals and power-sharing arrangements with local warlords, particularly those associated with the former Northern Alliance, such as Abdul Rashid Dostum, and Mohammed Fahim. Further, despite the unitary nature of the state, the central government does not really control much (as of 2010) outside of the capital city Kabul. The current government's reputation as an imposed regime, backed by the United States and the West, makes it less legitimate in the eyes of many Afghans, particularly among Pashtuns in the south (where the Taliban insurgency is strongest).

Nonetheless, the design of the constitutional framework in Afghanistan illustrates the different types of institutional solutions that can be applied to the problem of promoting political democracy and stability in places that have notoriously lacked both. Whether they work will depend heavily on the future contextual development of Afghanistan.

More questions, not more answers

At the beginning of this book, I held out the idea that an effective teaching and learning approach is *problem-based learning*, which essentially involves students thinking about application of principles to open-ended problems. An open-ended problem means that there is really not a "right" or "correct" answer or solution – only a best effort, based upon information we know (or we think we know). Sometimes this is hard for students to grasp, especially after years of testing for the "right" or "correct" answer. The reality is that there is no correct answer when applying principles to solving complex political problems – only your "best shot."

This book, thus, has not been designed to provide answers, but to provide a way to think about problems, and to ponder a variety of institutional solutions to the problem of building democracy. By doing so, it is hoped that this will help students think about political problems in more nuanced and complex ways, and to realize that to understand the principles of comparative politics is to understand that it is about asking the right questions, not providing the right answers.

References

Afghan Constitution (2004) at http://www.afghan-web.com/politics/current_constitution.html.

Afghanistan: A Country Study, at http://memory.loc.gov/frd/cs/aftoc.html.

CIA World Factbook, 2004–2009, at https://www.cia.gov/library/publications/the-world-factbook/.

Collins, Kathleen (2002) "Clans, Pacts, and Politics in Central Asia," *Journal of Democracy*, 13: 137–152.

Dupree, Louis (1973) *Afghanistan*, Princeton, NJ: Princeton University Press.

Edwards, David B. (2002) *Before Taliban: Genealogies of the Afghan Jihad*, Berkeley and Los Angeles: University of California Press.

Ishiyama, John (2005) "The Sickle and the Minaret: The Communist Successor Parties in Yemen and Afghanistan after the End of the Cold War," *Middle East Review of International Affairs*, 9: 7–29.

Rubin, Barnett (2002) *The Fragmentation of Afghanistan: State Formation and Collapse in the International System*. New Haven, CT: Yale University Press.

Sabahuddin, Abdul (2008) *History of Afghanistan*, London: Global Vision Publishing House.

Vogelsang, Willem (2002) *The Afghans*. Oxford: Blackwell Publishing.

World Bank (2010) *World Development of Indicators*, at http://data.worldbank.org/indicator.

Index

Note: page numbers in italics denote a figure and page numbers in bold denote a table.

Comparative Politics: Principles of Democracy and Democratization, First Edition.
John T. Ishiyama.
© 2012 John T. Ishiyama. Published 2012 by Blackwell Publishing Ltd.